W9-AQH-362

Masterworks of the French Cinema

Masterworks of the French Cinema

Introduction by John Weightman

The Italian Straw Hat
Grand Illusion · La Ronde
The Wages of Fear

Icon Editions
Harper & Row, Publishers
New York, Evanston, San Francisco, London

FIRST US EDITION

ISBN: 0-06-435331-1 (cloth)   0-06-430051-X (paper)

LIBRARY OF CONGRESS CATALOG CARD NUMBER: 73-21853

CONTENTS

ACKNOWLEDGEMENTS

The publishers wish to thank the following individuals and organisations for their help in the preparation of this volume: Mr. Jacques Charrière of L'Avant-Scène du Cinéma, for the loan of stills; the British Film Institute and Westfield College, University of London, for the provision of viewing facilities; *Sight and Sound* for permission to reprint articles on *The Italian Straw Hat, La Ronde* and *The Wages of Fear;* Mr. Joel Finler, for permission to print an extract from his unpublished manuscript on Renoir; Dr. Roger Manvell, for permission to reprint his article on *The Italian Straw Hat;* Mr. Karel Reisz, for permission to reprint his review of *The Wages of Fear.* Translations by: Marianne Alexandre, Andrew Sinclair, Nicholas Fry and Robert Adkinson.

INTRODUCTION

by John Weightman

The four films, the scenarios of which are included in this book, span a quarter of a century of French cinema. Two were made before the Second World War: *The Italian Straw Hat (Un Chapeau de paille d'Italie)* in 1927 and *Grand Illusion (La Grande Illusion)* in 1937; and two after it: *La Ronde* in 1950 and *The Wages of Fear (Le Salaire de la peur)* in 1953; the first is a silent film and the other three talkies; the subject-matter of the four varies widely from bedroom farce to international tragedy. Yet what struck me first on seeing them all again in a group was a certain family air which differentiates them from the French New Wave films of the later fifties and sixties. René Clair, Jean Renoir, the late Max Ophuls and Henri Clouzot all belong to the older tradition of what one might call " the well-made film ", by analogy with the well-made play, *la pièce bien faite*. It would not occur to them to echo Jean-Luc Godard's notorious remark about a film needing a beginning, a middle and an end " but not necessarily in that order ". They show no sign of the New Wave predilection for improvisation, obscurely insistent sequences, loose ends, jumpy camera-work or jumbled sound-tracks as devices for getting closer to " reality " or the modern consciousness. They are all openly and unashamedly old-fashioned in their aesthetic principles. Indeed, both Clair and Renoir, who are writers as well as directors, have expressed their disbelief in avant-gardism as a conscious ideal. The first, referring to literature, has criticized some modern writers for "taking themselves too seriously", and he adds a comment which might apply equally well to the cinema: " One does not bear witness to the times because one has decided to do so. One may, perhaps, turn out to have been a witness, if posterity thinks one worthy of the title." (*Comédies et Commentaires*, 1959, p. 340). Renoir makes an almost identical statement: " If one starts by saying: ' I am going to turn everything upside down, I am going to be modern ', I am sure that one will not be modern. . . . However, in spite of oneself, if one is gifted that way, one will be modern, even if one is not trying to be so." (*Cahiers du*

9

Clearly, what Clair and Renoir depended upon, although they were pioneers in the new medium of the cinema, was the old French tradition of craftsmanship, with its respect for firm intellectual structures and carefully calculated effects. It is not an accident that Renoir was the son of a painter and tried his hand at pottery before becoming a film-maker; his endeavour, as he himself explains, is to create film-objects solid enough to exist independently of their creator. One might add that, in France, the craftsman or artisan was, and perhaps still is, very close to the *bricoleur,* the do-it-yourself handyman, and that Clouzot's *The Wages of Fear* is not only a remarkable piece of craftsmanship in itself but also takes as one of its themes the celebration of the *artisan-bricoleur* by presenting the handling of the lorries as a triumph of human ingenuity. Ophuls is not fully in the same tradition; he belonged to the Jewish middle-class of Saarbrücken and began his career as an actor and film-maker in Germany, before opting for French nationality at the time of the Saar plebiscite in 1934, but some, if not all, of the episodes of *La Ronde* are worked out with a comparable attention to general meaning and accuracy of detail. In short, we are dealing here with " square " films, and the critical problem is to decide whether they can still produce a full impact on the contemporary film-goer, who has been exposed to a looser and perhaps more complex aesthetic.

There is another sense, too, in which they do not belong to what some people would regard as pure cinema. All four are very literary in conception. Three are adaptations of pre-existing works — *The Italian Straw Hat* is a famous vaudeville by Labiche and Augier, first produced in 1851, *La Ronde* is based on *Der Reigen,* an episodic play written in 1896 by the Viennese Jewish dramatist, Arthur Schnitzler, and *The Wages of Fear* is a transposition of a book by the contemporary novelist, Georges Arnaud. Only *Grand Illusion* was composed specifically as a film-script, but it was a development of a real-life story that Renoir had been told by one of his *ancien combattant* friends, and it interested him in the first place because of its human appeal. Consequently, in these four films, the cinematographic effects are not intended to operate, as it were, in their own right; they are meant to convey a definable psychological content. The film-maker is interpreting a body of already existing material, and however he may adapt, simplify or complicate it, it is still the dominant feature of the work and is open to the kind of critical discussion that would be appropriate in the case of any recognized classic of literature or drama. I would not go so far as to say that each film has a precise message to convey; perhaps a successful work of art is never a vehicle but always a system of ambiguities; but each relates to a world-view or metaphysic which gives it its particular resonance.

As it happens, the four films fall neatly into two pairs. *The Italian Straw Hat* and *La Ronde* are comedies about sexual relations and social conventions among the European bourgeoisie of the 19th century. *Grand Illusion* and *The Wages of Fear* are concerned with virile friendship or rivalry in extreme situations — during war-time or in a bleak, pioneering area of South America — from which women are virtually excluded. The themes are, then, men with women and men without women; life within the constraints of average urban society, and life as a heroic struggle outside the bounds of normality.

Of course, the normality with which Clair and Renoir are dealing retrospectively has now long been dead and gone. It was the world of arranged marriages and institutionalized adultery, of *garçonnières* and champagne suppers in the private rooms of discreet restaurants, of *grisettes, cocottes,* actress-prostitutes and all the other varieties of kept women. Precisely because it was so stereotyped, it gave rise to a form of stylized comedy, of which the two great French exponents were Eugène Labiche and, later, Georges Feydeau. The action of this kind of comedy, the speed and suspense of which can still be appreciated by theatre-audiences today in the ingenious revivals put on by eminent theatrical companies both in France and England, always depends on one main question: How to save appearances? How to give a comic representation of the sordid expedients of bourgeois life and then re-establish its respectable façade by the end of the play?

The Italian Straw Hat is an especially clever example of the genre, since it intertwines a marriage of convenience and an act of adultery in the most inextricable way, and makes the resolution of the problem depend on the replacement of a purely ornamental, yet indispensible, bourgeois appurtenance, a woman's hat. Fadinard, a young man about to settle down to respectability, is concluding an advantageous marriage with the daughter of a rich, but rather crass, nursery-gardener. As he is driving through the Bois de Vincennes on his wedding-day, his horse accidentally chews the straw-hat of a lady who has retired into the bushes with an army-officer. The officer, to protect the honour of the lady who cannot return to her husband without her badge of respectability, demands, with threats of violence and destruction, that Fadinard should find an identical hat as soon as possible. The wedding procession consequently turns into a mad chase from one place to another in search of headgear until, in the final scene, a hat of the required sort is found among the wedding-presents, so that the adultress can be saved and the marriage be consummated.

Although the film is now nearly fifty years old, it does not seem to me to have dated at all and, indeed, I suggest that it can be reinterpreted quite easily in terms of Existentialist psychology and the modern French obsession with the *object*. One can only marvel at the fact that René Clair, who was under thirty at the time of making the film, should have brought out the social and psychological implications of the Labiche-Augier vaudeville with such mastery. His work is a creative adaptation which turns the characters into Chaplinesque puppets, rushing this way and that to preserve their collapsing bourgeois rituals. He removes one or two episodes of the original to give himself more room to make visual humour out of the way the bourgeois objects — boots, gloves, wedding-presents and furniture — keep impeding, or fusing with, the action. There is one particularly telling scene in which the top-hats of the wedding party go up and down in a frenzy of salutation independently, as it were, of the people beneath them, which is very reminiscent of the orgy of greetings in the great, anti-bourgeois, Sunday-morning episode in Jean-Paul Sartre's novel, *La Nausée* (1938). It is not impossible that Sartre had seen the film and been inspired by it. No doubt, in 1851, Labiche had been quite instinctive and unconscious in his dehumanizing of the characters and his exploitation of objects. Clair was able to profit from Chaplin's more systematic treatment of the same devices, so that, for instance, when the adultress falls into a faint (a psychosomatic manifestation of *mauvaise foi*), her rigid body passes rapidly and significantly between the three or four men in the room as an object that they clasp in a pseudo-erotic embrace. It would not be difficult to interpret the joke as a comment on the automatism

12

and superficiality of bourgeois relationships.

Above all, Clair manages to suggest something that would probably escape the average reader of the Labiche text. The essence of the plot, behind the social dance, is that a bridegroom, who urgently needs to placate his future father-in-law and is itching to settle down for the night with his bride, is repeatedly frustrated by the obligation to find a particular object before he can consolidate his position and consummate his marriage. He should be " subject ", because he is a husband about to come into his own, but he is constantly reduced to the status of " object " by the complexities of the search for the object. The tingling rhythm that Clair keeps up with such skill from beginning to end conveys to perfection that this apparently frivolous vaudeville is, in its deeper implications, a comic nightmare, an anxiety dream connected with sexual desire or performance, a protracted orgasmic fear of failure or *ejaculatio praecox*. It thus easily transcends the social circumstances of the period in which it is set and appeals directly to the unconscious of the modern spectator.

When *La Ronde* was first shown in France in 1951, it did not receive very good notices, perhaps because it seemed too frothy and superficial at a time when " commitment " was still the dominant fashion on the Parisian cultural scene. It deals with human types in old Vienna, but presents them in a purely human, not a political, light. The " round " of sexual passion links all the classes, from the aristocracy to the proletariat, but once the connection has taken place each individual reverts to the position that he or she had previously occupied in the social hierarchy. Love is just " the contact of two epidermises ", the satisfying of a particular urge, an exercise in vanity or a temporary palliative to boredom; it does not change personalities or act as a social leaven. Actually, the tone of the original work by Schnitzler is quite bitter and pessimistic, so much so indeed that it caused a scandal in Vienna in 1896 and had to wait no less than a quarter of a century for its first public performance in 1921. The text is not included in the commonest edition of Schnitzler's works, presumably because of its shocking nature. The suggestion has been made, although I have not been able to substantiate it, that Schnitzler meant to imply not only that " love " is a fuzz of deceit or self-delusion around the sexual act, but also that the true link

13

between individuals is venereal disease, which is transmitted from the prostitute to the soldier in the opening scene and is brought back by the Count to the prostitute in the final episode. If so, the original play is a black comedy of the bleakest sort, a virulent comment on life in general, not a stylized manipulation of social forms for the purposes of entertainment, like French bedroom farce.

However, Ophuls has clearly aimed at giving the film an aura of Viennese charm. He introduces Anton Walbrook as a suave master of ceremonies, and replaces the idea of the round as a dance by the image of the merry-go-round, with its reassuring Verlainian associations of " *Tournez, tournez, bons chevaux de bois!* " Walbrook, a sort of Great God Pan in evening dress, is present, it would seem, to remind us that it is love which makes the world go round, an optimistic doctrine somewhat at variance with Schnitzler's intentions. Ophuls keeps some of the bitterness of the original — for instance, the crass male chauvinism of the soldier is retained in the first two episodes — but he is careful to poeticize as much as possible, and I confess that, to my mind, he is sometimes too obviously sugaring the pill. Not all the episodes are equally good, either because his taste is uncertain or because he cannot always get the best out of his star performers. Jean-Louis Barrault over-acts wildly as the poet, and Gérard Philipe, as the Count, is, for once, strangely stiff and unconvincing. Incidentally, the last sequence, between the Count and the prostitute, remained unintelligible to me until I read, in a commentary on Schnitzler, that the Count is meant to be drunk and dissipated through social conformity, but has a nostalgia for purity and would have liked to think that his encounter with the prostitute had remained platonic. I suspect that, for most film-goers, the significance of this episode remains obscure.

So, if *La Ronde* is a classic, I would say that it is an imperfect one, in which some of the characters — the poet, the Count, the actress — never come quite alive, either because Ophuls' direction is at fault or because French actors cannot really manage the German types.

But the film contains three episodes which make it memorable in the annals of the cinema, because of the performances of Daniel Gélin, Danielle Darrieux and Fernand Gravey as the young man, the adulterous wife and the commonplace husband. It is sad to think that Gélin, whose first film this was, achieved such elegance and subtlety only once again, in Jacques Becker's charming *Edouard et Caroline*, and then declined into a series of secondary roles. The high point of the film is undoubtedly the fiasco scene between Gélin and Darrieux, in which he is so naïvely lyrical and she so delicately ironic. Almost as good is the bedroom conversation between husband and wife on the varying tensions of bourgeois marriage, as the very phallic clock swings its pendulous genitalia from side to side. The tone here, which is appreciably lighter than in Schnitzler's play, is not one of bitterness but of amused acceptance of the vagaries of human nature.

When we move on from *La Ronde* to *Grand Illusion*, we do not find ourselves in a radically different atmosphere. Renoir, too, is an amused observer of human types, and although he is dealing with the drama of the war-time atmosphere in the prison-camps of the First World War, he does not allow his traditional French sense of human fellowship to become too cloying or simplistic. Of course, since he made *Grand Illusion*, there have been innumerable films on the same theme in connection with the Second World War — some of them very successful, such as *The Bridge on the River Kwai*, *King Rat* and *The Colditz Story* — and it is an obvious proof of Renoir's talent that one can still sit through *Grand Illusion* with complete absorption, in spite of being now so familiar with the various possibilities of the human situation. He has got the details right with such care that every sequence in the film is rich in meaning. Gabin starts out as a typically jaunty young Frenchman of plebeian origins who, through the experience of imprisonment and escape, gradually comes to understand the mentality of people remote from himself — an aristocrat, a Jew, a German widow, etc. — so that his war-time life is an accelerated education. Renoir does not reject patriotism, but he shows it in perspective as an ultimately pathetic attempt to bestow an absolute value on relative concepts, as when the British and French prisoners sing the Marseillaise to mark the capture of Douaumont, only to be frustrated a day or two later by the news that Douaumont has fallen again to the Germans. He can be explicit, but he also knows how to suggest a great deal in an implicit, intuitive way. Two of the most moving moments are, first, the sudden recollection of femininity in a purely masculine society when the prisoners dress up in women's clothes for the Christmas entertainment, and, second, the expression of the innocence and vulnerability of childhood through a back view of the little German girl sitting at the farmhouse table. Perhaps some of the symbols are a shade too obvious for modern tastes — Von Stroheim treasuring the geranium, which is the only concession to gratuitous beauty in the stark world of internment, or Gabin and his companion struggling hopefully through the snow in the final sequence — but they serve their purpose and one cannot say that they are overworked.

It is rather more difficult to determine how, in general, the title is to be understood. Renoir took it from Norman Angell's book, in which " the great illusion " is the belief that war achieves any of the ends for which it is undertaken. But Renoir's film is not specifically about the war, or at least not about the fighting. Nor can *la grande illusion* be despair about human nature as a whole, since the work gives a bracing impression of the resilience of different kinds of men under extreme stress. It might even be argued that Renoir had too nice a nature to sense the appalling evil of which mankind is sometimes capable, and which was already in evidence in Germany in 1937, had he known it; he remains, for the most part, within the average, warm-hearted, Left-Wing humanism of the French post-Enlightenment tradition. He may mean simply that the division of mankind into nations and classes is an illusion. The French and German aristocrats have, fundamentally, the same sense of honour, so why should they be divided against each other in the name of the nation state? The Frenchman and the Jew have to stick together, so do they not share a common humanity? The Frenchman comes to love the German woman, so what is the sense of national boundaries? Yet, at the same time as he suggests these questions, Renoir is realistic enough not to flinch at the tragedy. The aristocrats, for example, cannot be other than they are, since their whole behaviour, in the last resort, is governed by the military ideal, which supposes the existence of an enemy to be fought; their admirable moral code depends, then, on a tradition created by generations of warfare; out of the evil of war has come good; but this good is consumed again by war; evil and good engender each other and then combat each other in ironic reciprocity. When he implies this view of things, Renoir goes beyond any typically Left-Wing philosophy into a more Absurdist attitude, which supposes a positive struggle within a wider context of sceptical clarity.

16

With Clouzot, we are in a peace-time world where the struggle between men is, however, a permanent form of warfare. Of the four film-makers, Clouzot is the one with the keenest sense of evil, as we know not only from *The Wages of Fear* but also from *Le Corbeau* and *Les Diaboliques*. This is not to say that he is entirely devoid of Renoir's appreciation of human fellowship and goodness; the warmhearted Luigi and the loving Linda are like devoted lambs among a pack of ravenous wolves. But his real interest is in the lengths to which men and women will go in order to assert their pure aggressivity, and he is using Luigi and Linda mainly as foils. Here he is dealing with marginal or criminal types, of the sort that have always aroused great interest in French literature, from the time when Balzac created the character of Vautrin in the early 19th century right up to the publication of *Papillon,* a best-seller of two or three years ago. In fact, on seeing *The Wages of Fear* again, one is reminded very much of Papillon's adventures in Guiana and Venezuela after his escape from the French penal colony. Monsieur Jo is a kind of Papillon, an ex-denizen of Montmartre with a cult of virility and impassibility, who is admired by the younger tough, Mario, over whom he establishes his ascendancy. With exquisite precision, Clouzot brings out all the horror of the situation: the remote South American town, vegetating in squalor next to the enclave of the U.S. oil company; the international riff-raff, who can neither make a living nor put together the air-fare to make their escape; the attachment of Luigi and Linda to Mario, who still has a puppy-like charm, although he is prepared to sacrifice both of them to become Jo's buddy, and in any case has never had any qualms about sharing Linda with her employer. It is characteristic of the tough that, for him, women should be expendable or interchangeable, but that he treasures a *métro* ticket to remind himself of Pigalle and presents this ticket to Jo as a token of his esteem.

Once the appalling journey begins, *The Wages of Fear* becomes one of the most effective suspense films ever made, which turns long-distance lorry-driving into an epic experience. But it is much more than that. The extensive introductory episode is necessary to establish the character of Jo and the master/disciple, father/son or male/semi-female relationship between him and Mario. The public humiliation of Luigi by Jo is a virility display in which Jo wins Luigi's " man ", Mario, almost as if he were a female object, although there is no doubt about his masculinity; this is a subtly sadistic scene, in which goodness and generosity are made to appear almost as effeminate attributes. Subsequently, the psychological interest of the lorry-journey lies in the reversal of roles. Jo collapses through age or hidden inner weakness; even Luigi turns out to be naturally courageous in a way Jo is not; eventually Jo is struck by Mario in the kind of classic episode in which the son repudiates, and takes over from, the father; after the shaming, Jo has to " *pisser en Suisse* ", i.e. he is is not even invited to urinate with the true men. All the symbolism of this sequence dovetails beautifully together: when the wooden platform crashes into the valley as the lorry lurches back onto the road, Jo's prestige crumbles with it for good, and Mario is now a total adult who drives the lorry as he wishes and treats Jo as a subordinate; he is man, alone against the universe and carrying the older generation with him as a burden of responsibility; when he drives over Jo's leg, he is youth sacrificing age to ensure its own survival.

The Wages of Fear was dubbed " an atheistic film " by one of the French critics, and I have no doubt that it is. It depicts a world of material necessity and pure appetites, roughly organized according to virile codes. But what are these codes but a futile gesturing in the face of the unknown? As the dying Jo mutters significantly to himself, he never got to know what lay " *derrière la palissade* ", behind the fence. And it is a particularly fine touch, I think, to make the exhausted Mario, a temporary hero, stagger out of the lorry into the glare of the burning oil-well. The blaze represents the senseless energy of the universe, which man can harness in little ways — Mario's achievement will allow the engineers to put out this particular fire — but which will reassert itself against man in the long run. In any case, there is really nothing Mario can do with his triumph except exult in it so gleefully that he swings his empty lorry off the road and is killed without the help of explosives. He commits suicide, we might say, through high spirits, a form of *hybris* no less dangerous in the godless, than in the god-ridden, world.

Looking back over the four films, I note that they are all, in the final analysis, quite harsh, as French works are inclined to be. Yet they leave no feeling of depression in the spectator, but rather a

18

sense of elation, because of the intelligence and vitality with which they are conducted. There are very few soft or indefinite parts, except in the episodes of *La Ronde* I have already criticized; no concessions to sentimentality or muddle or happy endings, but instead a desire to see life clearly and to express the findings with wit and poetry. If I had to establish an order of merit, I would put *The Italian Straw Hat* and *The Wages of Fear* first, as having the absolute hardness of internal logic, but I think it is also legitimate to appreciate the more human vibrations of *La Ronde* and *Grand Illusion*.

CREDITS:

Produced by	Films Albatros-Kamenka
Directed by	René Clair
Scenario by	René Clair, from the play by Eugène Labiche
Camera operators	M. Desfassiaux, N. Roudakoff
Designed by	Lazare Meerson
Date	1928

CAST:

Fadinard	Albert Préjean
Lieutenant Tavernier	Vital Geymond
Anaïs Beauperthuis	Olga Tchekowa
Bobin	Pré fils
The cousins	Alice Tissot, Bondireff
Uncle Vésinet	Paul Olivier
Beauperthuis	Jim Gérald
Lady customer	Lucienne Bogaert
Valet	Alex Allin
Mayor	Velbert

THE ITALIAN STRAW HAT

On a marriage announcement card we read the following: "Monsieur Antoine Nonancourt, nurseryman of Charentonneau (Seine) is pleased to announce the wedding of his daughter Hélène to Monsieur Jules Fadinard, gentleman. The wedding ceremony will take place on June 11th, 1889, at the church of. . . ."

A wreath of orange blossom is lying on top of some article of furniture. Two hands protruding from white sleeves take hold of it.
The hands belong to a prim-looking lady (MME. A.) who is gazing tenderly at the wreath through her pince-nez; she shows it to her husband (MR. A.) who is carefully straightening his made-up tie on his wife's instructions.
HELENE comes in, seemingly in a great hurry, sees her cousins, runs across to kiss them. MME. A. turns round, while HELENE picks up her wedding veil.
NONANCOURT is standing in the doorway, holding his boots in one hand and pulling out his watch with the other. He comes into the room.
He goes to greet MR. and MME. A., then withdraws, urging the others to hurry. HELENE replies:

TITLE: *Yes, daddy. My cousin's going to help me . . . I'm ready.*

NONANCOURT goes to his bedroom and sits down to put his boots on. BOBIN comes in and greets him; the newcomer places his hat on an armchair and goes to stand in front of the mirror, gloves in hand.
MME. A. has put the orange blossom down again, and is pinning the veil. She shows what she has done to . . .
MR. A., whose tie has fallen off and who is striving to put it back on. In the bedroom, BOBIN is looking smugly at his gloves; he removes the label and puts them on with some difficulty.
NONANCOURT is trying desperately to put his shoes on, without success.
He calls to BOBIN, who comes across to help him. MR. A., having entered the bedroom, embraces BOBIN and offers his advice to NON-

21

ancourt, who attempts once more to pull his boots on.

The story moves to the Bois de Vincennes, on the outskirts of Paris.

Title: *The groom sets off for his new home.*

A cabriolet passes down a road through the Bois de Vincennes. Fadinard, the bridegroom, looking very pleased with himself, cracks his whip in the air, twirls his moustaches and straightens his tie.

Mme. A., meanwhile, is still pinning the veil; Mr. A. appears again, but his wife sends him away. He goes out, hat in hand.
Bobin is kneeling in front of Nonancourt. He has removed his gloves, and one of them can be seen lying on the floor close by. Nonancourt is visibly suffering, as Bobin pushes and pulls (*Still*). Finally Nonancourt's foot goes into the boot, just as Mr. A. re-enters.
Mme. A.'s difficulties with the bridal veil persist (*Still*). Suddenly Helene turns round and signals that a pin has fallen down her back. Nonancourt starts to put the second boot on, as Bobin offers his advice. Mr. A. also adds his, but Bobin disagrees with it; Mr. A. goes away, visibly hurt.
Helene shows Mme. A. where the pin has fallen. The older woman begins to fuss and her pince-nez falls from her nose. At that moment. . . .
Mr. A. re-enters, but his wife sends him away again. She picks up her pince-nez and goes on looking for the pin.

Fadinard, riding on his cabriolet, cracks his whip again.
The lash of the whip passes through the air close to the branches of the trees which line the route.
Fadinard raises his whip to crack it again.
The whip strikes a branch and the lash wraps itself round it.
The whip is snatched from Fadinard's hands. . . .
And falls in the grass.
Fadinard turns round, pulling on the reins.
The cabriolet comes to a halt; Fadinard climbs down and runs back to look for the whip.
He goes towards the trees and starts to look for the whip among the branches.
His horse, now untended, slowly starts to walk away . . . down the avenue.

22

NONANCOURT has by now succeeded in putting on the boots. Apparently satisfied with the footwear, he gets up, then suddenly pulls an agonised face and clutches his foot. BOBIN looks up from his kneeling position on the floor, and MR. A. also watches NONANCOURT's pained movement.

HELENE is now quite ready, but still seems to be worried about the pin. MME. A. looks vexed.

NONANCOURT puts on his frock-coat and gingerly tries to walk; MR. A. helps him about the room.

FADINARD is still looking for the whip. Finally, he finds it among the undergrowth and turns to go back to the cabriolet; however, he looks in surprise to see. . . .

His horse in the distance, standing in front of a bush.

Furious, FADINARD runs in the direction of the horse.

The horse is ruminatively eating foliage from the bush, on which an unlikely object is hanging — a woman's straw hat.

FADINARD runs up to the cabriolet, then tries to get hold of the horse.

He pulls the horse to get it back on to the road.

Then FADINARD suddenly gazes with astonishment. . . .

As he sees the horse munching the straw hat (Still).

FADINARD looks at the horse, then looks towards. . . .

The bush; from behind which a man is peering angrily. The man (TAVERNIER), wearing military uniform, fixes FADINARD, then calls to him.

FADINARD picks up what is left of the hat and goes towards TAVERNIER, looking rather anxious. Does the hat belong to this man?

TAVERNIER indicates that the hat does in fact belong to him.

FADINARD smiles and questions TAVERNIER again.

TAVERNIER seems now to be denying something, and talking at the same time to someone who is hiding close by him. A woman's head (that of ANAIS) appears beside TAVERNIER; her hair is very untidy.

FADINARD approaches the couple behind the bush, still talking to TAVERNIER; the two men start to argue.

ANAIS, fearing a scandal, hides.

TAVERNIER looks very threatening.

FADINARD, looking rather frightened, holds the hat out to TAVERNIER.

FADINARD holds out some money to TAVERNIER, who throws it back in his face. FADINARD throws it back again, and the action is repeated by TAVERNIER. Finally, FADINARD keeps the money, throws the hat at TAVERNIER and turns to run.

FADINARD climbs quickly into his cabriolet and sets off.

Meanwhile, TAVERNIER has dashed out of the undergrowth with ANAIS. He puts on his képi and makes as though to run after FADINARD. ANAIS, anxious, holds him back.

FADINARD, using his whip again, turns to look back and sees. . . .

TAVERNIER and ANAIS in the distance — before they are hidden from sight by a bend in the road.

FADINARD looks pleased now; he laughs and starts to use his whip again, then suddenly thinks better of it and lays it down.

TAVERNIER and ANAIS gaze at the hat in horror. TAVERNIER, a desperate expression on his face, turns and sees. . . .

A hackney cab approaching. They stop it and climb in; the cab sets off again.

NONANCOURT glances at his watch and consults MR. A. about the exact time. NONANCOURT leaves in a great hurry, while BOBIN picks his glove up.

NONANCOURT enters the drawing-room and orders HELENE to hurry. HELENE goes with him and MME. A. follows. But HELENE suddenly stops again.

BOBIN is still looking for his other glove. He looks at his hands. . . . One of which is gloved and the other not.

MR. A. walks up to him and they both start looking for the other glove. BOBIN rummages in his coat pockets.

NONANCOURT, HELENE and MME. A. come in, very hurried. MME. A. drags her husband away, as he is dusting his tie. NONANCOURT shouts at BOBIN, who is kneeling on the floor looking for his glove. BOBIN displays his hands, but NONANCOURT makes him get up. Then NONANCOURT, with an expression of great suffering, clasps his foot again. He takes the myrtle, his hat and gloves.

The group pass one by one through the doorway. MR. A., still holding his tie, tries to allow his wife through first, but she shoves him and makes him go in front of her. She passes through, adjusting her pince-nez at the same time. She is followed by HELENE, who is scratching her back, then the suffering NONANCOURT with the myrtle, and finally BOBIN, still searching for the glove. The door closes behind them.

In the hackney cab, TAVERNIER is urging the coachman to greater speed. ANAÏS' hair is flying in all directions, so that she is forced to try to put the remains of the hat on her head.
But, as the cab goes by, we can see that she can't find a suitable position for it. TAVERNIER also tries to arrange the hat. A passer-by stops and starts to laugh; a cyclist also turns round and starts to laugh, almost knocking the pedestrian over. An argument breaks out between them.

In front of NONANCOURT's house, we have the impression of a gathering of top hats and elaborate ladies' hats (*Still*). The guests are busily embracing each other.
They begin to climb into the carriages, urged on by NONANCOURT, who is still holding the myrtle.
The first carriage starts off, followed by that containing NONANCOURT and HELENE. Then come MR. and MME. A., a number of other guests and their children. When the carriages have left, a number of small children gather to watch their progress down the street.

FELIX introduces VESINET into the drawing room of FADINARD's apartment; VESINET hands a packet to FELIX.
As he gives it to him, he says:

TITLE: *I'm the bride's uncle; it is here that the wedding party is meeting, isn't it?*

FELIX replies and shows VESINET to an armchair which has its back turned to the rest of the room. VESINET takes out his ear trumpet. Then FELIX runs towards the door, putting the packet down as he does so.
FADINARD enters looking very happy; he gives his hat and gloves to FELIX, who points out the seated VESINET.
FADINARD goes towards VESINET and speaks to him, but VESINET doesn't move. Surprised, FADINARD repeats what he has just said, but still VESINET remains motionless. FADINARD finally goes right up to VESINET, who now sees him and gets to his feet.
He picks up his ear trumpet which he had placed upon the table,

then embraces FADINARD, who seems to question him. VESINET signals that he is a little hard of hearing and shows FADINARD his ear trumpet.

VESINET takes FADINARD by the arm and admires the apartment. FELIX shows him the packet. FADINARD thanks VESINET, who tries to embrace him again, but FADINARD backs away. VESINET has to direct his trumpet towards FADINARD, who takes him on a tour of the apartment. FELIX puts the packet down again.

They open the door of the bedroom and look in.

A maidservant is just putting a second pillow in place.

FADINARD, rather moved by this sight, drags VESINET away, as the latter puts his trumpet in position again. He closes the door.

Outside the house, TAVERNIER stops the cab, because he has seen. . . .

FADINARD's cabriolet parked in front of its owner's house. FELIX is just about to lead the cabriolet away.

TAVERNIER pays the cabman and gets out of the hackney cab.

He goes into the house, dragging ANAIS with him. A number of passers-by start to laugh, while ANAIS tries to hide the hat.

In the house, FADINARD is leading VESINET back to his armchair, the back of which is still turned towards the door of the room. FADINARD moves to another part of the room, as VESINET picks up an album of photographs.

He looks at a portrait. . . .

Of HELENE.

FADINARD is looking absolutely delighted, when suddenly an expression of horror comes over his features, as he sees. . . .

ANAIS and TAVERNIER entering the apartment.

TAVERNIER, hard-faced and menacing, advances towards FADINARD. ANAIS has removed her hat and she tries to hold TAVERNIER back. He releases himself and greets FADINARD more or less correctly.

FADINARD, still confused, replies to his greeting.

TAVERNIER is now behaving very formally, but there is a touch of irony in his attitude to FADINARD. He signals to ANAIS to sit down, then sits down himself and invites FADINARD to do the same.

FADINARD sits down.

TAVERNIER shows him the hat again, and seems to be on the point of surrendering to his undoubted rage, but ANAIS succeeds in calming him each time this happens.

FADINARD looks gravely at the hat, but we suspect that he is only just preventing himself from bursting into laughter.

TAVERNIER rises angrily; ANAIS tries to hold him back again, but this time TAVERNIER goes up to FADINARD and grabs hold of him.

He starts shouting, as does FADINARD. TAVERNIER is working himself up into a terrible rage, when FADINARD suddenly makes him shut up by pointing to. . . .

His uncle VESINET, who has heard nothing and is smiling beatifically.

Uncle VESINET is in the foreground; TAVERNIER starts shouting again; ANAIS gets up and goes to him.

FADINARD supports ANAIS in her attempt to calm TAVERNIER, then, very serious, he asks if he can see her hands. He gazes at. . . .

The hands of ANAIS; his finger points to a wedding-ring.

He then asks the uncomprehending TAVERNIER to show him his hands too.

There is no wedding-ring on TAVERNIER's finger.

TAVERNIER looks very taken aback as FADINARD comes closer to him. . . .

Until we see him by TAVERNIER's shoulder.

There is some face powder on TAVERNIER's shoulder; FADINARD wipes it off with his finger and takes hold of a long hair at the same time (*Still*).

Watched by the amazed TAVERNIER, FADINARD goes up to ANAIS. . . .

He compares the colour of the powder and the hair to those of ANAIS.

Now FADINARD understands the situation; he smiles and wags a threatening finger at TAVERNIER and ANAIS. The furious TAVERNIER springs to the attack again.

TAVERNIER passes the hat to ANAIS, as FADINARD moves behind a chair which is promptly grasped by TAVERNIER.

Facing FADINARD, TAVERNIER starts to shake the chair violently.

The feet of the chair strike hard on the floor; TAVERNIER's feet move about nervously.

VESINET smiles and closes his book.

TAVERNIER, now brandishing the hat again, pushes FADINARD.

FADINARD backs up to the window, and TAVERNIER follows him, still waving the hat. But as FADINARD begs TAVERNIER to be quiet, he hears. . . .

The carriages which are drawing to a halt outside the front of the house.

FADINARD tries to explain what is happening to TAVERNIER.

ANAIS is worried about being seen without a hat in a strange house. She gets up. . . .

TITLE: *I don't want people I don't know to see me without a hat . . .*

TAVERNIER picks up his képi and they look for somewhere to hide.

NONANCOURT, HELENE and BOBIN are already on the stairs.

FADINARD shows TAVERNIER and ANAIS into the bedroom, then runs back to join VESINET. He says something to him, gives him his ear trumpet. Then he turns round. . . .

NONANCOURT, still carrying the myrtle, HELENE and BOBIN come in. FADINARD runs up to them.

He embraces HELENE. NONANCOURT, however, looks rather displeased and pulls FADINARD to one side and shows him his watch.

FADINARD smiles and assures him that all is well. But he sees. . . .

NONANCOURT, who is hopping from one foot to the other, HELENE, who seems to be constantly scratching herself, and BOBIN, who is still looking through his pockets and hiding his ungloved hand.

FADINARD becomes anxious and goes up to. . . .

HELENE. She smiles and explains the matter of the pin to him. He smiles and leads her to. . . .

The bedroom door. He looks at the back of her bodice. But HELENE, modest, wants to go into the room and starts to turn the handle of the door.

Within the bedroom, TAVERNIER and ANAIS are listening close to the door. The handle starts to turn and they look at each other. ANAIS takes the hat from TAVERNIER.

Suddenly another door opens and FELIX appears, much to the astonishment of ANAIS. FELIX advances oblivious into the room, carrying FADINARD's hat.

FELIX looks completely stupefied when he sees the occupants of the room and leaves immediately through the door by which he has just entered.

Meanwhile FADINARD is preventing HELENE from going into the bedroom.

NONANCOURT, still accompanied by BOBIN, looks at his watch, calls the others, and puts the myrtle down.

FADINARD agrees with NONANCOURT and takes HELENE along with him.

They all leave the room very quickly.

VESINET, forgotten by everybody, dozes in his chair.

FADINARD suddenly comes back into the room. He shouts to NONAN-COURT that he is coming back, then closes the door and runs towards that of the bedroom.

TAVERNIER and ANAIS, now almost fainting, come out of the room. TAVERNIER takes hold of a chair and bangs it on the floor. ANAIS faints completely, as FADINARD closes the door. TAVERNIER holds ANAIS with one arm, while he makes threatening gestures at FADIN-ARD with the other. FADINARD urges him to be quiet, then goes towards VESINET.

He sees that VESINET is dozing; he takes the ear trumpet from the table.

He blocks up the ear trumpet with a piece of paper.

He goes back to TAVERNIER, who picks up a chair and raises it over FADINARD. ANAIS comes to her senses.

FADINARD asks him exactly what he wants; TAVERNIER picks up the hat and says threateningly to FADINARD:

TITLE: *Madame is married. She can't go back home without a decent hat. Find one!*

FADINARD shrugs his shoulders and points through the window to. . . .

The wedding party in the street, which is waiting impatiently. NONAN-COURT looks especially agitated.

FADINARD tries to explain the situation, but TAVERNIER will have none of it. He insists . . .

TITLE: *The lady's in a terrible state. . . . I can't leave her. Get a move on! This is what it looks like . . .*

He tears a piece from the hat. FADINARD refuses to take it, but TAVERNIER thrusts it in his pocket all the same.

NONANCOURT, now very angry, leaves the wedding party and goes back into the house.

He calls to FADINARD as he climbs the stairs.

FADINARD hears him, makes TAVERNIER be quiet, then runs. . . .

To the door to prevent NONANCOURT from coming all the way up. He goes out, taking the myrtle with him.

29

ANAIS remains clasped in TAVERNIER's arms. FELIX comes in, carrying FADINARD's hat. He sees the couple.

Very surprised, he goes out again.

On the stairs, FADINARD is reassuring NONANCOURT and giving him the myrtle. He won't be a minute. NONANCOURT goes down the stairs again, while FADINARD goes back to his room.

TAVERNIER is still clasping the fainting ANAIS. When FADINARD comes up to them, TAVERNIER thrusts ANAIS into his arms, throws the hat to the floor and angrily walks over to a corner of the room near the bedroom door. This door is suddenly opened and FELIX appears again. TAVERNIER is hidden by the open door, so that. . . .

The astonished FELIX sees. . . .

FADINARD holding ANAIS in his arms.

FELIX closes the door again. TAVERNIER takes a chair and smashes it down on the floor. FADINARD wants to set ANAIS down, but when he tries to do so she almost falls.

TAVERNIER's anger is uncontrollable.

TITLE: *If you don't do what I say, I'll smash everything* . . .

FADINARD looks as though he is about to assault TAVERNIER, but ANAIS hinders him. He catches her as TAVERNIER overturns some furniture and goes out.

FELIX, hesitating to come in, is still standing behind the bedroom door, holding FADINARD's hat.

In the drawing room, VESINET wakes up, stretches, smiles, turns round and finally gets up.

He goes towards FADINARD, who thrusts ANAIS into his arms to go after TAVERNIER.

FELIX timidly opens the bedroom door a few inches, and sees. . . .

ANAIS in the arms of the excited VESINET.

FELIX closes the door again. TAVERNIER dashes back into the room; knocking against all the furniture, pursued by FADINARD. FADINARD takes ANAIS from VESINET and makes her sit down.

FADINARD begs TAVERNIER to be quiet in front of VESINET. TAVERNIER understands and they pretend to talk in a friendly fashion. FADINARD urges VESINET to go out.

VESINET goes and closes the door.

TAVERNIER continues his apparently friendly discussion with FADINARD, but as soon as the door closes he leaps at him.

Meanwhile, VESINET, on the stairs, finds that he has forgotten his ear trumpet, and he turns to go back.

TAVERNIER has grasped hold of FADINARD. VESINET comes back into the room; TAVERNIER sees him and lets go of FADINARD, who doesn't understand what is happening, and begins to talk in a more friendly fashion again. VESINET apologises and goes towards. . . .

The sofa, and picks up his ear trumpet.

VESINET goes out of the room. FADINARD leaps immediately from his chair, pursued by TAVERNIER.

Outside the door, VESINET, intrigued by the strange happenings, applies his ear trumpet to the key-hole.

TAVERNIER and FADINARD are arguing close to the door.

VESINET, however, can't hear a word they are saying, and, disappointed, he goes away.

TAVERNIER and FADINARD are on the point of coming to blows.

Still hiding behind the bedroom door, FELIX hesitates to enter the other room. Finally he goes in, carrying FADINARD's hat and gloves. He comes into the drawing-room, causing TAVERNIER to let go of FADINARD and to start talking quietly again. FELIX hands the hat and gloves to FADINARD, who takes advantage of this pause to take correct leave, watched by FELIX. But TAVERNIER stops him and shakes his hand (*Still*).

TAVERNIER holds on to FADINARD's hand and squeezes it hard, while continuing to smile.

By this time VESINET has reached the foot of the stairs, where he collides with NONANCOURT, now very angry, who interrogates him. VESINET puts his ear trumpet to his ear, but can't hear anything. NONANCOURT pushes him back, shoves the myrtle into his hands and goes back into the house.

TAVERNIER is still holding FADINARD by the hand. ANAIS comes to and gets up to go to them. FELIX, turning round, goes to pick up the chair which has been overturned.

On the staircase, NONANCOURT is calling to FADINARD. Hearing no reply, he starts to climb the stairs again.

FADINARD hears him coming, as does TAVERNIER, who lets go of FADINARD's hand.

TAVERNIER and ANAIS run to hide each on either side of the double door leading from the staircase. NONANCOURT opens one side of the door and FADINARD immediately opens the other, so that both

TAVERNIER and ANAIS are hidden. NONANCOURT comes into the room. FELIX turns round from his task of putting ornaments in order and sees. . . .

NONANCOURT cursing FADINARD, who, maintaining an air of correctness and calm, puts on his hat and follows him.

FELIX shakes his head and turns to look in the direction of the bedroom again.

As he leaves, FADINARD closes both halves of the door, revealing ANAIS and TAVERNIER. ANAIS promptly falls into her lover's arms. FELIX breathes again. Then he turns and sees. . . .

ANAIS in the arms of TAVERNIER.

TAVERNIER calls FELIX across and pushes ANAIS into his arms. Then he starts to write something very quickly on a card.

On the stairs, FADINARD is vainly trying to come back to the drawing room, but NONANCOURT drags him away.

TAVERNIER finishes writing and hands the card to FELIX. He takes ANAIS from the servant and tells him that the card must be given to FADINARD.

FADINARD is now outside the house, surrounded by members of the wedding party. NONANCOURT is still shouting angrily, while HELENE tries to calm him. FADINARD suddenly seems to make his mind up. He points to the windows, motions everyone to be quiet and says:

TITLE: *I can explain everything.* . . .

Just as he starts to speak, however, FELIX arrives on the scene and holds out TAVERNIER's card to FADINARD, who reads:

The following text written on a visiting card: "If you compromise the lady by a single word, I challenge you to a duel tomorrow, and I shall kill you. If you do not quickly return with a hat exactly similar to the first, I shall smash all your furniture today."

FADINARD reads the card closely. He is in fact very frightened, but he manages to summon a smile.

FADINARD feigns cheerfulness, then tells FELIX to go to TAVERNIER and tell him that he will do as he says. He then urges everyone to get into the carriages; FELIX goes back into the house.

TAVERNIER, holding ANAIS, goes into the bedroom. He lays her out on the bed, then nervously lights a cigarette.

In the street, the carriages draw away from the house.

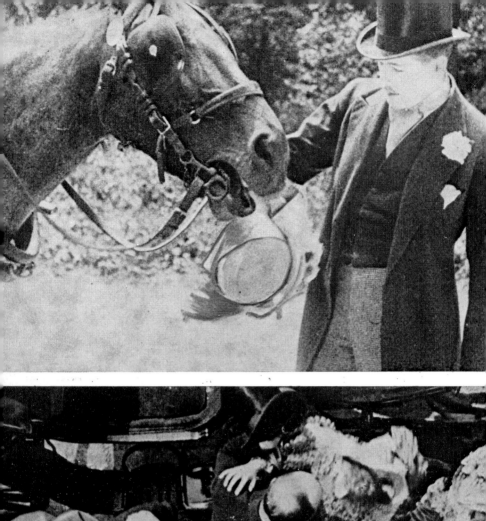
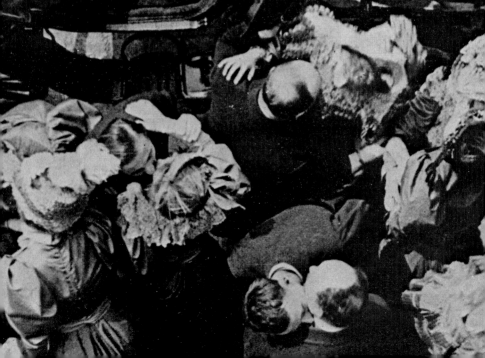

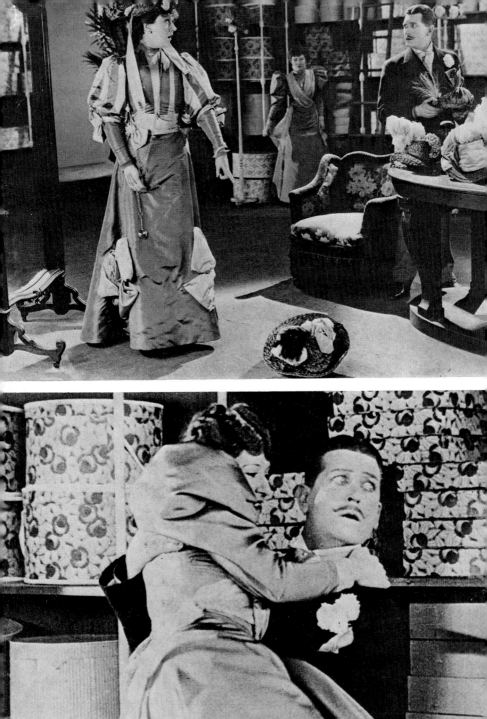

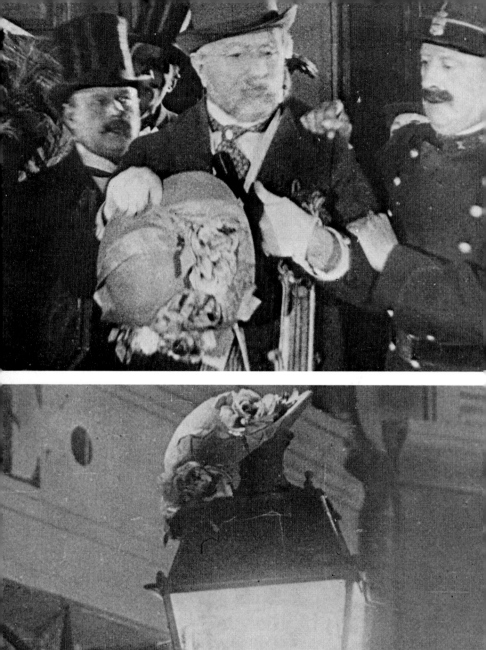

FELIX runs into the drawing-room, but sees nobody there.
In the bedroom, TAVERNIER is glaring and posturing furiously. FELIX
opens the door cautiously. TAVERNIER listens to what he has to say,
then clears him out of the room.
Outside, the last carriages draw away from the house.
FELIX sits down in the drawing-room, fed up. He looks down and
sees the half-eaten straw hat lying near his feet.

The carriages come to a halt in front of the town-hall. A number of
children begin to gather round, attracting more passers-by.
FADINARD is sitting next to MME. C., and on his right he sees. . . .
The façade of the town-hall.
And on the other side, FADINARD looks at. . . .
A fashion shop.
He looks longingly at the shop, but NONANCOURT is watching very
carefully and leads him away. He places the myrtle in the carriage.
The wedding party climbs the steps outside the town-hall. . . .
Past the bust representing the Republic.
FADINARD finally calms down. Then a horrified look suddenly comes
over his face as he thinks of. . . .
TAVERNIER kicking at a chair and knocking it over.
FADINARD glances hurriedly at his watch. The Mayor hasn't arrived
yet. Looking out, he sees. . . .
The empty square in front of the town-hall.
FADINARD makes an ambiguous sign to NONANCOURT and gets up.
He leaves his hat and gloves behind.
He quickly leaves the wedding party.
NONANCOURT is beside himself with anger and questions everybody
about FADINARD's strange behaviour. HELENE alone remains calm.
FADINARD, hatless, runs out of the town-hall, watched by the waiting
coachmen. . . .
Who start to talk and laugh as they see the prospective husband
apparently fleeing from his wedding.

FADINARD stops in front of the fashion shop. A lady, wearing a most
extraordinary hat, passes FADINARD, who stares hard at her.
FADINARD gazes at the hats in the shop window; superimposed on
them is the wavering image of the Italian straw hat. Then the image
fades and. . . .

41

FADINARD goes into the shop.

CLARA, the owner of the shop, is helping a customer to try on a hat. The customer's hands appear and place her own hat to one side. FADINARD suddenly interrupts them.

CLARA pushes FADINARD back and tells him to be quiet. She helps the woman to try on another hat. The customer seems absolutely delighted with it. CLARA agrees with her and turns for another opinion to FADINARD, who, in the circumstances, is forced to agree. But the customer decides to try yet another hat on.

FADINARD leaps to help her and gives her another two hats at the same time. Then he turns away and knocks the customer's own hat on the floor. The lady picks it up, looking very annoyed.

He starts hunting for a straw hat in the various hat boxes in the shop, but CLARA interrupts him. He tells her exactly what he is looking for, but CLARA doesn't seem to grasp immediately what it is he wants. Then suddenly she seems to remember something, and an expression of joy appears on FADINARD's face.

Meanwhile, in the town-hall, the MAYOR has finally appeared and he goes to sit in his official chair.

He looks around him at the assembled wedding party and notices. . . .

The empty place at HELEN's side. The only remaining traces of FADINARD are his hat and gloves.

The MAYOR looks absolutely dumbfounded.

NONANCOURT goes towards him, as though wishing to explain what has happened, then suddenly he changes his mind and dashes out. The MAYOR's air of astonishment increases.

Meanwhile, in the hat shop, CLARA is searching urgently, urged on by FADINARD, who is opening every hat box he can lay hands on; he throws a hat on the floor.

The lady customer, who is smiling at herself in the mirror, sees. . . .

That it is her hat which FADINARD has thrown on the floor. She complains to FADINARD (*Still*) and bends down to pick it up. FADINARD bends down at the same time and their heads meet violently. They both stagger back, slightly stunned, and the hat remains on the floor.

NONANCOURT dashes out of the town-hall and goes up to the waiting coachmen to ask them where the disappearing groom has gone. They tell him and NONANCOURT departs in the direction taken by FADIN-ARD. The coachmen start to laugh as he goes.

In the shop, CLARA is placing a ladder against a wall. She climbs up it and lays hold of a number of boxes which she passes down to FADINARD.

Then CLARA smiles as she comes to another pile of boxes.

Her obvious pleasure communicates itself to FADINARD. Can it be that she has found an identical hat? The boxes suddenly crash to the floor and FADINARD bends down to prevent their fall.

CLARA also loses her balance on the ladder and, clutching a box, falls straight into the arms of FADINARD.

At this moment, who should come into the shop but NONAN-COURT. . . .

Whose face becomes immediately contorted with rage.

CLARA, finding herself in FADINARD's arms, immediately begins to act coyly (Still).

Then, much to his dismay, FADINARD notices NONANCOURT and lets CLARA fall to the floor. NONANCOURT advances on his errant son-in-law.

But as he moves forward his foot is planted firmly on the lady customer's hat.

The lady stops NONANCOURT and demands an apology from him.

CLARA searches urgently in the hat box, but it turns out to be empty.

FADINARD becomes increasingly impatient, then CLARA says:

TITLE: *I did have a hat like that. . . . But I sold it . . .*

NONANCOURT throws himself at FADINARD and drags him away. FADINARD starts to follow, but collides with some furniture.

NONANCOURT shakes FADINARD, who says to CLARA:

TITLE: *Who did you sell it to?*

CLARA looks about for her sales ledger, finds the book and opens it. In the meantime, FADINARD has disappeared, dragged away by NONAN-COURT with brutal swiftness.

CLARA looks up and sees that he has gone.

She goes over to the lady client who, furious, is holding up her crushed hat. CLARA urges her to try another, enormous hat, and

43

the customer seems delighted with it.

In front of the town-hall, the waiting coachmen see NONANCOURT reappear with FADINARD. They laugh again as the ridiculous pair pass. Inside the town-hall the MAYOR looks very angry and makes as though to leave. BOBIN throws himself forward to prevent the MAYOR from leaving; he looks suddenly ashamed when he finds that he is restraining the MAYOR with his ungloved hand, and promptly switches to his gloved one.

FADINARD and NONANCOURT come back into the room and sit down. FADINARD turns to HELENE to apologise for his behaviour; she looks very upset.

The MAYOR rises pompously to his feet.

FADINARD and HELENE also rise.

In FADINARD's bedroom TAVERNIER gets angrily to his feet.
He calls out for the servant.

FELIX comes fearfully into the room carrying something to drink. TAVERNIER takes the drink from his hands and tells him to go and warn FADINARD again.

FELIX begins to protest, but TAVERNIER pushes him towards the door. And FELIX is thrust through the bedroom door, followed by TAVERNIER.

In the main hall of the town-hall, FADINARD and HELENE are standing, ready to continue the wedding ceremony.

HELENE takes the marriage oath first, then FADINARD.

They go back to their seats.

The front door of FADINARD's house suddenly opens and FELIX is sent flying out into the street. We just see TAVERNIER's foot thrust through the doorway behind him.

FELIX starts to argue from the street, when first a cushion, then a vase, are thrown at him. He decides to flee.

A chair follows, thrown from the house, but FELIX has already disappeared, and the missile almost hits a passing rag-and-bone man who is going by with his cart.

The rag-and-bone man looks round in amazement, then goes to pick up the chair and looks at it closely. . . .

44

. . . And adds it to his stock.

The MAYOR gets to his feet again and starts to make his wedding speech.

An unctuous smile spreads over his face.

FADINARD smiles at HELENE, as they listen to the MAYOR.

The MAYOR continues his conventional words of advice.

NONANCOURT listens to what the MAYOR is saying and smiles. Then NONANCOURT's shoes begin to cause him discomfort again. BOBIN suddenly becomes conscious that his ungloved hand is visible and hurriedly hides it. NONANCOURT orders him to listen to what the MAYOR is saying; they both start to pay attention again, smiling dutifully.

The MAYOR continues talking and smiling.

We see the first row of wedding guests from behind the MAYOR; they are all nodding and smiling dutifully, except VESINET, who doesn't react at all (*Still*).

Realising, perhaps, that he is taking no part in the service, VESINET starts to fidget with his ear trumpet, trying to clear it.

The MAYOR continues his long speech.

MR. and MME. A. listen dutifully. We notice, though, that MR. A.'s tie has fallen away from the collar. MME. A. looks at her husband and notices with irritation. . . .

The tie detached from the collar.

She jabs her husband with her elbow, but he takes no notice of her. She pushes him again, but this only has the effect of making him draw further away, towards his neighbour on the other side.

The man sitting next to him in turn draws away, pushing against his neighbour. . . .

Who pushes the man next to him; he, however, is sitting on the end of the bench, and protests and shoves everyone back again.

MR. A. is thus pushed back against his wife, who looks at him and pushes him again. He still doesn't take any notice.

The MAYOR is still talking and the first row goes on listening with apparent approval.

Infuriated by her husband, MME. A. pinches him, causing him to cry out loudly.

The MAYOR looks sternly at him, then carries on with his speech.

MME. A. signals to her husband to put his tie back in place. But he still doesn't understand.

As he talks, an anxious looks appears on the Mayor's face, as he sees. . . .

MME. A., still looking towards him, but signalling sideways to her husband that his tie is no longer in place.

The MAYOR is disturbed by this signal and immediately starts to straighten his own tie.

A number of the guests then start straightening their own ties, except MR. A.

Finally MME. A. manages to get her message through to her husband, who straightens his tie.

The MAYOR smiles and carries on with his speech.

The front row of guests listens politely, except VESINET, who is still trying to unblock his ear trumpet.

FADINARD looks approvingly in the direction of the MAYOR. VESINET abandons his attempt to unblock the ear-trumpet and pretends to listen.

And imitates the actions of FADINARD to give the impression that he really has heard what the MAYOR is saying.

Outside, FELIX has reached the town-hall and is talking to the waiting coachmen. He goes into the town-hall, where . . .

The MAYOR still hasn't finished his speech.

VESINET nods approvingly, imitating the movement of FADINARD's head.

FELIX comes into the room and sidles up to FADINARD.

He leans towards him and whispers in his ear, making FADINARD jump with fright.

The MAYOR glares at them.

FADINARD sends FELIX away and starts to listen to the MAYOR's speech again.

The MAYOR recommences his speech as FELIX leaves the room.

FADINARD, beginning to find that the MAYOR's speech is going on too long, takes out his watch and glances at it.

Meanwhile, we see that one of the children with the wedding party has fallen asleep.

FADINARD is now beginning to look distinctly agitated as the MAYOR shows no signs of stopping.

The MAYOR continues oblivious.

FADINARD nods his agreement with the MAYOR, but he is beginning to look very anxious. VESINET imitates him.

The MAYOR's oratory is now blossoming fully.

FADINARD, who can no longer stay in his seat, suddenly applauds and gets to his feet.

VESINET, who is leaning over his ear trumpet, doesn't see FADINARD's preparations to leave.

FADINARD drags HELENE away with him. The rest of the wedding guests applaud and follow them.

The sleeping child is suddenly woken up and begins to cry. A hand appears and slaps him, making him cry even louder.

The usher of the town-hall looks absolutely astonished as the wedding guests stream past him.

The MAYOR looks up in great surprise, clearly still with much to add to his speech.

VESINET raises his head to listen again.

He is now almost alone in the room with the MAYOR.

The MAYOR comes down from the daïs.

VESINET starts to applaud.

FADINARD has gone back to the hat shop; he hurries in.

The MAYOR upbraids VESINET for what he believes to be rudeness.

VESINET, not hearing a word, thanks the Mayor and turns to go.

Seeing FADINARD come back in the shop, the customer hurries to save her own hat from any further damage. FADINARD speaks urgently to CLARA.

NONANCOURT appears again in pursuit; the customer sees him and waves her crushed hat in front of him. NONANCOURT calls to FADINARD.

CLARA is giving FADINARD the address of the customer who has bought the Italian straw hat.

TITLE: *This is the address of Mme. Bauperthuis, who bought a very similar hat from me. . . .*

She gives him a box. FADINARD thanks CLARA and turns to rush from the shop.

As he turns, he knocks against the lady customer, causing her hat to fall on the floor. He jumps back to apologise and. . . .

Treads on the hat.

He leaves the shop with NONANCOURT, as the lady looks furiously after them. CLARA brings her another hat, which the customer refuses to look at. Instead, she clamps her own hat on her head and stalks out of the shop.

In FADINARD's bedroom: ANAIS is lying on the bed, while TAVERNIER is sitting close by, nervously pulling at a cigarette.
ANAIS seems very angry with him.
FELIX is anxiously climbing the stairs; he makes as though to open the bedroom door, thinks better of it, goes back.
In the bedroom, TAVERNIER gets to his feet and crushes out his cigarette in an ash-tray, in which there is already a pile of cigarette ends.
After some final hesitation, FELIX picks up a stick and goes into the flat.
FELIX enters the drawing-room, cane in hand, very military in bearing; he twirls his baton like a sergeant-major. TAVERNIER opens the door of the bedroom. FELIX doesn't notice him and continues his advance into the drawing-room. TAVERNIER draws closer to him, until they are only separated by the length of the baton.
They start to exchange words, FELIX telling TAVERNIER what FADINARD has said.

FADINARD and HELENE are now in church, undergoing the religious ceremony. They get to their feet from a kneeling position as the priest draws closer to them.

TAVERNIER, looking as angry as ever, snatches the baton from FELIX, waves it threateningly at him again, causing the servant to flee.
A messenger is bringing a bouquet of flowers to the house. He doesn't see anyone and waits for a moment on the staircase; then he hears some noise from the apartment.
FELIX is trying to escape from the drawing-room by the door which leads to the staircase, and TAVERNIER closes it firmly. Then the door opens again as the messenger comes in with the flowers. TAVERNIER seizes them and throws them at the messenger and pushes him out.
TAVERNIER pushes and kicks at the furniture in his anger.
ANAIS calls to him.
TAVERNIER comes out of the drawing-room. As soon as he goes out, FELIX, who has been hiding behind some furniture, reappears and dashes towards the staircase door.

48

He runs into the messenger, who has just thrown the flowers on the floor. An argument breaks out between them.

TAVERNIER has gone back into the bedroom, where ANAIS is having an emotional crisis and is very reproachful towards TAVERNIER. She tries to scratch him as he bends down to calm her.

In the church: FADINARD slips a wedding-ring on to HELENE's finger and slips one on to his own, but. . . . They have the wrong rings and have to change immediately.

FELIX, after arguing with the messenger, goes back into the drawing-room, but cautiously keeps his hand on the door-handle.

TAVERNIER comes back into the drawing-room and says to FELIX:

TITLE: *Go and tell your master I've waited long enough. The carnage is going to start.*

FELIX tries to start arguing again, but TAVERNIER takes a chair and throws it on the floor, then turns to threaten FELIX again, but the latter flees from the room.

On the staircase, FELIX passes the astonished errand-boy again, who turns to follow the fleeing servant.

The wedding guests are now being driven in their carriages through the streets.

FELIX runs out of the house. The messenger turns to watch him go, as a piece of furniture crashes into the street, causing the messenger to take to his heels.

TAVERNIER has just hurled some furniture from the window; he turns round and sees a cushion on an armchair. He seizes it, opens the window and throws it out.

He paces furiously up and down the room.

The cushion suddenly flies back through the window.

And lands, conveniently enough, on the same armchair.

TAVERNIER turns and sees the cushion again. He cannot understand what has happened, but he angrily grabs it again and throws it through the window.

Outside the house, a passer-by catches the cushion, balances it a moment in his hands.

TAVERNIER continues his pacing to and fro. As he passes by the window, the cushion flies in again and lands on ANAIS, who immediately wakes up. TAVERNIER is beside himself with anger.

ANAIS, thinking that TAVERNIER has thrown the cushion at her, also begins to get angry.

TAVERNIER tries to control himself and sits beside ANAIS, smiling. But the argument soon breaks out again.

The wedding party, apart from FADINARD, is sitting round a table in a restaurant. NONANCOURT, however, espies his fleeing son-in-law and runs after him.

FADINARD is crossing the dance floor of the restaurant in an attempt to escape from the others. NONANCOURT catches up with him and drags him back.

FADINARD, pulled along by NONANCOURT, eases himself from his father-in-law's grasp and pretends that he only intended to play a joke on the party. He sits down again and the eating starts again.

A clock — its hands at half-past four — is standing near a window. TAVERNIER is sitting opposite the clock, smoking nervously. He glances at it, extinguishes his cigarette, grasps a bronze ornament and makes as though to throw it at. . . .

The clock.

TAVERNIER is just about to throw the ornament, when ANAIS suddenly moves and TAVERNIER stops himself.

Outside the house, a carriage stops and the coachman gets down.

A lady and gentleman are sitting in the carriage; they give a box to the coachman and the man also gives him his visiting card which he places in an envelope.

INSERT written on the envelope: *Monsieur et Madame Fadinard.*

The coachman nods to show that he has understood his instructions, takes the box and goes into FADINARD's house.

The couple, very pleased with themselves and proud of their present, remain in the carriage.

The coachman climbs the stairs, then, seeing no one, hesitates. Then he goes on up the stairs.

We see his feet moving up the stairs.

TAVERNIER hears his steps on the stairs and his face lights up with hope. ANAIS also wakes up. Can this really be the hat? TAVERNIER strides eagerly out of the bedroom.

He goes into the drawing-room, just as the coachman enters carrying the box, upon which TAVERNIER's gaze fixes immediately.

The coachman holds out the box to TAVERNIER, who hurriedly opens it; a mass of wrapping paper flies out.

ANAIS is waiting impatiently on the bed.

The coachman, believing that he has carried out his commission faithfully, smiles. TAVERNIER wrestles anxiously with the complicated wrapping of the parcel, then he finally pulls out. . . .

A clock exactly similar to the one in the bedroom and showing exactly the same time.

Furious, TAVERNIER demands an explanation from the coachman, who holds the card out to him. TAVERNIER puts the clock down, takes the card, then hurls it at the coachman.

The coachman protests angrily, but, faced with TAVERNIER's fury, decides to leave. TAVERNIER snatches up the clock and goes back into the bedroom.

The couple, very self-satisfied, are waiting patiently in their carriage. The coachman strides angrily from FADINARD's house. He goes up to the carriage and hurls the card at his clients.

The two are utterly shocked at his behaviour; he explains angrily what has happened.

TAVERNIER is standing next to ANAIS. He angrily shows her the clock. . . .

We see it next to the other, exactly similar, clock.

The coachman, still very angry, ends his list of bitter complaints to the occupants of the carriage and climbs up on to his seat.

The man and the woman look at each other, very annoyed with what they consider to be FADINARD's outrageous behaviour. The man looks again at the house and the façade: there can be no doubt — it is FADINARD's house.

TAVERNIER, beside himself with anger, hurls the clock through the window.

The man in the carriage looks up in fright and grasps his hat. He looks, horrified, at his wife. Then they both look in complete amazement at. . . .

The smashed clock on the pavement.

They turn to look at each other again, their expression changing from stupefaction to indignation.

The coachman turns round and looks at them.

They signal that he can drive on. Their expressions of offended dignity remain. Obviously they will never have anything to do again with FADINARD.

The carriage draws away; as it goes we see that the rag-and-bone man has returned with his cart. He sees the clock on the pavement, picks it up, looks up at the extraordinary house from which such treasures rain down, then puts the clock on his cart and drives off.

We look down upon the wedding-guests, still at the banquet table, which is now in considerable disorder. BOBIN is singing (*Still*).

FADINARD is gazing lovingly at HELENE.

VESINET is sitting next to MME. B., who talks constantly; he nods in agreement. When the woman turns to talk to her neighbour on the other side, VESINET goes on nodding, until the woman turns back to him again.

NONANCOURT is talking with obvious pleasure to MME. A., when he suddenly grimaces and reaches under the table in the direction of his shoes. MME. A., embarrassed, gazes in front of her, as though she hasn't noticed anything.

Her husband, MR. A., is speaking with a very excitable woman, and looking very sad at the same time. Suddenly he sees. . . .

His wife glaring fixedly at him.

Believing that his tie has slipped again, MR. A. quickly raises his hand to his collar. In fact, the tie is still in place, but the brisk movement of his arm makes it fall again. MR. A. doesn't notice this and continues his conversation with the emotional lady.

BOBIN is fending off a child who is trying to take his glove away.

FADINARD is leaning amorously towards HELENE. Then he suddenly thinks of the hat again, looks at his watch in terror, apologises quickly to HELENE and gets to his feet.

No one notices that he is leaving. BOBIN continues singing; the other guests applaud.

FADINARD has so far managed to make his escape as far as the dance floor without being seen. He begins to brighten up as freedom seems possible.

Then suddenly he is stopped by the lady pianist and dragged towards the piano.

At this moment, NONANCOURT notices that FADINARD has disappeared and he gets to his feet and moves past BOBIN down the room.

FADINARD is desperately trying to escape from the pianist, who is urging him to choose which pieces she should play.

Everyone gets up from the banquet table and the singers fall silent. FADINARD pushes the pianist away from him, preparatory to flight. NONANCOURT appears, followed by the rest of the guests. NONANCOURT announces the dances and forms the guests into couples. Then he goes towards the piano.

The pianist ungraciously allows him to choose the music.

He holds the music for *The Lancers* in his hand.

He puts the score for the dance on the piano and rejoins the couples. Everyone takes his place for the dance: FADINARD with HELENE; VESINET opposite them with MME. B.; NONANCOURT with MME. A.; MR. A. opposite with MME. C.

The pianist secures her pince-nez and starts to play. A child comes and stands beside her to watch the movement of her hands.

The guests start to dance the first figure of *The Lancers* (*Still*).

They bow and curtsey.

The first figure comes to an end.

TAVERNIER is dozing in an armchair; suddenly he wakes up, leaps to his feet and goes to the window, from which he sees. . . .

An organ-grinder in the street.

He closes the window. ANAIS wakes up and complains. TAVERNIER sits down again.

The organ-grinder in the street.

TAVERNIER is rapidly becoming annoyed by the sound of the organ. ANAIS is also annoyed and they begin to argue.

The pianist at the reception is growing very angry with the child who is trying to run his hand along the keys.

The guests are dancing the second figure of *The Lancers*.

The figure continues. . . .

And finally comes to an end.

FELIX appears near the waiting carriages. He sees the coachmen and asks them a number of questions.

The child is now playing next to the pianist. The pianist pushes him away.

Nonancourt leads off on the third figure of the dance.

Nonancourt and Mme. C. bow gracefully to each other, then a sudden grimace contorts Nonancourt's face.

They return to their places and it is now the turn of Mr. and Mme. A. to lead off.

As they bow, however, Mr. A.'s tie falls.

Mme. A. makes a quick sign to her husband.

At this moment, however, Mr. A. turns to complete the figure and doesn't understand his wife's signal.

The pianist is still trying to push the child away from the piano.

Everyone is waiting for the dance to go on: it is Vesinet's turn, but he doesn't hear, though his partner, Mme. B., keeps up a constant barrage of conversation.

The child is still preventing the pianist from playing properly and she pushes him again. He still persists and the pianist pinches him, causing him to cry out.

The child starts crying, while we see the hands of the pianist as they start to play again.

The child's mother hears the crying and gets to her feet.

The mother goes to the pianist and starts to shout at her.

The pianist's hands stop playing.

The mother continues her argument with the pianist, while trying to comfort her child.

Vesinet, not hearing that the music has stopped, wants to go on dancing, in spite of desperate signals from the other guests.

The mother runs out of insults to hurl at the pianist, slaps the child and drags him away.

The pianist, very angry, starts to play again.

The quadrille starts again and Vesinet finishes his figure.

The door of the room opens and Felix comes in.

It is the turn of Fadinard and Helene; they bow to each other.

As they bow, Fadinard suddenly notices. . . .

Felix, looking very depressed, in a corner of the room.

Fadinard suddenly stops, the smile frozen on his face.

Nonancourt urges him to complete his figure.

Fadinard completes his turn and comes back to the same place and sees Felix again. He looks questioningly at him.

Felix raises his eyes heavenwards.

Fadinard understands the situation.

The fifth figure of the dance is just beginning.

FADINARD has dropped out of the dance and is questioning FELIX.

FELIX looks sad and makes a sign of acquiescence.

FADINARD begins to imagine the terrible things which might be happening to his house:

A window opens in FADINARD's house.

FADINARD starts to dance again.

An armchair flies out through the window.

The dance goes on.

FADINARD continues to dance, a horrified expression on his face as he thinks of. . . .

The armchair breaking up as it hits the pavement.

The dancers are taking up new positions.

FADINARD is lost in his anxiety.

Three chairs fly through the ground-floor window of FADINARD's house.

We return to the dancers and. . . .

The worried FADINARD.

We see a cupboard with a mirror. The mirror is suddenly smashed by a candelabra.

Return to the dancers.

FADINARD continues his reluctant parade.

The door of the house opens and a bed is shot out into the street.

Return to the dancers and . . .

FADINARD.

A group of passers-by jump on the bed, snatch the blankets and sheets off it, then break the bed up into small pieces and flee with their booty.

Return to the dancers.

FADINARD continues his dance, sighing deeply as his fears mount. . . .

All his furniture is suddenly thrown out through the door of his house (*Still*). As soon as it appears, it is carried away by passers-by.

Return to the dancers and. . . .

FADINARD.

A window breaks in FADINARD's house. TAVERNIER appears at the window and calls to the men in the street.

Return to the dancers.

FADINARD's house collapses completely in smoke.

The dancers pass by the bewildered FADINARD and take him with

55

them.

The quadrille turns.

FADINARD extricates himself.

He rejoins FELIX and they both quickly leave the room, leaving the door open behind them.

The quadrille is still continuing, when NONANCOURT notices that his son-in-law has escaped again.

Close to the carriages, FADINARD instructs FELIX:

TITLE: *Stop him from breaking everything; tell him I'm on the track of something very like the other.*

FADINARD gets in the first carriage and it drives off.

Inside the room, the guests begin to put their hats on.

In the carriage, FADINARD looks at the hat-box which CLARA has given him.

The address of Mme. Beauperthuis is written on the box.

FADINARD rouses the coachman and gives him the address.

NONANCOURT and VESINET appear, looking after the carriage.

TAVERNIER gets up from his chair; he is still smoking anxiously.

ANAIS tells him to be quiet.

TAVERNIER sits down again and stubs out his cigarette. . . .

In an ash-tray in which there are already about a dozen cigarette ends.

FADINARD's carriage stops in front of the Beauperthuis' house. He goes in.

Inside the drawing-room of the house: a screen is standing in the centre of the room. A hand throws a pair of trousers over it, then the hand appears again to take hold of a hot-water bottle.

FADINARD knocks on the door.

MR. BEAUPERTHUIS is pouring the hot water into a foot bath. The water is too hot and he hurriedly pulls his feet out and holds them in the air.

FADINARD waits outside. There is no reply, so he opens the door and goes into the room.

FADINARD hesitates in the doorway and sees. . . .

The screen standing in the centre of the room, from behind which BEAUPERTHUIS' naked feet protrude. The feet suddenly disappear.

BEAUPERTHUIS stands up in his bowl and looks round the screen.
FADINARD tries to explain what he is doing there. BEAUPERTHUIS
tells him to get out.
FADINARD's carriage is standing outside the house; the coachman
signals to someone.
NONANCOURT's carriage drives up and comes to a halt.
The whole of the wedding party draws up in front of BEAUPERTHUIS'
house.
Inside, BEAUPERTHUIS is still threatening FADINARD from behind the
screen.
FADINARD is still trying to explain his problem.

TITLE: *I am not a thief. I just want to ask your wife something.*

BEAUPERTHUIS doesn't want to listen and continues to threaten
FADINARD, who is rapidly growing impatient.
NONANCOURT is standing outside the house, surrounded by a number
of drunken wedding guests.
He looks up at. . . .
The house of BEAUPERTHUIS: it is very similar in appearance to
FADINARD's.
NONANCOURT advances towards the house.
FADINARD, in the meantime, is still trying to make BEAUPERTHUIS
understand what he wants.

TITLE: *I simply must have your wife's hat. If you won't give it to
me, I shall have to take it.*

BEAUPERTHUIS obviously thinks he is dealing with a madman. He
continues his threats and quickly dries his feet at the same time.
FADINARD hesitates for a moment, then suddenly turns and disappears
from the room.
BEAUPERTHUIS goes on wiping his feet and uttering threats, still
believing FADINARD to be in the room.
On the stairs NONANCOURT is supporting a rather drunken VESINET.

TITLE: *I know where I am. This is my son-in-law's flat. He must be
waiting for us.*

He goes in, while VESINET remains discreetly outside.
NONANCOURT, looking very drunk, goes in, and sees. . . .
The screen, BEAUPERTHUIS' slippers and trousers.

Smiling, NONANCOURT approaches.

FADINARD comes out of another door and crosses a corridor.

NONANCOURT sits down beside the screen and the socks suddenly disappear.

BEAUPERTHUIS quickly puts his socks on.

NONANCOURT puts the myrtle down and jokingly tugs the braces which hang from the trousers.

BEAUPERTHUIS is about to take his trousers when he suddenly sees them move. He mutters more threats and pulls at the trousers.

He and NONANCOURT pull from either side of the screen. NONANCOURT is finding this very funny indeed (*Still*).

FADINARD, meanwhile, is searching swiftly through a wardrobe for the hat.

Suddenly NONANCOURT looks down and sees. . . .

BEAUPERTHUIS' shoes, which are similar to his but much larger.

NONANCOURT quickly lets go of the braces and stares hard.

The braces spring back and hit BEAUPERTHUIS a stinging blow in the face.

Laughing, NONANCOURT removes the shoes and puts his own in their place.

FADINARD has turned out the whole of the wardrobe, but hasn't found anything. He runs out of the bedroom.

NONANCOURT has now put on BEAUPERTHUIS' shoes. He is enjoying this very much and grins slyly.

BEAUPERTHUIS has now put his trousers on and stretches his arm out from behind the screen.

He takes hold of NONANCOURT's shoes.

Very pleased with the trick he has played, NONANCOURT meets VESINET, who has just come into the room.

VESINET looks very uneasy about something and NONANCOURT leaves him immediately.

BEAUPERTHUIS, who has by now assumed NONANCOURT's shoes, stands up and immediately grimaces with pain. He looks at the shoes furiously, then leaps round the screen and falls on. . . .

VESINET, who collapses into his arms. BEAUPERTHUIS looks at him, then lets him fall and runs out of the room.

He goes into the bedroom and sees the disorder in which FADINARD has left the wardrobe.

NONANCOURT is on the staircase, calling to the other members of the wedding party.

FADINARD is in another bedroom pulling down great quantities of hats and hat-boxes.

BEAUPERTHUIS hears him from the corridor and dashes to the bedroom in spite of the pain which his shoes cause him.

He hurls himself at FADINARD, who jumps on a bed, bounces on it and dashes out of the room. BEAUPERTHUIS follows in hot pursuit. Meanwhile, the wedding-party has begun to gather in the drawing-room. NONANCOURT is ordering them to stand in certain positions and then starts to deliver a speech to them.

FADINARD hurries down the corridor. BEAUPERTHUIS follows. FADINARD hides behind a corner and sticks his foot out and trips BEAUPERTHUIS. When the latter gets up he pulls a bench across the corridor, blocking it.

FADINARD sticks his head round the drawing-room door, then pulls it back again. The door closes, making the guests turn round, but there is nothing to see.

FADINARD runs down the corridor, comes to the bench and jumps over it. BEAUPERTHUIS follows closely, still grimacing with pain from the shoes.

FADINARD runs into the bedroom and hastily begins to search among the hats again. BEAUPERTHUIS comes in and FADINARD turns round. BEAUPERTHUIS pulls out two pistols from a drawer and advances on FADINARD, who gives himself up.

BEAUPERTHUIS puts the pistols in his pockets and starts pushing back his sleeves.

He seizes FADINARD by the throat, while the latter simply pushes his hands in BEAUPERTHUIS' pockets, takes out the pistols and sticks them into his assailant's midriff. BEAUPERTHUIS recoils hurriedly.

FADINARD keeps him covered with the pistols.

TITLE: *Sir, you could be of immense service to me, with very little trouble to yourself.*

BEAUPERTHUIS seems very doubtful about this, but FADINARD starts his story:

TITLE: *Let me tell you a story and you will see why you must give me your wife's hat . . .*

FADINARD starts his story.

We see FADINARD approaching his horse which is holding the straw hat in its mouth. FADINARD takes the hat from the horse and laughs. TAVERNIER and ANAIS appear from behind a bush. FADINARD pulls back the bush to reveal ANAIS in bodice and petticoat, her head buried in her hands. FADINARD wags his finger at them, then holds out the hat. TAVERNIER looks at ANAIS, then they both look at the hat.

Smiling, FADINARD goes on with his story.

BEAUPERTHUIS laughs and questions him more closely.

FADINARD, seeing that his captive is in a good humour, begins to relate more details of his adventure.

TAVERNIER indicates that ANAIS is married by pointing to her wedding-ring. FADINARD laughs and TAVERNIER jumps at him, but FADINARD knocks him to the ground. ANAIS throws herself on her recumbent lover, then kneels in front of FADINARD. TAVERNIER also scrambles to his knees. ANAIS puts on the torn hat, but realises she cannot go back home dressed in this way. They beg FADINARD to find them another hat and give him a sample of the old one. FADINARD leaves them, still thanking him on their knees.

FADINARD tells his story and laughs.

BEAUPERTHUIS suddenly stops smiling.

FADINARD continues joking, unconscious of his captive's change of humour.

BEAUPERTHUIS is now thinking very hard about. . . .

ANAIS' hat.

We see ANAIS wearing the hat.

Then TAVERNIER.

Then ANAIS with half-eaten hat.

TAVERNIER twisting his moustaches.

The half-eaten hat.

BEAUPERTHUIS looking grimmer.

FADINARD continues his funny story. Then he stops and looks worried as he sees the changed expression on BEAUPERTHUIS' face.

BEAUPERTHUIS, now overtaken by some terrible anger, gets to his feet. FADINARD, bewildered, backs away and knocks against some furniture, causing a photograph to fall. He picks it up.

It is a photograph of ANAIS, wearing the straw hat, with BEAUPERTHUIS, her husband.

He stares anxiously at it. . . .

The photograph.

Now very frightened, he looks at it again.

BEAUPERTHUIS has at last understood the situation exactly.

FADINARD and BEAUPERTHUIS look at each other, both speechless. Then FADINARD tries to say something, but BEAUPERTHUIS makes him shut up immediately. Then FADINARD makes as though to leave.

NONANCOURT continues his speech. All the wedding-guests are weeping.

BEAUPERTHUIS, in a truly terrifying fit of rage, advances on FADINARD, takes the pistols from him, which FADINARD surrenders without fuss.

BEAUPERTHUIS addresses FADINARD:

TITLE: *You told me that this man and . . . this woman were at your house. What is your address?*

FADINARD pretends that he cannot remember.

He turns to run and BEAUPERTHUIS follows after in hot pursuit.

NONANCOURT has finished his speech. He leads HELENE towards the door of the bedroom. The doors opens and FADINARD and BEAUPERTHUIS appear.

NONANCOURT looks bewildered as FADINARD introduces BEAUPERTHUIS. FADINARD turns to the wedding-guests.

TITLE: *You are quite mistaken. This is not my house here. . . . Let us leave. . . .*

He pushes all the guests outside. In the meantime, BEAUPERTHUIS has cornered NONANCOURT.

BEAUPERTHUIS asks NONANCOURT:

TITLE: *Where does this gentleman live?*

FADINARD interrupts by pushing NONANCOURT away and making desperate signs to him not to tell. NONANCOURT makes the same sign to BEAUPERTHUIS, then picks his myrtle up again.

They go out, leaving BEAUPERTHUIS alone. He goes to get his hat, then sees VESINET.

VESINET has seen nothing of recent events; he is still trying to unblock his ear trumpet. BEAUPERTHUIS asks him what he is doing. VESINET merely grins and BEAUPERTHUIS grows angry. VESINET shows him the ear trumpet and BEAUPERTHUIS puts it to VESINET's ear.

BEAUPERTHUIS shouts into the trumpet, but VESINET only seems to hear when BEAUPERTHUIS isn't shouting. He looks at the trumpet again, then BEAUPERTHUIS takes it and examines it. He takes a paper-knife from the table.

He extricates the ball of papier-mâché from the trumpet.

BEAUPERTHUIS holds the trumpet out to VESINET, who listens. He smiles happily when he realises he can hear. BEAUPERTHUIS asks him where FADINARD lives and VESINET is only too pleased to reply.

BEAUPERTHUIS takes his hat and quickly leaves.

The wedding-guests are climbing into the carriages outside the house. Suddenly BEAUPERTHUIS appears, brandishing his pistols.

FADINARD, looking very anxious, sees BEAUPERTHUIS run past him. He is pondering this sight when the happy VESINET appears beside him and says:

TITLE: *My trumpet's been unblocked! I could hear what the gentleman was asking me. . . . I gave him your address.*

FADINARD is terrified. He throws the trumpet on the ground and makes as though to strike VESINET.

He runs quickly to kiss HELENE good-bye and says to NONANCOURT:

TITLE: *Go to my house. I'll join you later.*

And he dashes away.

BEAUPERTHUIS is still managing to run with reasonable speed, in spite of his tight shoes.

FADINARD is running after him.

BEAUPERTHUIS stops a cab; two policemen watch him as he gets into the cab and drives off. FADINARD appears, speaks to the policemen and all three dash in the direction taken by the cab.

Inside the cab, BEAUPERTHUIS grips his pistols tightly.

FADINARD leads the policemen after him.

BEAUPERTHUIS urges the coachman to greater speed.

The coachman turns round and sees. . . .

The pistols in BEAUPERTHUIS' hands.

He stops the cab, climbs down rapidly and flees. BEAUPERTHUIS gets out of the cab and starts running again, but his tight shoes hinder him and he is caught by FADINARD and the two policemen. He has already concealed the pistols in his pockets.

FADINARD urges the policemen to search him; they find the pistols and lead BEAUPERTHUIS away. The coachman joins them.

The group turns the corner of the street and disappears. Then we see FADINARD reappear, having given the others the slip. He sets off quickly in the opposite direction. Then the policemen, dragging BEAUPERTHUIS between them, also reappear, followed by the coachman.

The policemen watch FADINARD running away. The policemen hesitate, then start to lead BEAUPERTHUIS away. The coachman protests. The arguing group turns a corner. A mother and a child appear; the child laughs at something he sees round the corner. The mother tries to pull him along, but the child continues laughing at some comic scene he can see. The mother slaps him and leads him away.

The clock in FADINARD's bedroom strikes nine o'clock.

Close to the clock, we see TAVERNIER's hand stubbing out a cigarette in an ash-tray.

The ash-tray is already overflowing with cigarette ends.

Outside FADINARD's house; it is growing dark. The coaches of the wedding-guests arrive one by one.

NONANCOURT is ringing angrily at the door.

FELIX, who has been sleeping in the drawing-room, wakes up and goes out.

TAVERNIER gets to his feet and listens.

The front door opens and FELIX peers out. NONANCOURT asks him:

TITLE: *Is my son-in-law here?*

FELIX shakes his head. NONANCOURT looks very puzzled, then insists on coming into the house. FELIX stops him and NONANCOURT starts arguing with him.

NONANCOURT's angry face.

TITLE: *My master has forbidden me to allow anyone to enter while that woman is still here.*

FELIX prattles on to NONANCOURT.

ANAIS is lying down.

NONANCOURT is thunderstruck by what he hears; he turns towards the wedding-guests.

The wedding-guests stare back at him.

NONANCOURT makes a furious speech from the front of the house:

TITLE: *A woman in his house! On his wedding night! This is too much. I'm taking my daughter back!*

The wedding-guests approve, though HELENE wants to protest; she is silenced by BOBIN.
NONANCOURT goes on:

TITLE: *Since everything is finished, let us take back the wedding presents and my daughter's trousseau.*

The wedding-guests applaud his plan.
FELIX tries to stop them coming in, but NONANCOURT opens the door and forces his way in with VESINET and BOBIN.

Meanwhile BEAUPERTHUIS has reappeared, shouting at the policemen and straightening his clothes. He runs off, watched by the policemen and the coachman.

BOBIN comes out of the house carrying an armful of packages. Then he goes back into the house again.
Upstairs NONANCOURT is directing VESINET to carry certain articles of furniture away. They divide the last of the presents between them.
TAVERNIER, intrigued, looks through a chink next to the door. From his viewpoint, we see NONANCOURT going out carrying the present brought by VESINET, then VESINET loaded with other presents.
TAVERNIER is utterly astonished. What kind of house is this? He makes a sign to ANAIS not to move.
FADINARD appears out of breath in the street. He hurries up to HELENE.
He kisses her and apologises. He then glances anxiously behind her and sees. . . . .
NONANCOURT, VESINET and BOBIN loaded with furniture and presents. He goes up to them, but NONANCOURT has already started to pass the presents to the guests.
He tries to stop NONANCOURT, who pushes him away and says:

TITLE: *It's all finished. . . . We're leaving.*

The guests have taken all the presents; only VESINET's package remains. NONANCOURT is carrying it off, but FADINARD holds him back. NONANCOURT and FADINARD start arguing. They start to tug at the package, one at the lid, the other at the box itself.

VESINET runs towards them.

He tries to stop them tugging at the package, but only succeeds in opening it. FADINARD stares inside it and sees. . . . .

An Italian straw hat.

FADINARD, quite astonished, questions VESINET, who replies:

TITLE: *Yes, it's my wedding present.*

FADINARD hardly seems able to believe it. Then he draws himself up, a changed man.

He embraces HELENE, then dances and shouts for joy. He embraces NONANCOURT and VESINET, then turns again to HELENE.

Meanwhile, VESINET has taken the hat out of the box to show it to HELENE. NONANCOURT automatically puts the lid back on.

FADINARD, mad with joy, leaves HELENE and runs towards NONANCOURT.

TITLE: *Everything's going to be all right. Wait for me a minute.*

He seizes the hat-box — now empty — and runs into the house.

NONANCOURT and the guests watch him disappear, obviously thinking that FADINARD is mad; they start to leave.

But three policemen are watching the group closely; they see. . . .

The guests, partly hidden in the street shadows, taking away parcels and furniture.

The policemen consult among themselves, then run towards the guests.

They start to question the guests.

They ask for VESINET's papers and he tries to explain what is happening. The policemen become increasingly suspicious. VESINET takes out his ear trumpet and is immediately arrested.

The policemen then see. . . .

The guests loaded with packets and the myrtle.

The policemen arrest everybody, except HELENE. FELIX appears just in time to see them led away.

Upstairs, FADINARD has joined TAVERNIER and ANAIS. He tries to calm the latter, very tactlessly:

TITLE: *Your husband knows all about the hat! He's coming here. . . .*

TAVERNIER and ANAIS look terrified; ANAIS gets to her feet. TAVERNIER advances threateningly on FADINARD.

65

FADINARD pushes TAVERNIER back, smiles reassuringly:

TITLE: *But he won't be able to make head or tail of it. Because I've found a similar hat.*

TAVERNIER and ANAIS look on anxiously.

FADINARD triumphantly opens the hat-box and holds it towards the couple, so that he cannot see the inside. The box is, of course, quite empty.

FADINARD cannot understand what has happened as TAVERNIER starts to threaten him again, while ANAIS has an attack of hysterics.

The wedding-guests are herded into the police station. VESINET is holding the straw hat (*Still*).

BEAUPERTHUIS appears running down a street. He stops because of his shoes, then sets off again.

FADINARD dashes out of the room and TAVERNIER and ANAIS follow. BEAUPERTHUIS is running down the street, looking for the door of FADINARD's house. HELENE and FELIX, who have been left behind, see him. FADINARD is coming down the stairs, when he suddenly sees BEAUPERTHUIS and runs back up again.

FADINARD closes the door of the drawing-room. FADINARD explains what is happening to TAVERNIER and ANAIS. They hide one on each side of the door, so that they are hidden as the two halves are flung open, as BEAUPERTHUIS enters, to be received very correctly by FADINARD.

While BEAUPERTHUIS is searching the room. . . .

FADINARD goes up to the door behind which TAVERNIER is hiding and kicks it hard. . . .

BEAUPERTHUIS bounds into the bedroom.

He comes through the bedroom doorway.

FADINARD makes TAVERNIER and ANAIS leave immediately. He aims another kick at TAVERNIER, who turns round, thinks better of it, and dashes off.

BEAUPERTHUIS looks under the bed. FADINARD comes in and kicks him, BEAUPERTHUIS turns round and FADINARD bows, telling him to look everywhere. He goes out, leaving BEAUPERTHUIS to look in all the cupboards.

At the police station, VESINET is being interrogated. Most of the women guests are weeping.

FADINARD goes down the stairs to see what has happened to the straw hat.

He comes out of the house, watched by FELIX and HELENE.

In front of another part of the house façade, ANAIS has broken down again. She says to TAVERNIER:

TITLE: *I can't go back without the hat. . . . My husband will guess everything.*

FADINARD goes up to them. He turns to ask FELIX what has happened. FELIX points to. . . .

The police station, where NONANCOURT and BOBIN can be seen in the shadows.

TAVERNIER thinks for a moment, then cries out:

TITLE: *I'll go and get the hat. I know the inspector.*

He dashes away, keeping an eye on FADINARD, who looks as though he is about to kick him again.

The wedding-guests are trying to exculpate themselves at the police station. They are required to place their belongings on a table, including the myrtle. VESINET tries to pick it up again but a policeman pushes him away.

FADINARD runs to HELENE, who refuses to speak to him.

BEAUPERTHUIS comes back into the drawing-room and looks behind the door, then starts to search for his wife in every corner.

TAVERNIER is talking to the inspector's assistant; he is given permission to take the hat. VESINET tries to protest, but a policeman tells him to shut up. TAVERNIER goes to the window.

FADINARD and ANAIS see. . . .

TAVERNIER at the window.

BEAUPERTHUIS crosses the landing and starts to come down the stairs.

TAVERNIER throws the hat which catches on a street lamp (*Still*).

ANAIS and FADINARD panic. They can hear. . . .

The limping steps of BEAUPERTHUIS on the staircase.

FADINARD makes ANAIS hide behind HELENE, then disappears himself.

TAVERNIER appears and tries to unhook the hat.

FADINARD runs to the door.

An umbrella has been left behind by one of the guests. FADINARD picks it up. BEAUPERTHUIS appears and FADINARD greets him, holding out his hand as though it is raining. He opens the umbrella and holds it over the astonished BEAUPERTHUIS.

Anais is hiding behind Helene, who is looking at her scornfully. Helene is going to say something, but Anais pleads with her to be quiet.

Tavernier and a lamp-lighter are looking up at the hat.

Fadinard is holding Beauperthuis back to ask him if he has found anything. He holds the umbrella over him and leads him away from Anais. Beauperthuis is still looking carefully around him. Fadinard treads on his foot, causing even greater pain to Beauperthuis.

Tavernier is sawing at the hat cord with his sword.

Anais is trembling with fear behind Helene, who has at last understood her position. Anais thanks her.

The sword passes through the cord. The hat falls.

Fadinard, who is watching events closely, suddenly pretends to bend down and the umbrella collapses over Beauperthuis' head.

Tavernier runs across to Anais with the hat. She immediately runs away, and Tavernier follows. Helene is left alone.

Beauperthuis angrily limps away from Fadinard.

Anais calls a cab and climbs into it. Tavernier follows her; he is standing smiling in front of the cab, when the hand of Anais suddenly appears and slaps his face.

Vesinet is still arguing with the inspector, who, exasperated, sends the whole wedding party away.

A breathless Fadinard comes up to Helene, who says to him:

Title: *Everything has been explained to me. I forgive you.*

Fadinard, delighted, sweeps Helene up in his arms and goes into the house with her.

The wedding-guests come out of the police station and appear, carrying the presents, in front of Fadinard's house.

Nonancourt calls them together, then looks around for Helene. He sees. . . .

That the door of Fadinard's house has been closed, but that the bride's train is caught in the door.

Nonancourt and the guests stare as they see. . . .

The door open again.

Fadinard appears in the doorway, but Helene takes up her stance in front of him and says. . . .

Title: *Nothing is finished, daddy. I will explain everything. My husband is a gallant man.*

68

NONANCOURT and the guests stare in front of them, astonished. FELIX comes up to them and takes the presents back.

FADINARD and HELENE make farewell gestures, then go back into the house. FELIX carries the presents in after them.

NONANCOURT is completely at a loss. He finally lets go of his presents, which FELIX then carries into the house, and the rest of the guests do the same.

They turn to go.

Back at BEAUPERTHUIS' house, ANAIS is just getting into bed. BEAUPERTHUIS comes into the room and advances towards her.

He looks very angry, but very close to him, on a table, we can see. . . .

The Italian straw hat.

ANAIS glances towards it.

BEAUPERTHUIS cannot understand. He must be dreaming!

The guests start to climb back into the carriages which are standing beneath the street lamps.

BEAUPERTHUIS tries to speak, but ANAIS shows that she is tired and silences him. He gives in and looks at. . . .

The Italian straw hat.

All this is quite beyond him. He sits down and removes his shoes, uttering a cry of pain as he does so. He looks at his shoes, still not understanding why they hurt him so much, and holds them in his hands.

NONANCOURT and BOBIN are together in a carriage.

NONANCOURT looks at his shoes with deep satisfaction.

BOBIN suddenly shouts out with joy. He has just found his second glove in his pocket.

MME. B. is still talking to the sleeping VESINET.

MME. A. looks at her sleeping husband. She speaks to him. He jumps and reaches up to see if his tie is still in place. It falls down again.

In the marital bedroom, FADINARD goes up to HELENE and kisses her, but. . . .

A hand is seen knocking on the door.

TAVERNIER comes into the room and apologises: he has forgotten. . . .

His képi.

He takes it, but in the doorway he turns round and extends both hands to FADINARD and thanks him; he salutes HELENE and goes out. As he goes, he glances behind, fearing another kick. FADINARD, who had nothing of the sort in his head, takes up a threatening posture. TAVERNIER retreats and FADINARD comes back to HELENE.

We see the wheels of the guests' coaches moving away.
BOBIN's two gloved hands near NONANCOURT's crossed legs.
VESINET's ear trumpet falls on to his knees, while MME. B.'s hand fidgets as she talks.
MME. A.'s hand reaches up to put her husband's tie in place.
BEAUPERTHUIS' hand holds the Italian straw hat, while, in the other, he holds the shoes.

The clock shows midnight.
Beside the clock in FADINARD's bedroom, HELENE's hands can be seen laying down the orange blossom crown on a shelf. FADINARD's hands appear and place a glass globe over it.

CREDITS:

Scenario, adaptation and dialogue	Charles Spaak and Jean Renoir
Directed by	Jean Renoir
Produced by	Réalisations d'Art Cinématographique (R.A.C.) (Frank Rollmer, Albert Pinkovitch and Alexandre)
Music	Joseph Kosma
Lyrics	Vincent Telly and A. Valsien
(Si tu veux, Marguerite...)	(as sung by Fragson)
Technical Adviser	Carl Koch
Assistant Director	Jacques Becker
1st Operator	Christian Matras
2nd Operator	Claude Renoir
Set Designer	Eugène Lourié
Sound Engineer	Joseph de Bretagne
Orchestra	Vuillermoz (arranged by Smyth)
Editor	Marguerite Renoir

CAST:

von Rauffenstein	Erich von Stroheim
Maréchal	Jean Gabin
de Bœldieu	Pierre Fresnay
Rosenthal	Marcel Dalio
The Actor	Julien Carette
The Engineer	Gaston Modot
The Teacher	Jean Dasté
French Soldier	Georges Peclet
English Officer	Jacques Becker
Demolder	Sylvain Itkine
Elsa	Dita Parlo
Others	W. Florian, C. Sainval, etc.
Shot during	Winter 1936-1937
Studios	Billancourt and Eclair
Locations	In Alsace, the outskirts of Neuf-Brisach, in Haut-Koenigsburg and the barracks of Colmar

Titles: then the legend: THE EVENTS DESCRIBED IN THIS
FILM TOOK PLACE DURING THE WAR OF 1914–1918.
In the officers' mess of an air squadron on the French front,
camera tracks into close-up of a gramophone with a horn,
playing the music of the song ' Frou-Frou, Frou-Frou . . .', also
being hummed by a man's voice. Pan up to Lieutenant MARE-
CHAL who is bending over the gramophone as though hypno-
tized by the spinning record. He seems lost in distant memories,
as he sings the chorus.
MARECHAL close-up: *Frou-Frou . . . Frou-Frou-Frou . . . Tra la la
la . . . la . . . la . . . Frou-Frou . . .*

MARECHAL is a mechanic whom circumstance has made an
officer. He is wearing a uniform, his képi pushed slightly
towards the back of his head, his airman's jacket unbuttoned,
his scarf loosely knotted round his neck. It is winter, one of
the terrible winters of that war, and this officers' mess behind
the French front is not very warm. Behind MARECHAL in a
blurred background, a few officers are seen sitting at tables
near the bar, talking together. Suddenly, MARECHAL snaps out
of his reverie and lifts his head. Camera follows him towards
the bar, where he speaks to a soldier, HALPHEN.
MARECHAL: *Hey! I say, waiter, are you going to Epernay?*
HALPHEN: *Yes, of course.*
MARECHAL: *When?*
HALPHEN: *In half-an-hour.*
MARECHAL, near him now: *In the lorry?* HALPHEN nods. *Well then,
be a sport . . . try to wait for me.*
HALPHEN: *Joséphine.*
MARECHAL, as though it were obvious: *Well naturally . . . Joséphine.*
HALPHEN smiling: *You're not the only one.*
MARECHAL shrugging: *I don't care!*

Pan towards the door, revealing the other officers talking and
drinking together at different tables; the record plays the same
song. Captain RINGIS bursts in. Camera pans back with him as

he spots MARECHAL and goes over to speak with him.

RINGIS: *Hey, Maréchal . . . there's a fellow here from the General Staff. . . . You've got to show him around.*

MARECHAL disappointed: *A bloke from the General Staff? . . . Hmmm, well. . . . He's come at the wrong time.*

RINGIS ironically: *Joséphine?* Sceptically. *Where are you going to get with all that?*

MARECHAL follows him as far as the door.

MARECHAL: *All right. She'll wait. At your service, Captain!*

They go out together. Camera stays for the moment on the door. There is noise from the room and the record of ' *Frou-Frou* ' finishes playing. Pan back to the bar covered with the squadron flags. Camera holds and closes on the large sign on the bar, which has three drawings on it: a hunter, a crocodile, and a skull sketched round the following text: SQUADRON M F 902 — ALCOHOL KILLS — ALCOHOL DRIVES PEOPLE MAD — THE SQUADRON LEADER DRINKS IT. Captain RINGIS, followed by MARECHAL, comes in through the open door of his office. Camera tracks back and pans to the ' fellow from the General Staff.' This man wears a monocle and seems very haughty. He is waiting for them and examining the enlargement of an aerial photograph. He readjusts his monocle to have a better look . . . when RINGIS and MARECHAL come into shot. MARECHAL gives a military salute.

RINGIS to MARECHAL: *Captain de Bœldieu, of the Divisional Staff.*

MARECHAL saluting: *Maréchal.*

BŒLDIEU icily shaking the photograph: *I say, Monsieur Maréchal, do you know this photograph?*

He holds it out to MARECHAL, who looks at it.

MARECHAL: *Oh, yes, Captain . . . Ricord took it when he was with me.*

BŒLDIEU: *And is this Monsieur Ricord around?*

MARECHAL: *He's on leave.*

BŒLDIEU: *Of course!*

BŒLDIEU goes over to MARECHAL and points at the photograph. Behind them, Captain RINGIS stands on tip-toe to look at the document.

BŒLDIEU: *It's that grey spot which worries me. . . . There, below the road.*

RINGIS interrupting: *It's not a road, it's a canal.*

MARECHAL: *Is it? I thought it was some railway lines.*

BŒLDIEU ironically: *What touching unanimity! . . . This precise detail gives one a fine idea of the perfection of our photographic equipment.*

MARECHAL shrugging: *Well . . . it was misty that day.*

BŒLDIEU: *I would like to resolve this enigma.*

RINGIS: *As you wish. . . . I'll ask for a fighter.* As he speaks, he turns to pick up the telephone. *Hello! Hello! Give me the fighter squadron.*

> MARECHAL looks at the photograph again, then gives it to BŒLDIEU, and gets ready to leave.

MARECHAL: *I'll put on my stuff then, Captain.*

> He goes out. Camera stays on RINGIS and BŒLDIEU.

RINGIS: *What would you like to put on? A flying suit or a goat-skin?*

BŒLDIEU still examining the photograph: *I have no preference. . . . Flying suits smell rather and goatskins shed hairs.*

RINGIS on the telephone again: *Yes. . . . Give me the fighter squadron, please.*

> Through an open door of a German officers' mess, the German commander enters, followed by a few officers. Camera tracks back to show a part of the room, which is much the same as the officers' mess of Squadron M F 902. There is hardly any difference: a table set for a meal, a bar, bottles. The gramophone is playing a Viennese waltz by Strauss. But there are no drawings on the walls. Commander VON RAUFFENSTEIN, who has just come in, is still wearing his fighter-pilot's uniform. His back straight, his heels together, he takes a glass of spirits and downs it in one gulp, then he scratches his ear. He is small compared with the other officers surrounding him to congratulate him. His type is the Prussian squire: well-bred, strict, hard-faced. He speaks in German, as do the rest.

RAUFFENSTEIN to his orderly: *Herr Bredow, take a car and go and look in the direction of the sugar plant. . . . I shot down a Caudron. . . . If they are officers, invite them to lunch.*

BREDOW: *Very good, Commander.*

RAUFFENSTEIN to one of his officers: *Herr Fressler, this is the moment to distinguish yourself. . . . You are going to concoct for us one of your famous fruit punches. . . .* Pause. *We ought to celebrate my second kill.*

The other officers raise their glasses and surround him and toast his victory. RAUFFENSTEIN drinks at one gulp, bending backwards to do so.

FRESSLER: *With pleasure, Commander.* He turns to the barman. *Give me three bottles of Moselle, two of Rhine wine, one of champagne, a half of Martell, one box of pineapple, three lemons . . . and sugar, of course.*

During this list spoken partly off shot, pan along the bar to end on photographs of women pinned to the wall. Cut back to the door: BREDOW comes in again and salutes. The music of the Strauss waltz is loud.

BREDOW: *There's two officers. . . . One of them's got a bullet in his arm; I've just taken him to the ambulance.*

Shot of the whole room, taken slightly from above. After a time, BREDOW enters again, followed by BŒLDIEU, then by MARECHAL, whose arm is in a sling. BŒLDIEU is always pretty immaculate. MARECHAL seems tired; he is wearing a jersey, his jacket is over his shoulders, his head is bare, his arm in a sling. RAUFFENSTEIN makes a sign to BŒLDIEU to come in and clicks his heels together. His officers do the same. BŒLDIEU gives them a dignified salute.

RAUFFENSTEIN in strongly-accented French: *Captain von Rauffenstein, Commander of Squadron 21. . . . We are very honoured to receive French guests.* Introducing his men. *My officers. . . . Orderly. . . . Their coats.*

BŒLDIEU after saluting: *Captain de Bœldieu.*

They shake hands. RAUFFENSTEIN turns towards MARECHAL and bows more formally. He is not very interested in this second Frenchman, immediately guessing that MARECHAL is not a career officer.

[Long shot. RAUFFENSTEIN turns towards the barman. Hubbub.

RAUFFENSTEIN: *And your punch?*

MULLER: *May I serve you some?*

RAUFFENSTEIN: *Please do.*][1]

A German soldier removes BŒLDIEU's overcoat while RAUFFENSTEIN leads everyone to the table.

---

[1] Square brackets denote a cut in the final version of the film for the screen.

76

RAUFFENSTEIN, in French: *Gentlemen, please be seated.*

RAUFFENSTEIN seats BŒLDIEU on his right and indicates the chair on his left to MARECHAL. Everybody sits down. In a medium close-up, RAUFFENSTEIN leans over to BŒLDIEU and speaks in French to him, putting on his monocle.

RAUFFENSTEIN: *I used to know a de Bœldieu . . . a Count de Bœldieu. . . .*

BŒLDIEU interested: *Ah, yes. . . . That was my cousin Edmond de Bœldieu, military attaché in Berlin. . . .*

RAUFFENSTEIN in English: *He was a marvellous rider. . . .*

BŒLDIEU in English: *Yes, in the good old days. . . .*

Slow pan to MARECHAL and the GERMAN OFFICER sitting next to him. MARECHAL is looking at his plate.

GERMAN OFFICER: *Aren't you hungry? . . . You're not eating?*

MARECHAL: *Yes. . . . Yes . . . but . . .* He shows his arm in the sling. *I can't cut the meat. . . .*

GERMAN OFFICER: *Allow me.*

He takes MARECHAL's knife and fork at once and cuts up his meat for him.

MARECHAL: *You speak French well.*

GERMAN OFFICER: *I once worked at Gnome, in Lyons.*

MARECHAL joyfully: *No joking! Me too, I'm a mechanic! . . .*

All heads turn in the direction of the door which they have heard opening. Cut to a German soldier coming into the room carrying a wreath. Camera tracks before this imposing wreath in close-up to make visible the words written in gilt on the ribbon around it: TO CAPTAIN DE CRUSSOL, FRENCH AIR FORCE, SHOT DOWN IN FLAMES ON MARCH 12TH 1914. . . . FROM THE OFFICERS OF THE GERMAN SQUADRON F S 21. Quick cut back to the group shot at the moment when RAUFFENSTEIN rises abruptly at the table.

RAUFFENSTEIN stiffly: *Gentlemen . . .* To BŒLDIEU. *I apologise for this . . . coincidence.*

At a sign from RAUFFENSTEIN, the music from the gramophone is stopped. All the officers stand to attention in front of the table. Each bows his head.

RAUFFENSTEIN after a moment of silence: *May the earth lie lightly on our brave enemy.* All remain still (*Still*). *Thank you, gentlemen.*

Everybody sits down again. The Viennese waltz is replayed on the gramophone and, while everyone is eating, an old soldier appears at the door. He salutes, clicking his heels together. He is a military policeman without flashes, shown in medium close-up.

POLICEMAN in German: *Military police. I have come to take the officer prisoners into custody.*

Dissolve on sound of clicking heels becoming sound of train wheels.

Through the windows of a railway carriage, the countryside is seen as the train passes. There is snow on the ground; the sky is low and grey. Train sounds and music. The original screenplay gave the following details: it is the start of captivity, seen through the windows of a railway carriage: the fields and the forests go by. Winter landscape, frozen and mournful. Patches of snow here and there. It is far away, very far away. . . . The train stops at last. Close on the railway sign:

KRIEGSGEFANGENEN LAGER Nr 17
HALLBACH
OFFIZIERSLAGER C.K.VII

Very quick shot of a grey, drab, sad building, overlooking a barracks yard. In the distance, a detachment of some fifty hang-dog Germans marches by in step.

Pan past the prisoners in the camp, who stand in a group waiting for the convoy of new arrivals. Camera stays on the still group of new prisoners, whose faces show an extreme fatigue. There are French, English, Russian and Belgian army officers. In the middle of this group, BŒLDIEU and MARECHAL are brought out by the camera tracking towards them. They stand side by side, the first looking very haughty, the second tired and yawning in a vulgar way. Seeing MARECHAL's 'incorrect' behaviour, BŒLDIEU looks at him with a certain contempt from behind his monocle. . . . Resume long shot: a German officer barks out a dry and brutal order, an unintelligible yell that makes everybody freeze. This German is the Feldwebel KRANTZ. All the prisoners turn to look at him curiously, as he produces a piece of paper. Before he reads it, he gives the French officers in particular a hard look. He reads slowly in French with a strong German accent.

KRANTZ: *In the name of Camp Commander Krauss, officers will be treated with all due regard to their rank. Commander Krauss, however, reminds you that you are subject here to the authority of the German law. You will therefore, as of to-day, learn German discipline and obey it.*

Camera begins on KRANTZ at the start of his speech, then pans along the German soldiers and the grave faces of the prisoners.

KRANTZ off: *Every German soldier working in a camp has the right to give you orders and you will execute these without complaint. You will salute all officers according to German army regulations. In case of attempts at escape, the sentries are ordered to shoot any officer discovered outside the camp boundaries.* Pan continues past BŒLDIEU's quizzical look and MARECHAL's intrigued one. *It is strictly prohibited to dress in a slovenly manner, to congregate in groups, to speak loudly and disparagingly of the German nation, to leave your quarters after curfew, to communicate either verbally or in writing with civilians outside the camp.* Cut to KRANTZ who continues to read aloud from his text. *It is strictly prohibited to talk to the guards.* He folds up the paper he has been reading and places it in his pocket; he continues in jerky French, repeating the words by heart. *Now, gentlemen, we are going to make you proceed to an office for a small formality.*

Long shot of the barracks yard. The guards make the prisoners march towards a building. Cut to a group of long-time prisoners who have been watching the scene.

ONE OF THEM: *Hey, new boys!*

ANOTHER: *Hey, look, tip 'em off!*

They all begin to sing the tune of ' *Ange pur, ange radieux,*' improvising the words in chorus. In the group are certain characters who will be important later, ROSENTHAL, THE ENGINEER, and THE ACTOR.

THE GROUP: *Ange pur, ange radieux. . . . Conceal your gold. . . . Hide your watches. . . .*

THE ACTOR advancing: *Oh, yes, hide it well!*

Immediately, the German guards jump on these disturbers of the peace and break up the group. Pan towards BŒLDIEU and MARECHAL who are queuing in front of a shed.

MARECHAL: *Hey, what are they getting at?*

BŒLDIEU, as though it were self-evident: *They are telling us to hide our gold.*

KRANTZ intervenes and gets rid of the last of the singers.

Camera stays on the group containing BŒLDIEU and MARECHAL as they get ready to enter the control shed. Medium close-up of a German soldier searching a struggling English officer rather roughly in the control shed.

ENGLISH OFFICER in English: *Hands away! Don't touch me! . . . Do you want my watch? . . . Pick it up now.*

The officer takes his watch out of his pocket and throws it onto the floor. Tilt quickly down to show the watch being smashed under the heel of the officer's boot. The German soldier bends over, and camera follows his gestures as he picks up the broken watch and puts it on a ledger where another soldier examines it and enters it in his book . . . during this, a hubbub of voices:

VARIOUS VOICES: *Ah! Leave me alone! . . . Let me be! Those are mine! . . .*

The German soldier motions over MARECHAL who goes over, followed by BŒLDIEU.

GERMAN SOLDIER: *Look out!*

He feels the arm of MARECHAL that is in a sling, then rifles his clothes.

MARECHAL: *Sorry, mate. . . . Got nothing on me. . . . If I'd known I was coming here, I'd have brought along a little cash. . . . Sorry!*

GERMAN SOLDIER: *Nicht!*

After searching MARECHAL, the soldier turns to BŒLDIEU and gets ready to rifle the pockets of his fur coat. BŒLDIEU, very haughty with his monocle in his eye, stops the soldier and says in a glacial voice (*Still*).

BŒLDIEU: *But, I say, what sort of carry on is this?*

The soldier finds a cigarette case, opens it, then lifts his head.

A GERMAN N.C.O. in French: *I'm sorry, Captain, but it's our duty to search you. . . . That's war!*

BŒLDIEU very coldly: *I could not agree with you more, but there are polite ways of doing it. . . . Otherwise, I will be obliged to mention the matter to the Commander of the whole army corps.*

In their room, the French prisoners surround one of their number, Rosenthal, who is unpacking a large parcel that he has just received. A German guard watches it all carefully. Pan across the room in which several similar groups of men stand about.

A Guard: *Open it!*

Cut back to Rosenthal who has not finished taking out tin after tin. Behind him, The Actor taps him on the shoulder.

The Actor: *How are ya, pal? . . . Keep smilin' . . . ya're happy!*

Rosenthal still unwrapping things: *Look, chocolate!*

Off, an angry soldier begins to argue. Pan onto him: he is facing a sentry and he holds a wrapped tin.

The French Soldier: *The bastards! You opened my tin of ham. . . . You haven't the right to! . . . No, you don't. . . . It's in the rule book. . . . And now it's gone bad!*

Angrily and contemptuously, he throws the packet at the German, who does not budge. Cut back to Rosenthal as he finishes the unwrapping of his parcel.

Rosenthal: *Well, as for me, I'm always amazed and delighted every time I get a parcel from my parents. . . . When I think, here we are, in the middle of Germany, separated from our own kind by a line of fire we can't cross . . . and yet, here's a tin of peas for me straight from Paris!*

The Teacher: *What surprises me most is the incredible honesty of our gaolers.*

Cartier, another prisoner: *Hey . . . that's true!*

The Actor interrupting him in a Paris slang accent: *He's a sort of feldwebel, Arthur. He gets cabbage every day. He loathes it. . . . It sits on his stomach. . . . He told me so himself! I bet you he'd rather scoff your peas!*

The Engineer: *Think it over for a second. If they had a go at our peas, people would stop sending us parcels. Then they'd have to feed us. They've already got enough trouble feeding themselves!*

Rosenthal: *Come. . . . Let's get a move on. Our guests must be hungry. . . .*

Tilt slightly onto a table where three German N.C.O.'s are eating their lean rations. On a wall, a portrait of Kaiser William II. They speak in German.

Leininger: *Ugh! It tastes like old galoshes.*

Zins: *What do the Frenchmen get to eat?*

ZACH: *Cabbage . . . but they don't give a damn, they've got their tins!*

ZINS: *And the Russians?*

ZACH: *Cabbage roots . . . minus the tins.*

    They all laugh.

ZINS: *And the English?*

ZACH: *Plum pudding!*

    All three shrug and continue eating.

    In the prisoners' room, MARECHAL lights a cigarette with a bit of burning paper which THE ACTOR is holding out to him. They both smoke as they wait for CAMILLE, who serves as ROSENTHAL's orderly, to finish setting the table.

THE ACTOR to MARECHAL: *In peacetime, I used to act at the Bouffes du Nord. Ever see my turn?*

MARECHAL: *Well, you know, I never go to the theatre. It's heavy stuff. Are you interested in the Tour de France? Well, I tell you, I've seen Chabert, then Petit-Breton, then those chaps. . . .*

    He goes on talking while camera pans around the room. Some of the men are moving towards the table. THE ENGINEER goes over to BŒLDIEU. Near them, ROSENTHAL takes out food which he puts on the table.

BŒLDIEU a little surprised: *Are we allowed to buy everything we want, in town?*

THE ENGINEER: *Just about anything we want, through the canteen.*

BŒLDIEU: *Perfect. In that case, I will buy the English sort of armchair, some books, playing cards, English cigarettes. . . .*

THE ENGINEER interrupting him: *Oh, those. . . . You won't find that!*

BŒLDIEU: *No?*

    In the background, CAMILLE hands a packet of cigarettes to ROSENTHAL.

CAMILLE: *Here they are, lieutenant . . . I'll try to come back tomorrow.* He salutes him in a friendly way.

ROSENTHAL: *Thanks, Camille.* He turns towards the two groups and waves them over to the table. *And now, my friends, if you'll be so kind, please be seated!* Hubbub; everybody sits down. ROSENTHAL continues, partly off shot. *Let me see, what will you have to start with? Cold chicken, paté de foie gras with truffles from Périgord or, Captain Cook's pickled mackerel?*

    The dinner sequence is made up of many shots of the various

diners, taken slightly from above — only the more important shots are indicated.

BŒLDIEU sitting down: *You keep a good table, as far as I can see!*

MARECHAL: *But don't we get fed here?*

A NEIGHBOUR: *In theory, yes. In practice, no. What they give us isn't eatable. Our parcels are enough* . . . laughing . . . *especially Rosenthal's.*

ROSENTHAL: *Come off it, it's nothing, really!* To his neighbour BŒLDIEU. *A little brandy, Captain, as an apéritif?*

BŒLDIEU haughtily: *Why not?*

Quick dissolve to a few minutes later. Slight tilt onto MARECHAL and his neighbour at table, THE TEACHER.

THE TEACHER: *I've never had such a good meal in my life* . . . holding out a plate to MARECHAL . . . *Have a bit more fish.*

MARECHAL: *Yes, please.*

THE TEACHER: *And I'm beginning to get used to Rosenthal being so generous* . . . *that just shows what adaptable creatures we are!*

Pan to THE ACTOR sitting opposite THE TEACHER; he is listening and making funny faces. He has a cigarette in his mouth and brandishes a bottle. He makes broad jokes, always in his strong Parisian slang.

THE ACTOR: *Needless to say, the lieutenant is a teacher.* . . . *Sister Ann* . . . *anagram* . . . *grand-daughter* . . . *Waterloo* . . . laughing at his own joke . . . *Shit! That's a good one!*

MARECHAL ironically, beginning off: *You, you're quite a funny man, aren't you?*

THE ACTOR stops laughing, as camera shows the whole table. BŒLDIEU, always stiff and unamused, leans towards THE ACTOR.

BŒLDIEU: *Do the rules of the game require that we pretend to find that funny?* He turns back to ROSENTHAL. *Congratulations, old boy, the brandy is quite up to scratch.*

THE ENGINEER taking the brandy: *Oh, it's the tip of the top, well worth it!*

Cut back to THE ACTOR who surreptitiously picks up BŒLDIEU's monocle from the table and tries to screw it in his eye and mimic BŒLDIEU while ROSENTHAL answers.

ROSENTHAL to BŒLDIEU: *It's the barman at Fouquet's who sent it to me in a bottle for mouthwash.*

THE TEACHER not understanding: *Fouquet's?*

MARECHAL to THE TEACHER: *Yes . . . a bar on the Champs-Elysées.*
THE TEACHER: *When I used to go to Paris, I'd eat my meals at my brother-in-law's. . . . It's much cheaper than a restaurant.*

Cut back to BŒLDIEU and ROSENTHAL.
ROSENTHAL whispering to BŒLDIEU: *How long ago were you last in Paris?*
BŒLDIEU: *A week.*
ROSENTHAL: *I envy you. Was everybody there?*
BŒLDIEU: *The other day, Maxim's was choc-a-bloc.*

Cut back to MARECHAL and THE TEACHER.
MARECHAL relaxed: *Oh, me . . . I never go to spots like that . . . Fouquet's . . . Maxim's . . . I like a good cheap little bistro better where there's a good line in wine. . . .*
A VOICE off: *A bit of chicken?*
THE TEACHER in close-up, thoughtfully: *Maxim . . . I don't know him either. . . .*
MARECHAL: *No loss to you, I can tell you.*
THE ACTOR in a quick close-up: *We know! We know! We all know you scoff at your brother-in-law's . . .* sings *. . . Frère Jacques . . . Frère Jacques. . . . Dormez-vous? . . .*

As he sings, he slaps BŒLDIEU on the shoulder. BŒLDIEU puts on his monocle and looks at him rather contemptuously.

French prisoners are walking about the camp yard. They are seen from above through the glass of a window in one of the camp buildings. THE ACTOR goes by and turns towards the window: with the fingers of his left hand raised to his eye, he imitates seeing through a monocle. . . . In the courtyard, ROSENTHAL meets him.

THE ACTOR: *Hey, just a sec. . . .*
ROSENTHAL: *What is it?*
THE ACTOR: *Is the . . .* continuing to imitate BŒLDIEU crudely *. . . monocle around?*
ROSENTHAL: *No, I haven't seen him.*
THE ACTOR: *Because I just came from the canteen. You can tell him . . . his English-type chair . . .* gesticulates *. . . pie in the sky. . . .*
ROSENTHAL leaving: *All right, I'll tell him.*

Camera tracks back from the window into medium shot of MARECHAL sitting among the baths and showers of the wash room. He still has his arm in a sling and THE ENGINEER is washing his feet. He looks out of the window.

MARECHAL: *Must say, he's nice, the chap with the tins* . . . pause . . *He must be rolling in civvy street.*

THE ENGINEER: *I'll say.* . . . *You know the big bankers Rosenthal?*

MARECHAL nods. *Well, mate, they're his mum and dad. Cross my heart, they really are.*

As he rubs MARECHAL's feet to dry them, MARECHAL shivers.

MARECHAL: *Hey, that tickles* . . . pause . . . *And what does he do?*

THE ENGINEER: *He owns a big dress designer's.*

MARECHAL: *That so? Funny.* . . . *If I had the cash, I wouldn't be in that line. What about you, what do you do outside this lot?*

THE ENGINEER: *Me, I'm an engineer for the ordnance survey.*

MARECHAL thinking: *Yes . . . on the ordnance survey.*

Close-up of THE ENGINEER, then a series of shots of the two men as each speaks. Off, the sound of singing German soldiers.

THE ENGINEER getting up: *Eh, between you and me, your mate with the monocle, can we trust him?*

MARECHAL is surprised by the question and THE ENGINEER looks as if there were a plot in the air.

MARECHAL: *Well . . . he's a bit lah-di-dah . . . but all the same, he's a good bloke! Yes, you can trust him.* . . .

THE ENGINEER speaking softly: *All right, then.* . . . After a pause, he bends over to speak in MARECHAL's ear in medium close-up. *Because, you know . . . at night . . . we dig a hole.*

MARECHAL surprised: *A hole? What for?*

THE ENGINEER as if it were obvious: *To escape!*

MARECHAL: *Impossible! But what do you dig your hole with?*

THE ENGINEER: *With the coal shovel and old tins. If my plans are right, we should come out at the other end in a garden, behind the buildings you can see over there . . . right out in open country.*

MARECHAL: *You can't get a move on with that.*

THE ENGINEER: *We've been working on it for two months. A few weeks more and we'll have it done.*

MARECHAL mocking: *Pooh.* . . . *The war'll be over by then.*

THE ENGINEER: *You think? You're under an illusion . . . besides, we like to get it ready just in case.*

Camera tracks back as THE ENGINEER finishes wiping MARE-CHAL's feet.

MARECHAL, both interested and sceptical: *And where are you digging this hole of yours?*

THE ENGINEER: *You'll see this evening, after roll-call.*

MARECHAL wondering at the thought: *A hole? . . . So you're digging a hole! Like Monte Cristo. I think that's very funny.*

> THE ENGINEER finishes his task and gets up. MARECHAL also jumps up.

MARECHAL: *Thanks, mate, you've done me a favour.*

THE ENGINEER: *Come off it, it's only natural, with your arm.*

> Camera tracks forward into close-up on MARECHAL.

MARECHAL: *Look. . . . If you don't mind, I'd like to ask you something.*

THE ENGINEER off: *Go on.*

MARECHAL: *In fact . . . what's it mean, the ordnance survey?*

> After dinner. Before lights out, the German N.C.O. ZACH goes by calling the roll. Medium shot of him, in front of the door of the prisoners' room. He reads off the list he holds in his hand.

ZACH: *Maréchal?*

MARECHAL off: *Present.*

ZACH: *Bœldieu?*

BŒLDIEU off: *You ought to say, Captain de Bœldieu.*

ZACH: *Rosenthal?*

ROSENTHAL off: *Hmmm. . . .*

ZACH: *Rémy?*

THE ACTOR off: *Here . . . we go round the mulberry bush!*

ALL off: *Good night, Arthur.*

> ZACH has folded up the list of prisoners. He scans the room one last time and goes out, closing the door behind him. Quick pan onto the prisoners who get up quickly from their beds and listen to the sound of ZACH's footsteps growing fainter. They all have solemn and wary looks on their faces. Each one gets ready in silence — this is obviously their routine every night at this hour — while MARECHAL on one side and BŒLDIEU on his bed look at them with surprise. THE ACTOR goes and barricades the door with a chair, then THE ENGINEER helps him to screen the window with a blanket.

THE ENGINEER: *Whose turn is it?*

THE ACTOR: *It's mine.*

THE ENGINEER and THE TEACHER go to a corner of the room. Tilt on them as they pull a bed aside and lift the floorboards, revealing a hole.

Cut back to THE ACTOR as he gets ready. He ties a string round his wrist. Cut to the other end of the string tied round an old tin which somebody else is balancing on a shelf.

MARECHAL coming closer: *What's that?*

As he speaks, he points to another empty tin which THE ACTOR is shoving into his pocket. On the side, there are more tins tied together (*Still*).

THE ACTOR: *It's to get the earth out.*

MARECHAL: *And this string?*

THE ACTOR: *If I'm stifling, I pull it . . . and the tin falls over. It's the alarm signal. Then the lads pull me out by the feet . . . feet . . . feet . . . sings . . . marching up and down again! . . . pause . . . Right. Off I go. . . . To play the mole . . . ecule!*

Pan to BŒLDIEU near THE ENGINEER. BŒLDIEU is holding some cards and seems to be playing patience.

BŒLDIEU: *Will it hold, your tunnel?*

THE ENGINEER: *It's got the right props, wood we've borrowed from the theatre.*

BŒLDIEU: *What do you do about the earth?*

THE ENGINEER: *We began by packing it under the floorboards, but now it's full up. You couldn't stick a pin in there. So now we put the earth in bags and take it for a walk with us.*

Pan to THE ACTOR who is ready for his job underground and slides on his belly into the tunnel. He soon vanishes completely, letting the string trail after him. A few seconds later, the string stops moving and lies loosely along the edge of the wall.

Cut inside the hole where THE ACTOR is face to face with his job. He sighs and attacks the earth.

Cut back to the men leaning over the hole. They straighten up again, sighing. Still solemn, they smile as they silently remember THE ACTOR's bad jokes.

Pan towards MARECHAL who is acting as look-out. Suddenly he seems worried and makes a gesture as if he wants the others to be quiet.

MARECHAL in a very low voice, troubled: *Didn't you hear anything?*

THE TEACHER coming closer: *No.*

MARECHAL: *I heard something all right.*

The others all listen and seem to indicate that MARECHAL is dreaming.

MARECHAL: *I tell you, I did . . .* pause. *. . . There, there it is again. . . .*

THE ENGINEER intrigued: *We'll send somebody out to scout around.* To THE TEACHER. *Hey you, with that babyface of yours . . . you go and see what's up.*

THE TEACHER: *I'll say I'm going to the lavatory.*

THE ENGINEER pushes THE TEACHER towards the door.

Cut to THE ACTOR underground. He is digging and breathing with difficulty near his candle.

It is night as THE TEACHER nervously leaves the barracks and reaches the yard. He meets two German stretcher-bearers carrying a man and watches them in surprise, while the N.C.O. ZACH comes up to him on sentry duty with his gun at the ready. THE TEACHER pretends to be completely at ease.

THE TEACHER: *Arthur, I mean, what happened just now?*

ZACH: *It's someone who tried to escape. We caught up with him in the gardens behind the buildings . . . so we shot him down.*

THE TEACHER worried: *Behind the buildings? Is he . . . dead?*

ZACH: *I think so . . .* He begins to shout at THE TEACHER *. . . You, what are you doing out here?*

THE TEACHER looking stupid: *Me? I'm off to the lavatory.*

He goes off.

Cut to THE ACTOR, who drops his tool and begins to suffocate more and more and pulls the string.

Close-up of the tin on the shelf. It falls onto a bed without a sound. Pan onto the group of prisoners at the window, anxiously waiting for THE TEACHER to come back. They are so absorbed they do not notice the fall of the tin for the alarm.

Cut to the door as it opens. THE TEACHER comes in and the others rush over to him.

THE ENGINEER: *Well, what happened?*

THE TEACHER whispering: *Some one tried to escape. I don't know how. . . . They killed him . . . in the gardens . . . behind the buildings!*

Dead silence. They are all very upset by the news. Suddenly, THE TEACHER starts; he has just noticed that the tin for the alarm has fallen on the bed.

THE TEACHER: *The alarm!*

Camera shoots from above as they rush over to the hole and struggle to get THE ACTOR out.

Cut to MARECHAL near them, embarrassed not to be able to help because of his arm. Cut back to the prisoners pulling on the rope. . . . THE ACTOR's feet appear. He is pulled out of the hole and carried over to a bed, where he gasps for breath.

THE TEACHER: *Does it hurt?*

THE ACTOR goes on gasping and shakes his head, while ROSEN-THAL comes over with a bottle in his hand and puts it to THE ACTOR's lips.

ROSENTHAL: *Drink some of this, old chap . . . drop of brandy!*

THE TEACHER: *It's the one from Fouquet's!*

THE ACTOR begins to stir on the bed as he feels better. He turns to ROSENTHAL, takes the bottle of brandy, has a swig, then sighs.

THE ACTOR singing: *" I had a little drop about an hour ago "*. . . . *Don't break it!*

He drinks some more. Pan to BŒLDIEU, THE ENGINEER and MARECHAL standing; they sigh and look at each other with relief.

BŒLDIEU: *Whose turn is it tomorrow?*

THE ENGINEER: *Yours then, Captain, if you'd really care to!*

BŒLDIEU: *I'd be delighted. People have told me that crawling is simply marvellous as exercise.*

Next morning. Mail is delivered at this time. Slight tilt up at the Feldwebel KRANTZ guarding the yard. Behind him stands a German soldier.

KRANTZ: *I remind you that it is strictly forbidden to have clothes sent to you which are not military dress.*

Cut to the yard. Many prisoners stand in groups, waiting for the mail to be delivered. Medium shot of a group made up of MARECHAL, BŒLDIEU, THE TEACHER and THE ENGINEER.

MARECHAL to ROSENTHAL: *Anything new?*

ROSENTHAL without looking up: *A letter from my aunt in Bordeaux.*

She says there's an incredible crowd down there.

THE ENGINEER leafing through the paper: *If I were them, I'd watch it. The Frankfurt Gazette announces a fantastic advance.*

MARECHAL sceptically: *Oh, right! They haven't even run up any flags. . . . They're not ringing the bells. . . . It can't be much!*

BŒLDIEU putting on his monocle: *Gentlemen, shall we proceed to more important matters?*

THE OTHERS: *Yes . . . yes, of course!*

ROSENTHAL: *Yes, but not all at the same time.*

They split up. A sideways tracking shot follows THE TEACHER and MARECHAL. . . . THE ACTOR catches up with them from behind, whistling between his teeth.

THE TEACHER: *I disapprove of this mania for exaggeration in the German news items.*

MARECHAL gruffly: *Well . . . what about our papers? Remember, right at the start, how the Russian steam-roller was going to crush them?*

Shock cut to THE ACTOR and THE ENGINEER reaching a corner of the yard set aside for gardening. They stop in front of a dug patch of earth, but a sudden sound of singing makes them turn their heads. Pan to what they see: a group of young German conscripts marching off to squad drill.

Cut back to THE ACTOR and THE ENGINEER, as they hold a spade and a shovel and continue their previous conversation.

THE ENGINEER: *And what about famous General Winter, the one who was going to kill off all the bad Jerries with bronchitis and brace up the Allies?*

THE ACTOR bantering: *And what about Turpinite? Remember Turpinite? With a little bottle as . . . big . . . as a radish, we were going to kill off a whole army corps. They even tried it out on a flock of sheep!*

THE TEACHER passes near them. As he walks, he shakes out the earth from under his greatcoat.

THE TEACHER: *Pity they didn't stop right there with the sheep!*

While THE ACTOR watches out for the sentry who is standing beyond them with his back turned, THE TEACHER continues shaking the earth out of his coat, while THE ENGINEER conscientiously pats the fallen earth into place with his shovel. They sing a little tune. After THE TEACHER has finished, he walks off and his place is taken by the relaxed MARECHAL, who also begins to get rid of the earth in his clothing.

MARECHAL pretending to be interested: *Well then? What are you planting here?*

THE ENGINEER getting up: *Dandelions, my boy. Yes, I dream of making myself a dandelion salad with lard.*

MARECHAL: *Go on! . . . The war'll be over before your dandelions even poke their heads out.*

> BŒLDIEU, full of dignity, comes up to them. Cautiously, he takes a bag of earth from below his armpit and empties it. Then he folds up the bag meticulously, taking care not to get his gloves too dirty.

BŒLDIEU haughtily: *If we go on with this odd business, we'll end up with hands like navvies.*

> As he finishes folding up his bag, ROSENTHAL comes up and empties his bag, only more discreetly. Quick pan to a French prisoner, soldier DRYANT, who comes running up to them.

DRYANT: *Oy, Oy! Rosenthal! . . . The crates are here.*

ROSENTHAL delighted: *The costumes?*

DRYANT: *Yes . . . three crates, sent by your firm. We've taken them to the theatre.*

ROSENTHAL to the others: *Let's go there, boys. There must be one crate full of women's clothes . . . real ones! . . .* He leads the others off . . . *Are you coming, Captain?*

> THE ACTOR is already on his way to the buildings: he hums and he walks waggling his hips and mincing crudely like a woman. BŒLDIEU does not move.

BŒLDIEU: *No thank you. My competence in theatrical matters is very slight indeed. Besides, I have something else to do. . . .*

> They all go off except for MARECHAL and BŒLDIEU who remain standing face to face.

MARECHAL ironically: *A little game of patience, aren't I right?*

BŒLDIEU: *Exactly . . . I happen to be a realist. . . .* He takes the opposite direction, then turns round. *I'll see you later.*

MARECHAL: *See you later!* He laughs mockingly.

Camera begins on English prisoners who are in a line on the stage of the entertainment hall, dancing and singing together ' *Tipperary* '. Camera tracks back slightly to show the whole

91

rehearsal; everyone wears either a soldier's or an officer's uniform. Circular pan round the hall past the orchestra and past some groups busily making sets; pan ends on a German sentry who is keeping close watch on ROSENTHAL and his friends, as he undoes the crates which have just arrived. These crates contain dresses, silk stockings, every sort of feminine finery. The sentry examines a corset.

THE ACTOR to the sentry: *Well, Arthur, found anything?*

THE SENTRY in a strong German accent: *No, I have found nothing.* The sentry takes a last look, about turns and goes off. Camera follows him to the door. [In the complete version, there is a cut to the sentry leaving the room and saying good-night in French. THE ACTOR wearing the hat of a marquis replies with the rest, but he says good-night in German with a strong Parisian accent.]

VOICES off: *Good-bye. . . . Bye for now, Arthur!*

Cut back to the group leaning avidly over the crates. ROSENTHAL waves an evening gown in the air and holds it on himself.

ROSENTHAL: *Ah! These things have to be handled with kid gloves . . . and your eyes shut.*

All are disturbed at the sight of this dress which they look at with great intensity.

MARECHAL: *Real dresses. . . .*

THE TEACHER: *Look how short it is. Like a dress for a little girl.*

MARECHAL shrugging: *Eh, didn't you know? All the girls are wearing short dresses now* . . . looking at the dress again and sighing . . . *My! . . .*

ROSENTHAL ecstatically: *Just below the knee!*

THE ACTOR: *My old lady wrote and told me, but I didn't believe it.*

MARECHAL: *Hey, you! Put one on so we can see what it looks like. . . .*

ROSENTHAL reacts strongly and stops THE ACTOR.

ROSENTHAL: *No, not him. . . . He hasn't shaved properly. What about you, Maisonneuve, with your angel face? . . .*

MAISONNEUVE: *If you think that's funny. . . .*

MAISONNEUVE goes off with the dress on his arm.

MARECHAL: *It isn't only their dresses that are short. They've cut their hair too!*

Cut to concentrate on MARECHAL, THE ACTOR and THE

TEACHER.

THE ACTOR astounded: *You don't say. . . . It must be like going to bed with a boy!*

THE TEACHER: *Really, when we aren't around to keep an eye on them, women go and do such foolish things. When I think of my wife, all these new-fangled things worry me. . . .*

AN N.C.O., an ageing professional soldier: *Well, I'm sure my wife hasn't had her hair cut off. . . . Bah, all that rot's only good for tarts!*

They laugh while ROSENTHAL takes some women's shoes out of the crate.

THE ENGINEER: *Oh, shit . . . shoes!*

ROSENTHAL happily: *We'd forgotten how small they were.*

ROSENTHAL goes on digging into the crate and pulls out some stockings.

THE ENGINEER overcome: *Stockings!*

THE ACTOR simultaneously: *Hey . . . stockings! Stockings!*

THE TEACHER, taking a stocking: *Silk! I've never felt silk like that before. . . .*

Quick cut to another soldier gaping at a pair of black stockings. Slight pan to the soldier MAISONNEUVE who appears dressed as a woman — skirt and top — and also wearing a wig. All the men turn to look at him and fall silent, curiously disturbed. How many memories and hopes are there. . . . MAISONNEUVE feels uneasy to see their intense looks on him (*Still*).

MARECHAL, with forced laughter: *Don't you think it's funny?*

MAISONNEUVE: *Funny?*

ROSENTHAL: *Yes, it's funny. . . .*

MARECHAL, very sane and a little sad: *It's really funny. . . . You look like a real girl.*

They fall into a heavy silence again. . . . They cannot find anything to say as they look at this soldier in a woman's dress. Very slow pan across the soldier's faces staring at MAISONNEUVE in absolute silence. Pan ends on the soldier in drag who has come forward to the middle of the hall and cannot help making a few feminine gestures.

VOICES off: *Yes. . . . It's funny!*

The barracks entrance. The main gate opens and a large cart

comes out, pulled by two horses and driven by a German soldier. The cart seems loaded with crudely-made coffins. As it goes by, camera stays on the civilians who have followed the cart up to this point. Cut to two old grandmothers dressed in black, seen slightly from below in medium close-up. One of the old women sighs, then speaks in German.

OLD WOMAN: *Poor lads!*

Cut to the young recruits drilling in the yard. Orders in German are heard off: *Attention! Eyes front! At ease!* The recruits run off in step.

In an annexe of the entertainment hall, which ROSENTHAL and his friends have converted into a sewing workshop, they are cutting out pieces of cloth and dresses to make stage costumes for the performance. Camera tilts onto the table where they are cutting and sewing. In the background, MARECHAL is seen standing near the window, not participating in these feverish and feminine activities. At the window, BŒLDIEU stands and looks out. Cut to a close-up of his expression of interest in the scene outside — the young recruits at drill. Cut back to the group shot, then cut back again to the close-up of BŒLDIEU, as he looks out of the window, turns to THE ACTOR who is singing and the others who are sewing, and then turns back to the window with the words:

BŒLDIEU: *On one side, children playing at soldiers. On the other, soldiers playing at children.* [*It doesn't really round things off!*]

THE TEACHER still sewing: *I'd like to know what's going on back home.*

THE ENGINEER: *Still no news?*

THE TEACHER mournfully: *Nothing.*

THE ACTOR cheerfully: *I couldn't care less what my old lady's up to. . . . What makes me want to slope off is, it's such a bloody bore. Ah, the Trocadero! . . . Cadet Rousselle, and la . . . la . . . la . . . he hums. . . . .*

ROSENTHAL interrupting: *In other words, you want to escape for the fun of it. . . .*

THE ACTOR with silly pleasure: *That's it!*

THE ENGINEER in close-up: *With me, it's just being contrary. Ever since they've stopped me fighting, I've been dying to get back and fight.*

94

Pan towards Bœldieu and Marechal, seen in medium shot.
Marechal as though talking to himself: *I just want to do like
everyone else . . .* more loudly. . . . *Besides, it gets me down to be
here while the others are all getting knocked off!*
Bœldieu turning to him: *As far as I'm concerned, the question
does not come up.* Medium close-up of him. *What is the purpose
of a golf course? To play golf. A tennis court? To play tennis. Well,
a prison camp is there to escape from. . . . What do you think,
Rosenthal? You're a sportsman.*
[Rosenthal: *I want to escape so I can go on fighting for my
country.*]
The Actor: [*Your country?*] *He's no sportsman! Why, he was born
in Jerusalem!*

> In the medium shot of the group, The Actor stands between
> Bœldieu and Rosenthal, who sits in the foreground with his
> back to both of them, facing camera with his head apparently
> lowered over his work. He looks down in the mouth, then he
> unenthusiastically puts on the panache of Bœldieu to answer
> back rather timidly.

Rosenthal: *Excuse me, I was born in Vienna, capital of Austria.
My mother was Danish, my father Polish, both naturalized citizens
of France.*
Marechal in a new shot: *Old Breton lords and ladies, eh?*
Rosenthal in a new shot: *Perhaps!* . . . still not looking at them
. . . *But the rest of you, Frenchmen from way back, you don't own
a hundred square metres of your country. Well, the Rosenthals in
thirty-five years have managed to get hold of three historic castles
with shoots, lakes, fields, orchards, rabbit warrens, fishing rights,
pheasants, stud farms . . . and three picture galleries full of ances-
tors, every one guaranteed!* Rosenthal has obviously reached the
end of his tether; he turns on the rest of them. *If you think that
isn't worth escaping for, to go and defend!*
Bœldieu looking surprised: *I must say, I had never thought of
patriotism from that angle. How odd!*
Marechal: *Rabbit warrens! Fishing rights! Pheasants! Those
flunkies of yours, I bet they scoff a lot of game.*

> Cut to a shot from above of The Teacher; he has his pipe in
> his mouth and tries to follow the conversation. A hand pulls
> off the stage wig which he has been wearing.

THE TEACHER chewing his pipe: *I got into action in a funny way. Believe it or not, I got into the army because I'm a vegetarian!*

Cut to the surprised MARECHAL and BŒLDIEU.

MARECHAL: *Vegetarian?*

THE TEACHER in close-up: *I'm not joking. My brother and I both had something wrong with our stomachs. So then the doctor told us . . . he told my parents first, of course: 'If you eat meat, you're done for.'* Hands put a clown's ruff round his neck. *Well, I became a vegetarian . . . and I got better. My brother went on eating meat . . . he became very ill. . . . He wasn't taken for the army.*

While he finishes speaking, there is the sound of the boots of German soldiers, marching in step. BŒLDIEU bows a little towards THE TEACHER.

BŒLDIEU: *I can see from your decorations . . . being a vegetarian has not stopped you from doing your duty.*

THE TEACHER nodding: *Nor did it stop my wife from sleeping with somebody else!*

Suddenly a military band starts up: fifes, big drums, trombones. The heavy marching pace of the conscripts blends in with the sound of martial music. BŒLDIEU goes back to the window, followed by all the others. Camera tracks back to frame them all as they watch the parade which is invisible. THE ACTOR, who is short, lifts himself onto the shoulders of THE ENGINEER. Pan in close-up from face to face during the following dialogue, as each watches the march-past.

THE ENGINEER: *I must say, it's a good show!*

BŒLDIEU coldly: *I hate fifes.*

THE TEACHER: *Whatever they say, it really stirs you up!*

MARECHAL with the pan ending on his face: *What stirs you, mate, isn't the music . . . nor the instruments. . . . It's the noise. . . . [The sound of the march, just like in every army.]*

The sound of marching grows louder. Dissolve to another shot of the group. THE ACTOR, still resting on THE ENGINEER's shoulders, turns and sees smoke in the room. Camera tracks in front of him as he dashes over to the ironing board.

THE ACTOR: *Blast! Burning. . . .* He picks up the hot iron from his trousers, which now have a hole in them. Furious, he waves the iron in the air. *With all your fancy chat and all, my trousers are done for!*

Cut to close-up of the ironing board marked by the hot iron. THE ACTOR lifts up the burned trousers to show them to everybody and begins to dance and sing.

Outside, the young German recruits are marching past.

Resume on THE ACTOR, who walks backwards as he sings until he bumps into the door which opens. In comes a sentry who takes a look round the room, then turns towards THE ACTOR. Seeing them all more or less dressed as women, and THE ACTOR now humming to himself, he taps his forehead with his finger and leaves the room.

Night in the yard. Start on a close-up of a poster in German and French, which has just been put up by a feldwebel. In French, the headline reads:

Official Communiqué   General Headquarters
                                          20 February, 1916
                  DOUAUMONT IS CAPTURED

This is followed by a text that is hardly readable. All the bells of the town nearby start pealing wildly.

Pan towards a lighted window and track forwards to show German officers celebrating the victory in their mess. They are drinking, singing, and playing the guitar. One of them rises, singing gaily, and leaves the room. Camera follows him: after a wave to the others, he closes the door. As he walks in the cold night air, he goes on singing, rubbing his hands together. Pan after him briefly in the yard, then tilt up one of the walls of the camp to stop on a window, where the French prisoners are staring in dismay at the joy and the celebrations. Camera tracks, towards them; the group includes THE ACTOR, BŒLDIEU, MARECHAL, THE ENGINEER, THE TEACHER, and ROSENTHAL, as they look down into the yard. Suddenly, THE ACTOR, speaking gravely, breaks the silence.

THE ACTOR: *With all that, are we still going to put on our show?*

MARECHAL: *And how! More so now than ever! I'd even suggest we invite, for once, the camp commandant and all his officers, just to show them our morale's all right.*

THE TEACHER: *Things are going badly, if they've taken Douaumont....*

97

MARECHAL annoyed: *Who's saying no to that? All the more reason not to cave in.*

BŒLDIEU turning to MARECHAL: *For once I agree with you, Maréchal. I may not participate in your theatrical ventures, but allow me to congratulate you all the same. . . . Good show!*

Pan past German soldiers singing and toasting the victory in their canteen. One of them is playing the guitar very loudly.

The wooden barracks hall has been turned into a theatre for the show. Medium shot of THE ACTOR on stage. He is wearing tails; the suit is a little too large for him, so that the actual tails of the coat dangle too low. Even though his costume does not fit, he sings and makes gestures with great gusto.

THE ACTOR singing: *Si tu veux faire mon bonheur, Marguerite! . . . Marguerite! . . .*

Camera stays on THE ACTOR singing and moving about on stage, as he periodically takes the carnation from his buttonhole to sniff it voluptuously, and as he tries to make everybody join in the chorus. Then camera tracks back on a crane to show the whole crowded hall. Prisoners from all the camp are there. In the front row, satisfied German officers. At the back, a few armed sentries stand, as if at the back of a music hall.

Cut back to a close-up of THE ACTOR, singing and miming another verse of the song. A shot of him from the rear shows the audience laughing. Cut back to him as he makes the audience take up the refrain. [The original script added — In the hall, the men laugh and temporarily seem to forget their troubles and their imprisonment. THE ACTOR is pretty bad and the song he sings is vulgar. But he is so much a Parisian that all the Frenchmen are overcome by the number. As for the German officers, they stay rather stiff and scornful, hardly open to this little song from Paris.]

THE ACTOR still singing: *Si tu veux faire mon bonheur, Marguerite, donne-moi ton coeur!*

Everyone joins in the chorus now, even the Germans, caught up in the enthusiasm of the audience. All laugh out loud, except the German officers, who clap politely. Cut back to THE ACTOR on stage, as he wriggles with pleasure while he acknowledges the loud applause.

The curtain closes. Cut to the rudimentary orchestra, then cut back to the stage as the curtain rises again. THE ACTOR bows once more to a loud crash of music, then goes back-stage to lift a flap and usher in the ' girls '. These come on stage, dancing a sort of can-can. The ' girls ' are five English prisoners, dressed in wigs, short dresses, jewels, and feathers. They dance and mince about in a poor imitation of women's airs and graces. They are a huge success! In comes the ' star ', fanning himself with a lace fan and going up to the footlights to dance the finale to ' *Tipperary* ' and then to a song like ' *Frou-Frou* '. Cut to a pan across the whole audience joining in the chorus, then back to THE ACTOR reappearing on stage, sitting on a cardboard motor-car, and also singing.

Cut to the wings, where ROSENTHAL opens a newspaper; he is very surprised, and makes a sign to MARECHAL and THE ENGINEER.

Cut back to the stage. Everyone is singing along with the ' girls '. All are having a good time . . . when MARECHAL, dressed normally, suddenly bursts onto the scene, pushing the ' girls ' aside. He is overcome; he raises his arms to get silence, the newspaper in his hand.

MARECHAL: *Stop! Stop!*

The orchestra stops playing. Everybody falls silent. MARECHAL yells in the total hush.

MARECHAL: *We've recaptured Douaumont! . . . It's the boche news which says it!*

For a few seconds, everybody in the audience is frozen. Then the orchestra strikes up ' *The Marseillaise* '. Everyone bursts into song and gets up at the same instant. The English ' girls ' pull off their wigs and lead the anthem in French with strong English accents. Pan round the hall at all the prisoners singing with great feeling, while the German officers rise and leave hastily. Pan after the officers as they go out, then return to the men happily chanting in the hall.

Dissolve to a shot of German soldiers outside, as they run towards a building.

There is the sound of boots advancing in the dark; they seem to be walking down the steps that lead to the detention cells.

MARECHAL is sitting on a prison bed, wrapped up in his army greatcoat. He is violently scratching away at the damp slimy wall with a spoon; the cell itself is dark and bare, having a bed, a blanket, and a door with a spyhole in it that lets in a sparse light. Pan towards the door as it opens. In comes the sentry ZACH to investigate the noise that MARECHAL is making. MARE-CHAL turns wearily towards ZACH and says nothing, but his face is angry. ZACH stares at him, surprised and bewildered.

ZACH in German: *What are you doing there?*

MARECHAL stupidly: *There? A hole. . . . . Yes, yes, yes! I'm digging a hole to escape!* He shouts the last word.

ZACH leans further forwards to look, and MARECHAL takes the opportunity to leap up, shove ZACH onto the ground and run out of the door, which he slams behind him. Camera stays on the door, while the sound of struggling is heard on its far side.

MARECHAL yelling off: *Keep your bloody hands off! Let me bloody be! Bloody . . . be!*

The door opens again. Three soldiers carry in the half-conscious MARECHAL and lay him out on the bed. Camera tracks in and tilts down on a close-up of MARECHAL.

The shadow of a soldier falls on a poster freshly stuck to a wall in the yard. The poster reads:

DOUAUMONT RECAPTURED BY
GERMAN TROOPS

German forces once again occupy the fortress of Douaumont after a battle which caused heavy losses to the enemy. We have taken 3,700 prisoners. The fortress is now safely in German hands.

Camera tracks backwards to show, from the rear, some French prisoners and German sentries or soldiers reading the poster which is in both the languages.

THE TEACHER: *There can't be much of it left.*

A PRISONER: *Oh, you've seen it? It's terrible. Who'd have thought so?*

A SENTRY in German: *They don't say how many got killed taking it. . . .*

In fact, the news by now hardly affects anyone. If the Germans take Douaumont or the French retake it, the war still goes on. . . .

Close-up from above of a mess-tin full of soup, then pan up to MARECHAL still in his cell. He is sitting down, his back against the wall, dirty, unshaven, glass-eyed. Sound of a key in the lock. He does not move. Pan to the door as it opens and admits an OLD GERMAN SOLDIER, who goes over to MARECHAL. A medium shot shows him looking at the untouched soup, shaking his head sadly, and slapping MARECHAL on the shoulder.

THE OLD SOLDIER in German: *Not feeling well today? Not hungry?*
MARECHAL, not understanding and shutting him up by shouting: *Stuff it, d'you hear?*

THE OLD SOLDIER moves away, but MARECHAL overcome by depression and rage, yells:

MARECHAL: *I'm fed up, d'you hear. . . . Fed up! I want to see day-light, for god's sake! I want to see the light! Shit to this hole! I want to see the light, hear somebody speaking French . . . French, d'you get me, speaking French!*

THE OLD SOLDIER, feeling sorry for MARECHAL and sensing that the crisis is nearly over, sits down beside him. He would very much like to do something for the Frenchman. . . . He looks about in his pockets and takes out three cigarettes. Without speaking, he offers them to MARECHAL, who refuses them. He puts the cigarettes down next to MARECHAL and goes on searching his own pockets, this time pulling out a mouth-organ to offer to MARECHAL.

[MARECHAL: *You want to make a bloody fool out of me?*]

MARECHAL turns towards the wall. THE OLD SOLDIER, very sorry for him, gets up and leaves behind the cigarettes and the mouth-organ. Camera follows THE OLD SOLDIER as he leaves the cell.

THE OLD SOLDIER triple-locks the door of the cell, then noise-lessly lifts the hatch over the peep-hole in the door to look inside.

MARECHAL picks up the mouth-organ in the end, lifts it to his lips, plays it.

Cut back to THE OLD SOLDIER. He is satisfied and shuts up

the peep-hole and walks down the corridor, humming ' Frou-Frou '. He meets a guard.

THE GUARD in German: *Why did he shout like that?*

THE OLD SOLDIER in German: *Because the war is lasting too long.*

Medium shot of THE ENGINEER, THE TEACHER and THE ACTOR who are smoking and talking softly together in their room.

THE ENGINEER: *If I calculated correctly, we'll be under the garden wall in four days' time. . . . Think of all those sacks of earth!*

THE TEACHER: *Now there's a chance of getting away and back to France. I'm worried about what's waiting for me back home.*

THE ACTOR: *Ah, there's more than one woman in the world.*

THE TEACHER: *There's only one for me.*

THE ACTOR as though stating the obvious: *That's why she sleeps around!*

Pan towards the seated ROSENTHAL.

ROSENTHAL sadly: *As for me, I can't bear to think we'll be leaving Maréchal behind.*

Pan ends on BŒLDIEU who is playing patience. He turns his head towards ROSENTHAL, takes out his monocle, and still keeps a card in his hand.

BŒLDIEU: *I too find it a bit depressing. It's really too bad, but that's war. . . . Feelings have nothing to do with it.*

Quick pan to the door as it opens. MARECHAL stands in the doorway with a soldier. He has just come out of the detention cell; he needs a shave, a wash, a comb; he is exhausted and dazzled by the daylight. BŒLDIEU dashes forward to greet him. Shot of the two men face to face.

BŒLDIEU: *Delighted to see you again, old chap.*

All the others surround MARECHAL to hold him up, for he is about to fall. They make him sit down.

ROSENTHAL fussing over MARECHAL: *Do you want to rest? Do you want something to drink?*

MARECHAL in a whisper: *I want to eat. . . . I want to eat. . . . I'm hungry.*

Medium close-up of ROSENTHAL hastily opening a tin and turning his head away to hide the fact that he is wiping a tear off his cheek.

THE ACTOR off: *Hey, come and sit here,* [*you'll be better off.*]

Dissolve to the same place, a few days later. The prisoners seem nervous and pace up and down the room. Clearly, tonight is the night they are going to try and escape through the tunnel which they have dug with such effort.

MARECHAL: *What's the time?*

ROSENTHAL: *Eleven o'clock.*

MARECHAL: *Time's pretty fast today.*

THE ACTOR acting: *Yes, but this evening, auf wiedersehen!*

THE ENGINEER: *Rendez-vous in Amsterdam, then!*

Medium close-up of THE TEACHER and THE ACTOR.

THE TEACHER: *I've always wanted to visit Holland because of the tulips.*

THE ACTOR: *I prefer their cheese. Ah, Dutch cheese!* . . . Pause. *Don't you like Dutch cheese?*

THE TEACHER: *Yes, but tulips are pretty. They say there are whole fields of them, as far as the eye can see.*

Pan to BŒLDIEU playing patience.

BŒLDIEU turning to THE TEACHER: *Really, my dear fellow, you have the taste of a parlour-maid.*

MARECHAL, who is beside the door, sees ZACH enter. Shot first shows the two men, then the others clustering around.

ZACH in his strongly-accented French: *General roll-call at three o'clock. All officers are changing camps. Get your kits ready.*

The prisoners stare at each other, dismayed, as ZACH leaves the room, closing the door behind him.

Pan across English officers grouped in one corner of the yard, then across ranks of French officers looking at them. Among the French are MARECHAL, THE ACTOR, THE ENGINEER, ROSENTHAL and BŒLDIEU. They have just answered roll-call in the afternoon, and are standing there with their kits, ready to leave.

THE GERMAN OFFICER in his strong accent: *Gentlemen, I wish you a pleasant journey and I hope you will see your wives again soon.*

He salutes them, and the little squad of men begin to march away, waving to ZACH as they pass by.

THE ACTOR: *Bye bye, Arthur!*

GERMAN OFFICERS' VOICES, in poor English: *English officers, 'shun!*
. . . English officers!

BŒLDIEU: *Perhaps we ought to warn them.*

MARECHAL: *What about?*

THE ACTOR: *'Bout the tunnel, what else? That it's all ready for them.*

When the two squads pass each other, ROSENTHAL and THE ACTOR try to get closer to the English.

THE GERMAN OFFICER pushing them back: *Back to your ranks!*

Cut to the English marching by. The suitcase of one of them springs open, its contents fall to the ground. Tilt down as the English officer bends, puts down his tennis racket, and begins putting back his things in his case.

Cut to MARECHAL who profits from this little mix-up to worm his way to the English officer's side, as if to help him repack his case.

MARECHAL whispering in French: *Colonel. . . . . Dans la chambrée numero sept.*

THE ENGLISHMAN: *It's really too kind of you. . . .*

MARECHAL: *Laisse-moi parler. . . . Il y a un trou creusé. . . . Préviens les copains.*

THE ENGLISHMAN: *I'm sorry, I don't understand French.*

MARECHAL: *Vous ne comprenez pas le français?*

THE ENGLISHMAN: *Thank you . . . thank you. . . .*

MARECHAL, annoyed and making signs: *Trou . . . un trou . . . dans le plancher. . . .*

THE ENGLISHMAN straightening up again: *Bon voyage!*

A feldwebel comes up and puts an end to this conversation, roughly pushing MARECHAL back to his squad.

THE FELDWEBEL: *Nicht aus der Reihe treten!*

(The English and the French are allies in the war, but the English — who are going to be sleeping in the quarters vacated by the French — will never know about the tunnel beneath the floorboards.)

Through the window of a train compartment,[1] the flat, mourn-

---

[1] A still showing BŒLDIEU and MARECHAL sitting in a train compartment and guarded by the old soldier, who had the mouth-organ, suggests that Renoir did shoot some scenes inside the train, which were edited from the final version.

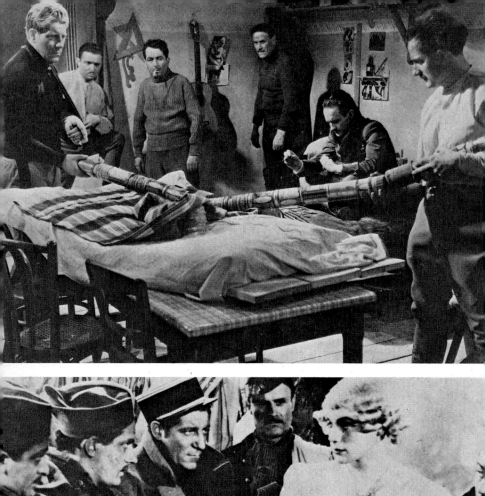

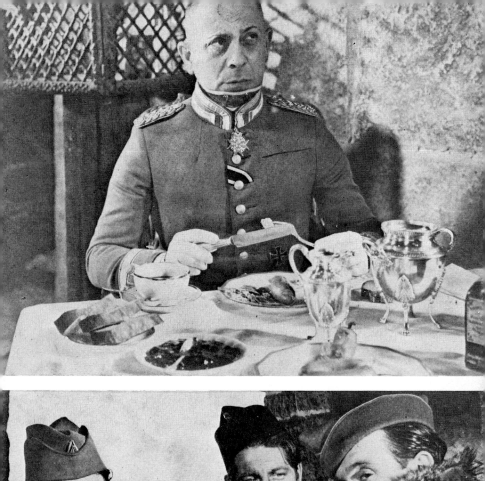

ful countryside moves by. The train speeds through a station without stopping, then rolls on past more countryside. When the train seems to be slowing down, a large sign for a prison camp appears and stays on screen:

KRIEGSGEFANGENEN   LAGER No 2
ALSHEIM
OFFIZIERSLAGER   C. K. V

Dissolve to more shots of countryside seen from a moving train for a few moments. Then the train slows again and another sign appears and stays on screen:

KRIEGSGEFANGENEN   LAGER No 9
SENTE
OFFIZIERSLAGER   C. K. XI

Slow dissolve to yet more countryside seen from a moving train. Finally the train begins to slow down, as the officers move from camp to camp.

Night is falling. In the distance, a great fortress perches like an eagle's nest on sheer slopes. The walls are in massive grey stone, very thick; above them, a fortified keep rises; above it, the imperial German flag.

The train halts in front of yet another sign:

KRIEGSGEFANGENEN   LAGER No 14
WINTERSBORN
OFFIZIERSLAGER   B. G. K. III

Camera starts on a huge wooden crucifix, then pans down to its base to show an altar. On this altar is a framed photograph of Kaiser William II. Pan in close-up round the room to show the personal possessions of its occupant — the camp commandant, who now lives in the old chapel of the fortress. (He is Von Rauffenstein, who shot down Marechal and Bœldieu and acted as their host in the German officers' mess at the front. The architecture, stained-glass windows, and carved stone of this curious room show its original purpose. The camp-bed of the officer, his collection of riding crops and spurs, his weapons, his valuable china and silverware look odd in this room where the mass was once said. . . . Von Rauffenstein's plane has gone down in flames. He now wears a steel corset and moves with difficulty. He walks stiffly, like a puppet. He could have left the army, especially as he is an officer of the old school and despises the sort of work he now has to do; but he has stayed on for his country's sake. He continues to serve, mutilated as he is, in pain, the shadow of the man he was. . . .)

Pan on past the commandant's belongings, including geraniums in a pot, a pair of binoculars and some daggers. There is a champagne bucket with a bottle in it, a leather-bound copy of ' Casanova ' with a pistol lying on it, a framed portrait of a young woman, all resting on a small table. Pan ends on the commandant's orderly in the act of blowing into his master's white gloves to open up their fingers. They speak in German to each other.

RAUFFENSTEIN off: *Open the window. It stinks in here! Enough to make you throw up.*

ORDERLY standing to attention: *Yes, sir!*

Camera tracks with the ORDERLY as he goes over to the window, opens it to the sound of a bugle call, then returns to where he was.

ORDERLY: *May I bring it to your attention, sir, if you don't mind, sir, that we have only two pairs of white gloves left.*

He shows the gloves in question.

RAUFFENSTEIN off: *Too complicated to have some more come from Paris! Try to make those last out until the end of the war.*

ORDERLY standing at attention: *As you wish, sir. Would you require another cup of coffee, sir?*

Tilt down in close-up on RAUFFENSTEIN's hand setting down a cup on the table where he is being served a large breakfast.

RAUFFENSTEIN: *If you must baptise this slop with the name of coffee. . . . I resign myself. . . . It'll warm my innards.*

ORDERLY: *As you wish, sir.*

The ORDERLY moves way, then returns, and, as he pours out another cup of coffee, he gives RAUFFENSTEIN a dossier. RAUFFENSTEIN takes it and begins to read as he drinks his coffee. Front shot of RAUFFENSTEIN, putting his monocle in his eye to read. There is a knock at the door (*Still*). Cut to outside the room where a German soldier is waiting in front of the door which opens.

ORDERLY: *What is it?*

114

SOLDIER: *The new ones are there!*

Cut back to the room. The orderly leaves the door ajar and walks over to RAUFFENSTEIN.

ORDERLY clicking his heels: *The new prisoners are in your office.*

MARECHAL, BŒLDIEU, and another French officer, Lieutenant DEMOLDER, are standing in the middle of the office. All three are looking at the half-open door. Pan with their gaze: through the doorway, RAUFFENSTEIN is seen as he gets up and sprays himself with scent, while his ORDERLY fusses over him and tidies his uniform. Finally, RAUFFENSTEIN picks up his sabre, his gloves and the dossier he has just been reading, then he walks into his office. He goes directly up to BŒLDIEU and bows and speaks in French.

RAUFFENSTEIN: *Delighted to see you again, Bœldieu.*

BŒLDIEU salutes, then shakes RAUFFENSTEIN's hand as it is stretched towards him.

RAUFFENSTEIN: *I much regret seeing you again here.*

BŒLDIEU: *[We share your regrets.] So do we.*

MARECHAL muttering: *Yes, a bit!*

RAUFFENSTEIN glances at MARECHAL, then addresses all three men.

RAUFFENSTEIN: *Will you be seated?*

MARECHAL: *No thanks, sir.*

RAUFFENSTEIN: *At ease, then.*

Very stiffly, RAUFFENSTEIN walks over to his desk, sits down and opens the dossier. Tilt up on him as he reads aloud: there is a different shot of each man as he speaks.

RAUFFENSTEIN: *Captain de Bœldieu, four attempts at escape: via the heating-system, in a refuse cart, through a drain, and in a laundry basket.*

BŒLDIEU smiling: *There are times when one has to make oneself rather tiny.*

RAUFFENSTEIN with a hint of a smile: *I quite understand. . . .* Returns to the dossier. *. . . Lieutenant Maréchal, five attempts at escape: disguised as a chimney-sweep. . . .*

MARECHAL: *You might say, sir, trying to win the sweepstakes. . . .*

RAUFFENSTEIN continuing: *Disguised as a German soldier, disguised as a woman. . . . That is amusing!* His mouth twitches ironically. *Very amusing!*

MARECHAL: *Yes, but what was much less amusing, sir, was that an N.C.O. really took me for a woman . . . and I didn't fancy that at all!*

RAUFFENSTEIN ironically: *Really?*

MARECHAL: *Right! Absolutely right!*

RAUFFENSTEIN: *Lieutenant Demolder, three attempts. . . .*

RAUFFENSTEIN gets up and walks in front of the three men as he speaks, smoking all the time.

RAUFFENSTEIN: *Gentlemen, your courage and patriotism earns my respect, but here the situation is something else. No one escapes from this fortress. You understand. . . .*

The three officers nod. RAUFFENSTEIN sits down on the edge of his desk, facing them.

RAUFFENSTEIN: *So that no one can complain of German brutality, I have decided to use French rules and regulations here. . . .* He takes booklets from his desk, distributes them. . . . *Here is a copy of them. They will make good reading for you when you cannot go to sleep. And now, gentlemen, would you be so kind as to give me the pleasure of your company. . . .* He rises and calls his ORDERLY. . . . *Oswald!*

ORDERLY off: *Zu Befehl, Herr Major!*

RAUFFENSTEIN: *Mantel!*

The ORDERLY hurries to pass RAUFFENSTEIN his cape, then his muff. . . . Dissolve to RAUFFENSTEIN as he comes into the fortress, followed by the three French officers whom he is showing around the place. The little group goes through courtyards and corridors, often patrolled by armed soldiers on guard. They even meet soldiers walking some guard-dogs on their leashes, as well as young conscripts at drill. There are various shots of them going up and down stairs until they finally reach an inner courtyard dominated by a watch-tower and mounted machine-guns. Some men present arms.

RAUFFENSTEIN: *My men are not young, but they are amused when they play at soldiers.*

Various commands in German are heard, off. The group goes down some steps, then halts in front of more soldiers standing at attention near machine-guns and field guns.

RAUFFENSTEIN showing off his field guns: *I have twenty-five of those.*

BŒLDIEU: *Hm, really?*

RAUFFENSTEIN: *I suppose you know Maxims. . . . Excellent machine-guns.*

MARECHAL mimicking BŒLDIEU: *Why, of course, sir. Personally, I prefer the restaurant Maxim's. . . .*

BŒLDIEU tight-lipped: *Touché.*

> They all smile . . . then continue their tour. BŒLDIEU and RAUFFENSTEIN walk side by side.

RAUFFENSTEIN: *I used to know a pretty gel at Maxim's . . . back in 1913. In English. . . . Her name was Fifi.*

BŒLDIEU also speaking English: *So did I.*

> They go by with MARECHAL and DEMOLDER following. DEMOLDER stops MARECHAL to point out something. Quick pan to the wall to show a niche cut into the stone; it holds a small statue of the Virgin. Return on the two men.

DEMOLDER admiringly: *Twelfth century!*

> MARECHAL shrugs. They go on until they catch up with the other two just as police dogs pass them again.

MARECHAL to RAUFFENSTEIN: *I beg your pardon, sir, but was this little home from home built just to put up me and Captain de Bœldieu?*

RAUFFENSTEIN, not understanding and adjusting his monocle: *Excuse me?*

BŒLDIEU: *Are we your only guests?*

RAUFFENSTEIN stretching out his hand: *Of course not! Your comrades are behind there. . . .*

> Cut to a gigantic wall, then cut back to the group which continues its visit, passing a statue set into the stone.

DEMOLDER ecstatically: *Thirteenth century!*

MARECHAL bewildered: *Is that so?*

> But MARECHAL does not give a damn for these details on the style of the prison. What he notices is the huge height of the fortress walls. Quick pan up this height.
>
> Cut back to the group which has reached the ramparts. RAUFFENSTEIN leans over the edge of the precipice and shows the perpendicular fall of the walls down to the moat. Quick pan down.

RAUFFENSTEIN: *A drop of one hundred and seventeen feet. No one will escape from here.*

The four men are back in the office after their guided tour. The prisoners are waiting to be taken to their quarters.

BŒLDIEU: *It was very pleasant of you, sir, to have shown us around your estate.*

MARECHAL joining in ironically: *Yes, it's a really pretty castle, sir. . . . Turning to* DEMOLDER. . . . *So ancient! . . . After a pause . . . . And so cheery!*

The door of the prisoners' quarters opens, showing RAUFFEN-STEIN and BŒLDIEU.

BŒLDIEU going in first: *I beg your pardon.*

RAUFFENSTEIN following him in: *I am sorry I could not have given you a room on your own.*

BŒLDIEU: *I am very grateful . . . but I could not have accepted in any case, sir.*

MARECHAL and DEMOLDER enter in their turn.

RAUFFENSTEIN: *Gentlemen, I hope that our little promenade did not overtire you?*

MARECHAL: *Not at all, sir . . . not at all.*

RAUFFENSTEIN bows, salutes and leaves the room by another door. Cut back to the three Frenchmen.

MARECHAL looking up: *Fourteenth century!*

BŒLDIEU unruffled: *Pure gothic!*

At this moment, two German soldiers and an N.C.O. come over to search them.

N.C.O.: *Do you mind? It's the search.*

While the soldiers search the pockets of the Frenchmen, the N.C.O. says to them with a smile:

N.C.O.: *You know, your friend, Lieutenant Rosenthal . . . he's here.*

MARECHAL delighted: *I don't believe it! Old Rosenthal!*

BŒLDIEU: *I see his luck was no better than ours.*

N.C.O.: *The Commandant has given me orders to put you in the same room. . . . He says you'll be better fed that way.*

They all laugh . . . but when one of the soldiers grabs MARE-CHAL's képi to turn it inside out and search it, MARECHAL loses his temper and snatches it back.

MARECHAL: *What's that? . . . Enough!*

The courtyard of the fortress is covered with snow. DEMOLDER, all bundled up, walks towards camera, reading something with

118

great concentration. A sentry goes over to him and speaks to him in German, although inaudibly. DEMOLDER looks up and gives a friendly wave before he retraces his steps.

DEMOLDER: *Thank you, my friend. . . . Very kind of you.*

In their new room, BŒLDIEU and MARECHAL have indeed found ROSENTHAL again, as well provisioned and generous as ever, sharing everything with his fellow prisoners: a LOCKSMITH, DEMOLDER who is a professor of Greek, a SENEGALESE NEGRO. . . . BŒLDIEU spends most of his days playing patience. . . . The others read, work, smoke, chat, and feel bored.

[The LOCKSMITH is telling the story of one of his ' amours '.

THE LOCKSMITH: *A good-looking blonde . . . big blue eyes. . . . An angel! Well, three days later I had to go and see the doctor. Don't trust a blonde!*]

ROSENTHAL is seated. Behind him, THE SENEGALESE, warmly dressed, is drawing carefully.

ROSENTHAL: *The same thing happened to me with a brunette.*

MARECHAL: *You can't trust anyone!*

ROSENTHAL: *She was a friend of my mother's! Ever so respectable. A real lady who did good works.*

MARECHAL: *It's usually clap which gets the posh people. . . .* Turning his head *. . . Isn't that so, Bœldieu?*

BŒLDIEU: *It used to be a question of class . . . as many other things were [believe you me]. But that, along with so much else, is becoming democratic. For the time being, the working class does not suffer from illnesses like gout or cancer . . . but it will some day, you wait and see. . . .*

A group shot of the room shows DEMOLDER as he comes in.

THE LOCKSMITH to DEMOLDER: *And the intellectuals?*

DEMOLDER: *For us, it's usually tuberculosis!*

ROSENTHAL at the same time: *Here comes Pindar!*

MARECHAL getting up and walking around: *And the bourgeois?*

ROSENTHAL: *Liver complaints. . . . Intestinal. . . . They eat too much. . . . In other words, all the different classes would die of their various diseases if wars didn't come along to reconcile the microbes.*

DEMOLDER goes over to the table where BŒLDIEU is playing patience and begins to set out all the books he is studying. As he does this, he gets in the way of BŒLDIEU's game and displaces the cards with his dictionaries.

Bœldieu coldly: *Excuse me. . . . He picks up two cards. . . . Do you mind? Your dictionaries are going to be in my way.*
Demolder rather shyly: *I'm sorry, but it's such difficult work. . . . Pindar has always been so badly translated.*
Bœldieu eyeing him through his monocle: *Really? I'm sorry to hear it. Rotten shame!*
Marechal coming over to talk to Demolder: *I never asked you before because basically I couldn't care less, but who is this chap of yours, Pindar?*
Demolder: *You can make fun of it if you like, but to me it's the most important thing in the whole world. . . . No joking, I care about it more than about the war or even my own life. . . . Pindar is the greatest of the Greek poets!*
Marechal: *The greatest Greek poet? Well, I never!*

Quick dissolve to a few days later, as Marechal goes off again to join Rosenthal, who is sitting on his bed consulting a large sheet of paper. The two friends, side by side, look at the map which Rosenthal has drawn.
Rosenthal: *Look. . . . Pointing with his finger. . . . We're here, above this curve, fifteen miles from the Mein. The only way to get to Switzerland without having to cross the Rhine is by Lake Constance. We'll have to walk two hundred miles.*
Marechal: *A nice little stroll.*
Rosenthal: *We'd have to walk for fifteen nights. We could hold out on six lumps of sugar and two biscuits a day.*
Marechal: *Really? A pause. . . . Want me to tell you something? You and your map, you're just as loony as him over there with his Pindar! Nodding his head. . . . Because, to get out of here. . . .*
Behind them, The Senegalese rises to come and show them his drawing.
The Senegalese: *There, I've finished. It's a picture of Justice hunting down Crime. I think it's pretty good.*
Marechal takes a vague look at the drawing, then begins to look at Rosenthal's map again.
Marechal: *No, but, I say, to get to your Constance. . . .*

Dissolve to a few days later, as Marechal's hands braid a rope in close-up. Pan to his face as he works. Rosenthal is by his

120

side, examining the rope.

ROSENTHAL: *Do you think it's strong eough?*

MARECHAL pulling at the rope: *Oh, yes. It'll take the weight of ten like you and five like me.*

Camera tracks back to show the whole room. THE SENEGALESE is posted by the door as a look-out. He suddenly turns round.

THE SENEGALESE: *Look out! They're going to search the rooms.*

At once, everybody gets to work concealing everything that is compromising; MARECHAL and ROSENTHAL dash over to a bed with their rope.

MARECHAL: *Under the mattress. . . . Yes. . . . Hurry up!*

BŒLDIEU: *Come, come, that's no good. It's infantile. . . . Allow me.*

As BŒLDIEU goes over to the window with the rope, cut to the stunned MARECHAL and ROSENTHAL.

MARECHAL: *Hey, well, I'd never have thought of that!*

BŒLDIEU dusting his fingers: *Out there the gutter's frightfully convenient.*

MARECHAL: *Look out! Here they come.*

Each one goes to his bed. Pan towards the door. Five German soldiers enter. Pan down to MARECHAL sitting on his mattress, reading a book aloud.

MARECHAL: *' Louise wrote to Victor: I am as tired as a girl who has made love twenty-two nights running.'*

As he reads, MARECHAL has his belongings searched by a German soldier. MARECHAL turns his head towards the man.

MARECHAL: *Twenty-two nights running! Think of that!*

Pan to another German soldier searching THE LOCKSMITH's pack. The Frenchman, who is stretched out on the bed, lifts his legs to make it easier for the searchers. Pan onto the table where DEMOLDER is absorbed in his work on Pindar. A German makes him rise and examines the stool beneath the scholar.

Cut to the door as RAUFFENSTEIN suddenly comes in, very dignified and smoking. He had not expected the prisoners to remain indifferent and seated. Quick shots of them all, intercut with medium close-ups of RAUFFENSTEIN walking to the centre of the room.

In medium shot, BŒLDIEU sits near his bed, while two German soldiers approach him to search his effects. He pays no attention to them and reads a book haughtily. Cut to RAUFFENSTEIN as he walks up to Bœldieu.

RAUFFENSTEIN: *Do not search that corner.*

Bœldieu gets up as RAUFFENSTEIN approaches, while the soldiers withdraw.

RAUFFENSTEIN (*Still*): *Give me your word of honour that there is nothing inside the room which is against regulations.*

Bœldieu after a pause: *I give you my word of honour. Thank you. But why* . . . He moves closer to RAUFFENSTEIN . . . *my word of honour rather than any of the others?*

RAUFFENSTEIN in close-up, ironical: *Hmm! The word of a Rosenthal . . . or a Maréchal?*

Bœldieu in reverse close-up: *It is as good as ours.*

RAUFFENSTEIN in a shot with Bœldieu: *Perhaps.*

They salute each other. Quick pan to DEMOLDER struggling with a soldier who has grabbed his dictionary.

DEMOLDER: *No, not that one! No! No, it's for Pindar! Don't!*

RAUFFENSTEIN goes over to the table and picks up the book which DEMOLDER is translating. He leafs through it, smiling. Then, with utter contempt, he throws it down on the table, examines with one hand DEMOLDER's face, and shrugs condescendingly.

RAUFFENSTEIN: *Pindar. . . . Poor old Pindar!*

He goes out, followed by the German soldiers. A few seconds later, the door opens to admit a prisoner from a nearby room.

PRISONER: *How did it go with you?*

ROSENTHAL: *Not too badly.*

PRISONER: *That's good.*

The prisoner goes out. Pan to Bœldieu who is coming back from the window with the rope, which he puts on MARECHAL's bed. MARECHAL immediately gets to work again.

Bœldieu and RAUFFENSTEIN, standing in the commandant's office in front of the crucifix and the altar, are talking rather nostalgically about the days when they were not enemies.

RAUFFENSTEIN: *Any news of your cousin, Edmond de Bœldieu, the military attaché I used to know in Berlin?*

Bœldieu walking about: *Yes, he's doing very well. He's happy. He was wounded. He has one arm less and has married a very wealthy woman.*

RAUFFENSTEIN: *I am so sorry. . . . Such a good horseman!*
While talking, they have gone over to the window and they sit down next to it. They suddenly talk in English.
BŒLDIEU seeing the miniature of a saddle: *Blue Minnie? Of course.*
RAUFFENSTEIN: *Do you remember?*
BŒLDIEU: *You were riding her when you won the Grand Military at Liverpool in 1909.*
RAUFFENSTEIN: *The Prince of Wales Cup!*
They switch back to speaking French. Alternate shots of the two.
RAUFFENSTEIN after a pause: *Hmm! . . . De Bœldieu, I would like to tell you something. Believe me, I feel nothing but distaste for my present job, as much as you do.*
BŒLDIEU: *You are hard on yourself.*
RAUFFENSTEIN: *I was a fighting man and, now, I am a bureaucrat, a policeman. It is the only way left for me to try and serve my country. . . .* He stresses the last word. *. . . Burned all over — that is why I wear these gloves. . . . My backbone fractured in two places, mended with silver plates. Silver strut in my chin, also a silver knee-cap. . . . I owe all this wealth to the misfortune of war.*
BŒLDIEU: *May I ask you something? Why do you make an exception for me by inviting me to your quarters?*
RAUFFENSTEIN in close-up: *Why? Because your name is Bœldieu, career officer in the French army, and my name is Rauffenstein, career officer in the imperial German army.*
BŒLDIEU in close-up: *But . . . all my friends are officers, too.*
RAUFFENSTEIN disdainfully: *You call Maréchal and Rosenthal . . . officers?*
BŒLDIEU: *They are very good soldiers.*
RAUFFENSTEIN with contempt: *Yes! . . . [Modern warfare, the nation in arms!] . . . The charming legacy of the French Revolution.*
BŒLDIEU smiling: *I am afraid we can do nothing to turn back the clock.*
RAUFFENSTEIN rises and puts out his cigarette by the window.
RAUFFENSTEIN: *I do not know who is going to win this war, but I know one thing: the end of it, whatever it may be, will be the end of the Rauffensteins and the Bœldieus.*
BŒLDIEU: *But perhaps there is no more need for us.*
RAUFFENSTEIN: *And don't you find that is a pity?*
BŒLDIEU: *Perhaps!*

RAUFFENSTEIN seems thoughtful as he looks at the window which opens on a sheer drop of one hundred and thirty feet. The pot of geraniums stands on the inner ledge, next to a small watering-can.

BŒLDIEU: *I do admire the way you look after your geranium.*

RAUFFENSTEIN turning back to him: *Do not think that I have turned into a botanist, but it's the only flower in the castle. . . .* He sits by BŒLDIEU. *. . . Ivy and nettles are the only plants growing here.*

MARECHAL and ROSENTHAL sit side by side, smoking as they talk in the prisoners' room.

MARECHAL: *I'm glad to be escaping with you.*

ROSENTHAL: *With us both.*

MARECHAL: *Yes, of course. Mind you, I really like Bœldieu. He's a good bloke, but you can't let yourself go with him, you can't feel free. . . . A different sort of education. . . .*

ROSENTHAL: *He's a fine chap.*

MARECHAL: *I agree, but you see, if ever you and I found ourselves in a bad spot, we'd just be a couple of poor down-and-outs, but him, he'd always be Monsieur de Bœldieu. . . . A pause . . . . Besides, you're a fine chap, too! Look at how you've fed us with all those food parcels from your family!*

ROSENTHAL: *It was only from vanity. When I fed you, it was my way of showing you how rich my family is. . . . People think Jews are mean, but they're wrong. If anything, we're often generous, because we suffer from the sin of pride.*

MARECHAL: *That's all rot! What's the sin of pride got to do with it! All I know is that you've been a good pal.*

A new shot of the room shows a tall shambling man, dressed in rags, as he bursts in. It is a RUSSIAN OFFICER, also a prisoner. He speaks French with a strong accent.

RUSSIAN OFFICER: *Comrades! We have been sent a big crate. . . . A present from the Tsarina. . . . Do us the honour of coming to share it with us.*

MARECHAL: *A present from the Tsarina? That means caviar, at least.*

In the great din rising in the room, the words, ' caviar ' and ' vodka ' are often heard.

The Russian prisoners' room is in a distant part of the fortress. Everybody is over-excited, speaking at once and exulting over

124

an enormous wooden crate stamped with the letter A. The officer who has invited the Frenchmen ushers in BŒLDIEU, who salutes, then MARECHAL and ROSENTHAL and DEMOLDER. They all shake hands and congratulate each other on their good luck.

RUSSIAN OFFICER cheerfully: *At last we may do something to thank you for your many kindnesses. The Tsarina* . . . He salutes . . . *has always been good-hearted.*

Cut back to the crate which three soldiers are trying to open with hammers and various other tools. Everybody falls silent as the wood begins to give. Finally, the top of the crate comes off. Tilt down in close-up on feverish hands pulling off the top layer of straw. There is a lot of sawdust and straw, which means that the contents must be fragile.

VOICE off: *Hurrah!*

The Tsarina's gifts are finally revealed: the crate is full of books. The Russians speak in Russian.

A RUSSIAN despairingly: *Books . . . books!*

ANOTHER: *What did you say?*

ANOTHER: *Books!*

ANOTHER: *Look underneath. . . . It isn't possible.*

Medium close-up of the hands turning over the books.

A RUSSIAN: *Nothing but moral treatises, grammars and Bibles!*

Cut to MARECHAL and BŒLDIEU and ROSENTHAL, who examines a book.

ROSENTHAL: *A cook book!*

MARECHAL: *Funny sort of grub!*

BŒLDIEU extremely haughtily: *Jolly poor joke.*

A RUSSIAN: *Let's set fire to it!*

ANOTHER: *Yes, fire! Burn the Tsarina's gift.*

Quick shots of angry Russians round the crate tossing books and straw about, until the whole place is in chaos. As they do this, they mutter and curse the Tsarina and swear obscenely. DEMOLDER tries to stop them from destroying the books.

DEMOLDER: *Stop! No, you don't have the right to burn books. For no reason at all!*

The furious Russians, not understanding what DEMOLDER is saying, shove him aside roughly and set fire to the crate. Cut to the Frenchmen.

MARECHAL: *Things are getting hot.*

125

ROSENTHAL: *We've got no place here.*

ROSENTHAL pushes his friends BŒLDIEU and MARECHAL towards the door. They leave just as German guards come running in to see what the racket is about. The guards try vainly to establish order, as flames begin to burst from the pile of straw and books.

Cut to the three Frenchmen in the corridors, as more German sentries rush by to try to put out the fire and the revolt. Soon they are all alone, walking down deserted corridors as they reach the sentries' posts. There is noise in the distance. The three Frenchmen look at the empty walls with envy.

ROSENTHAL: *All the sentries have left their posts! They've all gone to tame the Russians. . . . Look over there. . . . What a height, but nobody around!*

MARECHAL sighing: *If only we'd been ready, what a chance! We'd have thrown down the rope and in two secs. . . .*

ROSENTHAL: *Particularly as it's nearly night. . . .*

BŒLDIEU: *Well, we can try again another time. They've been good enough to organize a little rehearsal for us. . . . All we have to do would be to put them on a false scent. Now, we know that if one determined man got them to run after him, and if he could hold out for all of five minutes, his friends could escape during that time.*

ROSENTHAL: *That's a big risk.*

BŒLDIEU: *Oh, don't exaggerate. . . . A pause. . . . It would amuse me. When do you want to leave?*

MARECHAL: *Why us? You're coming too, old chap.*

BŒLDIEU: *No, Maréchal.*

MARECHAL: *Why not? Don't you think we can make it?*

BŒLDIEU: *Pfft! You know very well, that sort of thing wouldn't stop me going.*

MARECHAL: *Well, then?*

BŒLDIEU: *Your plan of escape can only work for two men, no more, and I know your preference as partners.*

ROSENTHAL: *That isn't fair.*

BŒLDIEU (*Still*): *And what is fair in a war?*

MARECHAL: *Oh, no, no, no and no, old chap. [You'd be risking your life for us.] We can't accept.*

BŒLDIEU: *I am not asking your advice. I have made up my mind.*

BŒLDIEU continues talking off, while there is a quick dissolve ending in a close-up of a squirrel in a cage in the prisoners' room.

BŒLDIEU continuing off: *I'm not against certain forms of entertainment. . . . In fact, I support them. . . . A pause. . . . Do you like music?*

Camera tracks back to show MARECHAL, seated on the left of a caged squirrel, playing with it through the bars with a straw. On the right of the cage, BŒLDIEU stands.

MARECHAL: *A bit, quite. A good waltz, yes.*

BŒLDIEU: *I'm extremely fond of the flute. We'll buy flutes for the whole camp and fix a date for a grand concert. This is the programme: at five o'clock, the full orchestra in all the rooms. That is when night falls. Five minutes later, our guards will confiscate the musical instruments. At quarter past five, there will be a new concert with all the instruments at our disposal — saucepans, animal calls, grinding teeth . . . and all you want. Result? We shall be summoned to a general roll-call.*

MARECHAL: *And then?*

BŒLDIEU: *Then? . . . A pause, as he amuses himself with the squirrel. . . . That is my affair. You will have five minutes to descend the walls and reach the woods.*

MARECHAL: *Listen, Bœldieu . . . I don't know how to say this. . . . For the first time in my life, I feel embarrassed.*

BŒLDIEU: *Come, come!*

MARECHAL: *Yes, I feel embarrassed.*

Dissolve to a few days later inside the room. Stay on BŒLDIEU's corner of the room, which can be recognised by its neatness and the photographs of horses pinned on the wall. BŒLDIEU is by his bed, bending over a basin full of water and washing his white gloves. MARECHAL comes and stands in front of him, looking embarrassed and moved, not knowing how to begin.

MARECHAL: *Bœldieu, I'd like to tell you something.*

BŒLDIEU barely raising his eyes: *Could you pour out a little warm water so I can rinse my gloves?*

MARECHAL takes a pitcher of water and does what BŒLDIEU asks.

MARECHAL: *Listen, whatever happens, I'd like you to know all the same. . . .*

BŒLDIEU cutting him short: *But I'm not doing . . . I'm not doing anything for you personally. That excuses us from the danger of getting emotional. . . .* He laughs drily.

MARECHAL: *There are certain times in life, all the same. . . .*

BŒLDIEU quite abruptly: *Let's avoid them, if you please.*

He has finished rinsing and squeezing out his gloves. He passes in front of MARECHAL to go and hang them on a line.

BŒLDIEU: *May I?*

MARECHAL follows him and points at the gloves.

MARECHAL: *Are you going to be wearing that stuff?*

BŒLDIEU: *If you have no objection.*

MARECHAL: *No, but I must admit that it wouldn't occur to me to put on a pair of white gloves for this sort of job.*

BŒLDIEU: *Each to his own taste.*

MARECHAL: *You can't do anything like the rest of us do. I've been with you every day for eighteen months, and you still say vous to me . . .*

BŒLDIEU combing his hair: *I say vous to my mother and my wife.*

MARECHAL: *No . . . then. . . .*

MARECHAL admires BŒLDIEU, but he is disconcerted because he cannot understand him. He would like, just this once, to get closer to him, to bridge the gap.

MARECHAL: *I'd like to explain it to you.*

BŒLDIEU pretending not to understand: *A cigarette?*

MARECHAL sits on BŒLDIEU's bed.

MARECHAL: *English tobacco makes my throat itch. Everything really, your gloves, even your tobacco, comes between us.*

These two men, who have faced the same ordeals equally bravely, will never be able to get along.

[Fortunately, ROSENTHAL comes to put an end to their embarrassment.

ROSENTHAL: *I've warned everybody. First concert at five o'clock.*

BŒLDIEU: *Perfect.*]

In a German mess, start on a close-up of an old ornate clock. The time is one minute to five. Pan to two seated German officers, as they smoke and speak in German. They are, in fact, promoted N.C.O.'s.

GERMAN OFFICER: *You can say what you like, but wherever there's* a German, there's order. Of course, I grant you the chief is a complete lunatic with his pot of flowers and all. . . . Lucky that I'm here. . . . I know how to keep that gang of devils in their place. Before I joined the army, I was a schoolmaster.

Night is about to fall on the fortress, perched like an eagle's nest on its summit. A flute concert strikes up in the distance. The two officers look up and go over to the window. The one who has not been talking bursts out laughing.

THE FIRST GERMAN furious: *Lieutenant von Frittwitz! Get those blasted flutes confiscated immediately!*

In the corridors, a succession of quick shots shows the German guards running to the prisoners' rooms. The corridor outside the Frenchmen's room is empty. Suddenly, THE LOCKSMITH, then DEMOLDER and a few others come out of the room dancing and playing the flute. Finally, when they hear the sound of running boots, they go back into their room, still playing. Cut quickly to various rooms as German soldiers storm inside and brutally confiscate the flutes.

In the room of the main characters, all are sitting around their big table, playing the flute for all they are worth. As soon as the German soldiers come in, they all stop at the same moment and raise their arms as one man to give up their flutes, which the German soldiers snatch away.

A SOLDIER leaving: *I wouldn't start up again if I were you.*

He goes out, slamming the door behind him.

MARECHAL: *That's what we're going to do in fifteen minutes.*

BŒLDIEU takes another flute out of his pocket and looks at it with an ironical expression.

At one of the sentry posts, the German officer, who has been a schoolmaster, walks up and down, looking satisfied because the noise has stopped. He rubs his hands with pleasure. He turns his head as he hears a door open. Soldiers enter and deposit flutes on the table.

A SOLDIER at attention: *Your orders carried out, Captain!*

THE OFFICER: *And now, parcels are not to be distributed until further orders. Only dry bread and water to be issued.*

At these words, a deafening racket starts up, making the Germans jump. Dissolve on noise to the following shots: In a succession of different rooms, including the Russian one, the

129

prisoners have picked up every object they can — saucepans, metal rods, forks, empty tin cans. All of them are doing their best to make as much noise as possible, while trying to keep time to the tune of ' Petit Navire ', a song they are all bellowing out at the top of their lungs.

Cut to various shots of soldiers, their arms at the ready, rushing down the corridors.

In the room of the Frenchmen, DEMOLDER is enthusiastically hitting the inside of a metal basin with a big spoon. The others also enjoy the din they are making.

Pan to ROSENTHAL who is winding the rope for escape round his waist. THE SENEGALESE is helping him do this. Pan continues round the room, showing MARECHAL also getting ready for the escape, and ends on BŒLDIEU in his best uniform putting on his white gloves.

Cut quickly from corridor to corridor. The Germans are trying to enforce order and push back the milling and shouting prisoners into the rooms.

Cut back to the Frenchmen's room. The door is shoved open by a German.

FELDWEBEL: *General roll-call!*

All the prisoners drop their noise-making bits and pieces to go out.

DEMOLDER: *At last I understand my students. I never had so much fun in my life.*

Last to leave is MARECHAL, followed by BŒLDIEU.

Camera tracks forward as MARECHAL turns to the other man at the door.

MARECHAL very embarrassed: *Well. . . .* He does not know what to say.

BŒLDIEU: *What?*

MARECHAL: *See you soon.*

With great dignity, BŒLDIEU holds out his gloved hand. MARECHAL shakes it and goes out. BŒLDIEU closes the door and stays in the room. Then he comes towards the camera, does up his gloves, and takes the flute which he fastens to his lapel. He seems to be smiling as he does so.

It is very dark in the courtyard of the fortress, and very cold. From above, all the prisoners are visible standing in rows under the searchlights and hemmed in by sentries. A certain disorder reigns, however, because of what has happened before. Many orders, given and cancelled, show that there is confusion among the Germans as well as the prisoners. RAUFFENSTEIN, dressed in his long army greatcoat, enters the courtyard. Everybody stands to attention. A FELDWEBEL begins to call out the roll. Intercut from a close-up of him to shots of prisoners answering ' Present '. As he begins to call out the names of the French prisoners, pan across the faces of THE LOCKSMITH, DEMOLDER, THE SENEGALESE, and the others. All reply in turn, ' Present ', including MARECHAL and ROSENTHAL.

FELDWEBEL: *Bœldieu!* No reply. *Bœldieu!* No reply. *Bœldieu!*

Cut to the nervous and surprised RAUFFENSTEIN, shot from below. At that moment, in the dimly-lit courtyard, a single flute begins to play the tune of ' Petit Navire '. Everyone, startled by the thin and shrill sound of the flute, looks upwards. Pan up to locate this odd music coming from the sky, just as more searchlights come on and move their beams about in the darkness along the walls, prying into every hidden recess of the fortress. Everybody anxiously follows with his gaze the beams of the searchlights as they locate a flight of steps leading to the sentry posts at the top of the ramparts. A beam climbs up the steps one by one in search of the flute-player. Suddenly, a French uniform appears in the circle of the light. Slowly playing ' Il était un petit navire . . .' over and over again, BŒLDIEU is seen from below sitting on the watch-tower. The soldiers look up. A close-up from below shows RAUFFENSTEIN, also looking upwards. He is trying to understand. From his angle, BŒLDIEU is seen, as he begins to climb higher (*Still*).

Cut to a corridor inside the fortress near a window, where ROSENTHAL unrolls the rope with the help of MARECHAL. They finally throw it out of the window, then ROSENTHAL lowers himself out while MARECHAL remains on the look-out.

Cut to the exterior wall of the fortress, down which ROSENTHAL is sliding on the rope.

Cut back to the corridors. Soldiers approach. MARECHAL closes the window and hides behind a column. The soldiers pass and, immediately afterwards, MARECHAL opens the window again and climbs out.

Cut back to the exterior wall. The two Frenchmen slide down their rope, drop from the end of it to the ground and flee towards the woods.

In the courtyard, pan past the sentries all ready to fire by the searchlight. Everyone is looking up, watching BŒLDIEU's antics. He stops a few times to play ' *Petit Navire* '. Camera cuts quickly to him as he plays, then cuts back to the yard.

AN OFFICER in German: *If he passes the limits of the camp, fire at will!*

Sound of rifles being cocked. Shot of BŒLDIEU, still climbing. He has fastened his flute to his jacket so he can use both hands to climb. Downward shot of the whole courtyard.

A GERMAN OFFICER: *Fire!*

Various soldiers fire. BŒLDIEU ducks and is not hit; he consults his watch, and goes on climbing higher. After the first volley, RAUFFENSTEIN stretches out his arm to halt the fire and walks to the centre of the courtyard to get a better view of BŒLDIEU.

RAUFFENSTEIN in medium close-up from above: *Bœldieu!* (Calling in English). *Listen!*

Cut back to BŒLDIEU, who straightens up and plays a few notes, then starts climbing again. There are a series of reverse angles.

RAUFFENSTEIN in English: *Bœldieu, have you really gone insane?*

BŒLDIEU in English: *I am perfectly sane.*

RAUFFENSTEIN, seen in medium close-up, is extremely upset; his voice trembles slightly.

RAUFFENSTEIN in English: *Bœldieu, you understand that if you do not obey at once and come down, I shall have to shoot. . . .* A pause, then he takes out his pistol. . . . *I dread to do that. I beg you . . . man to man, come back.*

BŒLDIEU has almost reached the ramparts and his voice seems to fall from the heights of the citadel.

BŒLDIEU in English: *It's damn nice of you, Rauffenstein, but it's impossible.*

From below, RAUFFENSTEIN is seen cocking his pistol, raising his arm, aiming and firing.

Cut to BŒLDIEU who has been hit. As he falls, he takes a glance at his wrist-watch.

Cut back to RAUFFENSTEIN, more still than ever. Very slowly, he puts his pistol back in his holster, then he walks about in the courtyard. After a time, a feldwebel goes up to him and comes to attention. Shot of the two speaking in German.

FELDWEBEL: *May I bring to your attention, sir, that Lieutenants Maréchal and Rosenthal have escaped.*

RAUFFENSTEIN: *Maréchal and Rosenthal!* He glances in the direction of BŒLDIEU's fallen body. *So that is why.* . . . . Sternly. . . . . *Call out the dog patrols, alert the stations, and the military and civilian authorities. Report to me about the progress of the search every quarter of an hour.* . . . *That is all.*

Very slowly, RAUFFENSTEIN begins walking towards the camera.

Close-up of a box containing the Extreme Unction, held by a military priest. Camera tracks backward to show BŒLDIEU, who is lying in RAUFFENSTEIN's room. The military priest, who has just given the wounded man the last sacraments, gets up and leaves on tip-toe, while a nurse takes up her place at BŒLDIEU's bedside. BŒLDIEU is obviously being looked after with great care, and every effort is being made to nurse the French officer back to life. Pan towards the door where the military priest is going. RAUFFENSTEIN stands there in silence; he helps the priest to put on his cape and opens the door. As the priest leaves, a German officer comes up to RAUFFENSTEIN and they begin to talk very quietly in German.

THE GERMAN OFFICER: *Your orders have been carried out, sir.* . . . *The patrols have not yet located the escaped prisoners.*

RAUFFENSTEIN: *Thank you.*

The officer leaves. RAUFFENSTEIN closes the door. Pan with him as he goes over to the bed. The nurse moves away a little to give her place to RAUFFENSTEIN. He looks with obvious pain at the man he has fatally wounded, and sits next to the bed. Camera tracks forward to show both men in medium close-up.

RAUFFENSTEIN: *Forgive me.*

BŒLDIEU: *I would have done the same thing. French or German . . . duty is duty.*

RAUFFENSTEIN: *Are you in pain?*

BŒLDIEU: *I would not have believed that a bullet in the stomach could hurt so much.*

RAUFFENSTEIN: *I was aiming at your leg.* . . . .

BŒLDIEU: *More than fifty yards away, very bad light.* . . . *And then*

I was running. . . .

RAUFFENSTEIN: *Please, no excuses! I was very clumsy.*

BŒLDIEU speaking with difficulty: *Of us two, it isn't I who should complain the most. I, I'll be finished soon, but you . . . you haven't finished. . . .*

RAUFFENSTEIN: *Not finished dragging out a useless existence.*

BŒLDIEU: *For a man of the people, it's terrible to die in the war. For you and me, it was a good solution.*

RAUFFENSTEIN: *I have missed it.*

THE NURSE interrupting in German: *You are talking too much.*

> The two men fall silent. Close-up of BŒLDIEU's face, strained with pain, gradually relaxing.
>
> RAUFFENSTEIN rises and goes to a corner of the room, opens a small closet, takes out a flask of spirits, and pours himself a glass.

THE NURSE off: *Sir!*

> RAUFFENSTEIN freezes for an instant, downs his drink in one gulp by arching his back, then goes over to the bed. THE NURSE is unscrewing the plasma bottle; she looks at her watch and notes the time of BŒLDIEU's death in her diary. Pan with RAUFFENSTEIN's hands as he closes BŒLDIEU's eye-lids gently. . . . After a while, RAUFFENSTEIN turns away and paces about the room, moving towards the window. He looks mournfully out of the window. It is snowing. Finally, he looks down at the pot of geraniums standing, as usual, on the sill. He looks at the only flower in the fortress for a moment, then takes a pair of scissors and lops off the flower.

> Long shot of the countryside beneath the ice and the snow. Everything seems dead, the trees, the earth, the sky. . . . Not a sound, not a breath. In the background, coming towards us along a road, a wrapped-up human figure leads a horse. Slow pan over the countryside by the roadside.

ROSENTHAL off: *God, he gave me a scare. . . . We ought not to have stayed so close to the road.*

> Pan continues down towards the voice. From above, MARECHAL and ROSENTHAL are seen, as they hide in a ditch near the road and wait for nightfall. Both men are dressed in shabby civilian clothes, dirty and worn out. They both wear felt hats.

134

MARECHAL: *So? We couldn't sleep in the rushes. They're full of water.*

ROSENTHAL sighing with relief: *He's gone.*

MARECHAL shrugging: *What, couldn't you see it was a woman?* He gets up. *Well, are you coming?*

ROSENTHAL: *Let's wait for night.*

MARECHAL is standing up, stamping and blowing on his fingers to warm himself.

MARECHAL: *Come off it, mate, I'm frozen solid. I've got to get a move on.*

He moves off. ROSENTHAL tries hard to stand up, but he has a swollen ankle. He finally gets up, slips, and painfully regains his balance again. MARECHAL, seen from below, advances towards the road. He turns his head towards ROSENTHAL.

MARECHAL: *Come on!*

Cut back to ROSENTHAL, looking pretty miserable as he finally manages to keep upright and reach MARECHAL. The two are seen slightly from below, as MARECHAL takes a tobacco-pouch from his pocket.

MARECHAL: *Do you want your sugar?*

ROSENTHAL takes his sugar lump and looks into the pouch.

ROSENTHAL: *Hey, there isn't much left.*

MARECHAL grumpily: *No . . . and we're not getting on much either!*

ROSENTHAL eating his sugar: *Don't you want some?*

MARECHAL closes the pouch and hands it to ROSENTHAL.

MARECHAL: *No, I had my share just now. . . . Here, I'd rather you took it. . . . Like that, I won't be tempted!*

ROSENTHAL looking at MARECHAL's shabby coat: *Have you been eating your buttons?*

MARECHAL: *Can you see they're missing?*

He shrugs and starts walking along the road which leads to a village; its church spire can be seen in the distance.

ROSENTHAL hesitating: *Are we going on, then? Not waiting till night?*

MARECHAL pointing to the village: *Course not, come along. We'll go round the dump.*

ROSENTHAL walks on, limping.

MARECHAL further off: *What's wrong? Foot hurting?*

ROSENTHAL in pain: *No, it's nothing . . . just a sprain!*

Dissolve to a new piece of countryside, less flat, but still covered with snow. Pan down from the top of a small hill to show the two Frenchmen sleeping side by side, ROSENTHAL's hands in MARECHAL's pockets. Suddenly, MARECHAL wakes up and rises, shoving ROSENTHAL a little.

MARECHAL: *Come along, off we go!*

ROSENTHAL gets up in his turn and follows MARECHAL with difficulty. He walks very slowly, helping himself with an ordinary stick which he uses as a crutch.

Dissolve to a mountain road covered with snow. MARECHAL is walking about five yards ahead of ROSENTHAL, who is having more and more trouble keeping up. He no longer even walks on his bad foot, but uses the stick to hop along on his other leg.

MARECHAL annoyed: *Well, are you coming or not?*

ROSENTHAL furious: *I'm doing what I can.*

They walk in silence for a time. MARECHAL has slowed down. They are side by side.

MARECHAL exploding: *You and your foot, you're getting on my nerves!*

ROSENTHAL pathetic: *I slipped, it wasn't my fault!* He almost shouts. *I slipped!*

The two men stop walking. Pan to show them face to face.

MARECHAL: *You slipped! We know you slipped! And when we get pinched for lagging like this, are you going to explain to them you slipped? Clumsy oaf! We've got nothing else left to eat, we might as well give ourselves up straightaway!*

As their tempers rise, the two men look at each other with exhaustion and hatred.

ROSENTHAL: *Willingly, because I'm fed up, too.* He yells. *Fed up! Fed up! Fed up! If you only knew how I loathe you!*

MARECHAL: *Believe me, it's mutual. Shall I tell you what you're for me? Baggage! Yes, baggage, a ball and chain tied to my leg. I never could stand Jews for a start, get it?*

ROSENTHAL trying to put on a brave show: *A bit late for you to find that out. . . .* Waving his arms and yelling. *. . . Shove off, will you? What are you waiting for? You're dying to get me off your hands.*

MARECHAL: *You won't be able to say that twice. . . .*

ROSENTHAL all worked up: *Go on then, shove off! Shove off! Shove*

off . . . quick! I don't want to see your ugly mug any more.
MARECHAL *shrugging: Right. Off I go. Try and get by on your own!
See you soon.*
ROSENTHAL: *I'm glad . . . so glad. I could sing. . . .*

MARECHAL turns away and walks off more quickly than before,
leaving behind the exhausted ROSENTHAL. Stay on ROSENTHAL,
seen slightly from above; he works at his leg to try to make it
better, but he is too far gone. He sinks onto a milestone by the
roadside and stretches out his leg (*Still*). His face is a mask of
exhaustion, dirt and despair. His expression remains frozen for a
time as he thinks of the awful end of this escape, so carefully
prepared with his friend. It is not fair, it is horrible! Full of
rage, ROSENTHAL begins to sing all by himself, just to show he
still has something left in him — and so as not to cry.

ROSENTHAL *singing: Il était un petit navire,*
　　　　　　Il était un petit navire,
　　　　　　Qui n'avait ja, ja, jamais navigué,
　　　　　　Qui n'avait ja, ja, jamais navigué,
　　　　　　Ohé! Ohé! . . .

Cut to MARECHAL, quite far away now, and walking with a
determined stride. He gives a flick of the head when he hears
ROSENTHAL begin to sing. Mechanically, he begins humming the
song also as he walks. Camera tracks after him in medium close-
up, as he sings and drowns out the more distant voice.

MARECHAL: *Au bout de cinq à six semaines,*
　　　　　　Au bout de cinq à six semaines,
　　　　　　Les vivres vin, vin, vinrent à manquer,
　　　　　　Les vivres vin, vin, vinrent à manquer,
　　　　　　Ohé! Ohé! . . .

MARECHAL, still walking, stops singing and can hardly hear
ROSENTHAL's voice, which still goes on singing stubbornly. Cut
back to ROSENTHAL, who is yelling out his song, his face increasingly distorted with sadness and fury.

ROSENTHAL *yelling: On tira à la courte paille,*
　　　　　　On tira à la courte paille,
　　　　　　Pour savoir qui, qui, qui serait mangé,
　　　　　　Pour savoir qui, qui, qui serait mangé,
　　　　　　Ohé! Ohé! . . .

Medium shot from above of ROSENTHAL who suddenly stops

singing, listens carefully, and can no longer hear MARECHAL. He is all alone now, abandoned. A pause. Both morally and physically exhausted, ROSENTHAL plunges his head in his hands and begins to sob; he does not notice MARECHAL's coat which is next to him in shot. MARECHAL has, in fact, turned back and is looking at his weeping companion. Camera tracks back to show both men in medium shot.

[ROSENTHAL almost pleading: *Why did you come back?*

MARECHAL does not reply.]

MARECHAL bends over and helps ROSENTHAL to raise himself up.

MARECHAL: *Come on, mate! Let's go.*

Held up by MARECHAL, ROSENTHAL walks a few steps. New shot of the two men, walking along the road on three legs with great difficulty. MARECHAL stops suddenly and looks at his companion. All his hatred and annoyance has gone from him.

MARECHAL: *You can't walk another step, can you?*

ROSENTHAL trying to be brave: *Oh, it's all right. I'm fine!*

MARECHAL: *Would you like us to stop at that little place over there?*

ROSENTHAL: *You're mad ... it's too dangerous!*

MARECHAL trying to convince himself: *It looks deserted. .... There's no smoke coming out.*

ROSENTHAL: *That's no reason.*

MARECHAL: *And when you're on a boat that's caught fire, what d'you do? Chuck yourself into the water, don't you?*

ROSENTHAL crying and laughing with joy: *You're right. Let's chuck ourselves into the water!*

[MARECHAL: *Let's go then, chum!*

And they start walking, step by slow step, towards a farmhouse.]

In a stable, MARECHAL and ROSENTHAL sleep, hidden in the hay. Circular pan shows the stable's small stalls, a feeding trough, a ladder against a wall going up to the loft, an old cart. Suddenly, the sound of footsteps is heard outside. Cut back to a close-up of the two friends, who start up and begin whispering.

MARECHAL: *Did you hear? ... Somebody....*

ROSENTHAL: *You get out by the window. You'll have time to get away while they're dealing with me.*

MARECHAL: *Come off it! I'll handle this one!* ROSENTHAL begins to protest. *And keep still!*

MARECHAL rises. Stay for a few seconds on ROSENTHAL who

cannot move. Cut to MARECHAL, who holds a thick log in his hands. He hides behind the door, waiting to knock out the first entrant. The stable door creaks, then opens to let in a cow. Behind the cow comes a young blonde woman. She looks so fragile that MARECHAL does not dare use his log, even though she can see him in the light of the lamp she is holding. When she sees the two men, she does not cry out, but remains quite still in her surprise (*Still*). In a reverse angle, the men look so filthy and tired that pity comes into her gaze.

She is young, dressed very decently in the style of all the local country women, yet slightly more elegantly and tastefully. Her face, framed by a kerchief, is delicate and beautiful. She looks gentle and rather sad. She shows no terror at seeing the two men and, as she closes the door behind her, she talks to them in German, as she knows no other language.

ELSA: *What are you doing here? Prisoners of war? Do you speak German?*

MARECHAL, who has not understood a word, gathers all the same what the last phrase means.

MARECHAL: *No!* On the defensive. *No! Not bandits! French.*

ELSA in German: *French. Who?*

ROSENTHAL seen from above in medium close-up: *She's asking us who we are.* He shows his ankle, turns towards ELSA and speaks in broken German. . . . *I've sprained my ankle. . . . We're terribly tired. . . . We're not robbers.*

ELSA: *I'm not frightened.*

ROSENTHAL in German: *Call the police! I refuse to go another step.* He shouts in French. *It hurts too much. . . . No, I won't go another step.*

ELSA: *A sprain.*

As she says this, she leans over ROSENTHAL and feels his ankle. Then she makes a decision and gets up.

ELSA: *Come into my house.*

MARECHAL: *What is she saying?*

ROSENTHAL to MARECHAL: *She's telling us to go to her house.*

The two men hesitate and look at each other, not knowing what to do. ROSENTHAL is exhausted, but MARECHAL shakes his head.

MARECHAL: *I don't trust her.*

ELSA: *I live alone.*

ROSENTHAL: *She says she lives all by herself.*

ELSA, carrying her lamp, leads the two men to the door of the farmhouse. They pause before entering.

ELSA: *Come in!*

MARECHAL shrugs and aids ROSENTHAL. All three enter. Shot of the door from the inside. The kitchen is lighted. ELSA turns to the two men and says specifically to ROSENTHAL, who understands her language.

ELSA: *Don't make a noise, my child is asleep.*

ROSENTHAL translating: *She says there's a child sleeping. Don't make any noise.*

MARECHAL helps her to seat ROSENTHAL carefully in an armchair next to the stove. MARECHAL remains standing, a little put out.

ELSA to MARECHAL: *Sit down, I'll be back at once.*

She goes into the next room. MARECHAL, who has not understood, remains on the defensive. Shot of ELSA, putting down her coat and leaving the room. Cut to ROSENTHAL, comfortably seated, and to MARECHAL, standing and looking worried. Pan back to ELSA who is returning, carrying a basin. She goes and fills the basin with water, and sets it down on the stove; then she puts down a bandage and a towel next to ROSENTHAL. While she waits for the water to heat up, she turns to MARECHAL.

ELSA: *Are you hungry?*

MARECHAL trying to understand: *Hmm. . . . Ah, yes! Hungry! . . . Yes. . . . Yes!*

Cut to medium close-up of ROSENTHAL, lying back in the armchair.

ROSENTHAL: *She's asking you if you're hungry.*

MARECHAL: *Yes. . . .* Impatiently. *. . . I understood.*

ELSA to ROSENTHAL: *What about you?*

ROSENTHAL stretching: *I only want to sleep.*

ELSA pours out some milk into a big glass held by MARECHAL. She then gives him a sandwich, which he begins gulping down. They all remain silent. After a moment, the sound of a battalion walking along the road can be heard. The soldiers are singing in the night.

140

MARECHAL looks urgently at ELSA, then at ROSENTHAL. The sound of marching feet can be heard distinctly over the singing. Suddenly, someone knocks on the shutters. Cut often from MARECHAL, alarmed, to ROSENTHAL, who gets up, to ELSA, who calmly goes over to the window, opens it, and pushes open the shutters. A young feldwebel is standing at the window. Shot of ELSA and the feldwebel talking in German.

FELDWEBEL: *Good evening.*

ELSA: *Good evening.*

FELDWEBEL saluting with one finger: *Sorry to disturb you, but how far is it to Wolfisheim?*

ELSA: *Seven and a half miles.*

FELDWEBEL sighing: *Seven and a half miles! Well, I'd rather be spending the night with you than on the bloody road to Wolfisheim! Still . . . He salutes . . . duty is duty. Thank you and good night.*

The feldwebel goes off. ELSA closes the shutters and the window again with great simplicity, and she turns towards the two Frenchmen, who are standing right by the door and staring at her in bewilderment. MARECHAL starts eating again, and ROSENTHAL sits down. ELSA goes over to the stove, picks up the basin and puts it down next to ROSENTHAL's leg. She picks up his leg and begins pulling at his foot to get the shoe off. ROSENTHAL cries out with pain. ELSA is very sorry for him, but is also worried about the child.

ELSA: *Hush! My child is asleep!*

Very slow pan to MARECHAL. He is watching the other two and understands their exchange.

Close-up of a framed photograph of an N.C.O. Above the frame is the ribbon given for the top German decoration. The photograph is standing on the mantelpiece. It is daylight, and, as ELSA's voice speaks off, pan to show another photograph next to the first one: a group of young men. ELSA's hand can be seen in shot, her finger pointing at various individuals.

ELSA: *My husband, killed at Verdun. My brothers, killed at Liège, Charleroi and Tannenberg. . . . She sighs. Our greatest victories! . . . Now the table is too large. . . .*

Pan to the table in the centre of the dining-room. ELSA's little girl, LOTTE, is finishing a slice of bread. She is five years old, brown-haired, blue-eyed, and looks very merry.

MARECHAL is looking after the cow; he is filling up her trough with hay. The fat cow, already used to him, comes to feed from his hand.

MARECHAL: *You're not scared, and you don't mind being fed by a Frenchman.* . . . Slapping the cow's side. *You were born in Wurtemberg and I was born in Paris; well, that doesn't stop us from being pals, does it? You're just a poor cow, and I'm just a poor soldier. And we're both doing our best, aren't we? Go on!*

He pushes the cow aside and leaves the stable. Stay for a moment on the cow, which turns her head towards the door and moos.

His back to camera, MARECHAL leaves the stable and goes over to take a look at the valley. He yawns and stretches luxuriously. The bells are ringing in the distance.

After a while, MARECHAL turns away and walks towards camera, humming. He goes off.

MARECHAL is now seen walking towards the farmhouse and, as he passes, he sinks his axe into the chopping block. He goes in. MARECHAL closes the door behind him and walks over to the oven to sniff at what is cooking. In the background, ROSENTHAL sits in an armchair in the dining-room. LOTTE, the little girl, is next to him, and the two are chattering in German. From a new angle, MARECHAL, seen from the front, has stopped at the doorway which divides the two rooms. He is looking at ROSENTHAL and LOTTE, who have not yet seen him. MARECHAL himself has not seen ELSA, who was scrubbing the floor behind him.

ROSENTHAL: *You're a very clever little girl.*

LOTTE coquettishly: *Mummy and I know everything.*

ROSENTHAL: *Really? Well then, tell me how much milk the cow gives every month?*

LOTTE: *Mummy's the one who knows that.* . . . Counting on her fingers. . . . *What I know is I've got five fingers. One . . . two . . . three . . . four . . . five. . . .*

Pan towards MARECHAL. ELSA, behind him, tenderly gazes at her daughter. The young woman already seems to have got used to the presence of the two strangers.

ELSA in German to MARECHAL: *Could you go and fetch me some water, please?*

142

MARECHAL not understanding and turning to ROSENTHAL: *What is she saying?*

ROSENTHAL: *She's asking you to go and get some water from the pump.*

MARECHAL: *Well, of course. It's a pleasure. . . .* Turning to ELSA. . . . *Wasser . . . wasser. . . .Ja!*

He and ELSA smile at each other. He cannot speak a word of German nor she of French. They enjoy this game which makes it easy for them to be friendly.

MARECHAL takes an empty bucket and goes out. Stay for a moment on the door, with ROSENTHAL in the background, stretching in the armchair. LOTTE skips over to her mother, who is smiling at her, and throws herself in ELSA's arms.

It is Christmas eve. MARECHAL and ROSENTHAL have put up a Christmas tree on the big table, shown in a long shot slightly from above. The tree consists of a big pine branch, which they are decorating with paper chains. ROSENTHAL is cutting out more pink paper, while MARECHAL fixes tiny candles onto the branches.

At the foot of the tree on the table is a manger which they have constructed out of cardboard and wood. A quick close-up inside the manger shows a rather odd-looking holy family. The baby Jesus and his parents are carved out of potatoes.

MARECHAL off: It's sweet, but it still looks a bit shoddy.

ROSENTHAL: *I did my best.*

MARECHAL: *Of course, you did. I was saying that to Father Christmas.*

ELSA enters on tip-toe and looks moved at the surprise the two foreigners have prepared. It is obviously the very humbleness and oddity of it which touches her.

ELSA in German: *Oh! The Virgin Mary!*

ROSENTHAL: *And baby Jesus . . .* Smiling *. . . my blood brother!*

He turns to MARECHAL. Shot of the three.

MARECHAL: *Touché, as poor Bœldieu would have said.*

ROSENTHAL suddenly sad as he remembers: *What, do you think he got knocked off?*

MARECHAL: *Better not to talk about it, all right?* He lights the candles on the Christmas tree. *It's ready. Shall we go and fetch Lotte?*

We ought to hurry, the candles won't last.

MARECHAL goes over to the bedroom with ELSA. Cut to ROSEN-THAL.

ROSENTHAL: *Just a moment!*

He goes over to the old-fashioned gramophone and winds it up. Cut back to MARECHAL and ELSA by the door, waiting and looking at each other tenderly. The lights go out. ELSA opens the door and goes up to her daughter's bed. MARECHAL remains in the foreground by the door, seen from the back.

ELSA waking up LOTTE: *Lotte! Hey, Lotte, Father Christmas has come!*

ELSA picks up her daughter and carries her into the dining-room. LOTTE's eyes begin to shine when she sees the tree and the lights. She slips out of her mother's arms and runs barefoot towards the tree and ROSENTHAL, who waits for her with open arms. Shot of LOTTE's face above the table, looking ecstatically at the tree and the nativity scene. The faces of ROSENTHAL, MARECHAL and ELSA appear behind hers.

LOTTE overjoyed: *Is it for me? Oh! I want baby Jesus!*

ELSA leaning towards her daughter: *Do you want to take him to bed with you?*

LOTTE: *No, I want to eat him.*

ELSA: *He's not to be eaten.*

MARECHAL smiles. ROSENTHAL is in the seventh heaven.

LOTTE reaching over to the manger: *I'll eat Joseph then.*

ELSA: *Eat Joseph, but in bed.*

LOTTE turns to ROSENTHAL and kisses him.

ROSENTHAL: *You're a very nice little girl. . . .*

He kisses the child again, very affectionately. Then MARECHAL catches LOTTE and picks her up to take her back to the bedroom. ROSENTHAL speaks to MARECHAL in German, pronouncing each syllable.

ROSENTHAL: *Lotte has blue eyes.*

MARECHAL is silent for an instant. In the background, leaning against the bedroom door, ELSA seems to be lost in thought.

MARECHAL repeats the phrase in German with a terrible accent.

MARECHAL: *Lotte — has — blue — eyes. . . .*

A quick close-up of ELSA shows her smiling and correcting MARECHAL's *frightful German.*

ELSA: ... *Blue eyes.*

MARECHAL: *Blue — eyes. ...*

ELSA goes into the bedroom, followed by MARECHAL carrying
LOTTE over to the little bed.

ROSENTHAL in the foreground at the door: *Goodnight, froglet!*

Once the child is in bed, MARECHAL comes back and looks at
the manger. ROSENTHAL is next to him. They look at each other
for a second, but say nothing and turn away as ELSA comes
back after closing the bedroom door. Group shot of the three
slightly from below.

ELSA embarrassed: *I ... don't know how to thank you.*

ROSENTHAL answering in German: *Thank us? When we owe you
everything!*

All three remain silent for a moment. But the silence is too
heavy, and ELSA breaks it.

ELSA first to ROSENTHAL: *Well then, goodnight.*

They shake hands affectionately and MARECHAL gets ready to
go to his room.

MARECHAL to ROSENTHAL: *Goodnight!*

Pan to the gramophone which is still playing. MARECHAL goes
and turns it off. ELSA is still standing in the middle of the
room, her eyes lowered.

MARECHAL to ELSA: *Goodnight.*

ELSA without raising her head and in French: *Goodnight.*

MARECHAL walks to the door of ROSENTHAL's room, then returns
before opening it. Casually, he goes over to the Christmas tree
and blows out the lighted candles. He then walks off again. Stay
on ELSA for a few seconds, then cut to MARECHAL who goes into
ROSENTHAL's room with the camera following him. MARECHAL
whispers, ' Goodnight ', and leaves by another door to go into
his own room. He closes the door behind him.

Medium close-up of MARECHAL, looking thoughtful. When he
has closed the door, he turns his head towards the dresser. On
the dresser is a tray full of apples set out to dry. He takes one
and begins eating it, as he walks about the room. Follow him
to show, at the same time as he notices it, that the door leading
from his room to the dining-room is ajar. In the background,
ELSA is still standing where he left her. MARECHAL, surprised,
goes up to her very slowly until he is standing right next to

her. She raises her face and he takes her in his arms (*Still*).

Cut to the snowy countryside seen by Rosenthal from the window of his room. Camera tracks backward to show Rosenthal, seen from the back, leaning against the windowsill. He moves away.

Rosenthal leaves the window. Follow him to the door which leads to the dining-room. He opens it and sees Marechal holding Elsa in his arms.

Taken by surprise, Marechal and Elsa move apart. Rosenthal goes over to Elsa and shakes her hand.

Rosenthal: *Hello . . . I'll do the coffee.*

Marechal a bit embarrassed: *We were waiting for you. . . . Coffee's ready*. He turns towards Elsa tenderly. *Tell him in French.*

Elsa, in close-up, shyly pronounces each syllable distinctly in French.

Elsa: *Coff . . . ee . . . is . . . read . . . ee. . . .*

This insignificant little phrase is her declaration of love. . . . And all three look at each other, laughing. . . . But Rosenthal's ankle has already healed. The two men will have to leave soon.

Quick dissolve to medium shot of the two men, seen from the back, leaning against the fence, which is the farm's boundary.

Rosenthal: *Have you warned her we're leaving?*

Marechal without turning round: *No, not yet.*

Rosenthal: *You must, you know. . . .*

Marechal embarrassed: *You go and tell her . . . [please . . . I can't bring myself to.]*

Rosenthal, extremely put out by the prospect, nonetheless goes off in the direction of the farm. Marechal, his back still turned, lowers his head a little.

Medium shot of Elsa: her expression shows that she is expecting the news. The door makes a noise as Rosenthal, looking downcast, comes in.

Rosenthal in German: *We'll be leaving this evening and. . . .*

Elsa interrupting him in German: *I knew it.*

Rosenthal: *Maréchal is so sad that he didn't dare tell you himself.*

Elsa: *Why? I always knew he would be leaving one of these days.*

She rushes out of the room. Rosenthal opens the window. In

the background is MARECHAL leaning against the fence.

ROSENTHAL: *Come in!*

MARECHAL, in the distance, straightens up and walks over to the farmhouse.

MARECHAL: *Yes. . . . Coming. . . .*

ROSENTHAL, in the foreground, closes the window.

LOTTE is eating by herself at the big table. Three other bowls are set on the table. ELSA, holding a coffee pot, comes into shot and pours out the coffee. MARECHAL, his head lowered, sits down, while ROSENTHAL goes over to the little girl and strokes her hair. ELSA speaks in German, showing some parcels with a gesture of her head.

ELSA: *Those parcels are for the. . . . You must eat something hot before you leave.*

ROSENTHAL to MARECHAL: *Well, we won't start till nightfall then?*

Cut to ELSA in medium close-up. She seems out of breath and sets down the coffee pot on the table to go quickly over into the corner. Follow her across the room, as she sits down and starts weeping.

Cut back to MARECHAL, who has immediately got up. He goes over to her. Medium close-up of the two, who remain silent for a moment.

Cut back to the table. ROSENTHAL, wanting to leave the lovers alone for the last time, begins to make discreetly for the door, then turns back to go and fetch LOTTE, whom he pulls towards the door.

ROSENTHAL: *Come along, Lotte. Let's go and say goodbye to the cow.*

They go out. Cut back to the couple, still sitting on the bench next to the fireplace, holding hands. ELSA speaks in German, MARECHAL in French. They speak at random, but they know that their words are words of love.

ELSA: *I was alone for such a long time. . . . I had stopped waiting. . . . You will never know the joy it gave me to hear your man's footsteps in this house. . . .*

She begins to sob.

MARECHAL: *Elsa, listen . . . when the war is over. . . . If I don't get killed, I'll come back. I'll take you and Lotte back to France. . . .*

147

Dissolve to a few hours later:

The moment of departure has come: the two friends are wearing the same old clothes — now clean and patched — and ROSEN-THAL has put ELSA's small parcels in his pockets.

ELSA stands very straight and dry-eyed. LOTTE is holding onto her skirt. ELSA speaks to MARECHAL.

ELSA in German: *Go quickly. . . . It's better that way!*

MARECHAL presses her hand for a long time; he would like to say something to soothe her, knowing how upset she is; but what can he say that she will understand? Suddenly, he picks up LOTTE and holds her in his arms. He speaks syllable by syllable in German with his execrable accent.

MARECHAL: *Lotte — has — blue — eyes.*

MARECHAL has put all his love, all his gratitude, and more still in this odd farewell. Quick cut to a close-up of ELSA, correcting him.

ELSA: *Lotte has blue eyes.*

Overwhelmed, MARECHAL leaves the room, followed by ROSEN-THAL.

Cut to a night exterior. The two men go forward.

MARECHAL hesitates to look back.

Cut back to the room. ELSA and LOTTE are standing at the open door, looking at the two friends walking away.

Cut to MARECHAL who looks back. In the background is the lighted door and ELSA, holding LOTTE against her. At that moment:

ROSENTHAL: *Look back!*

MARECHAL pretends not to have looked back.

MARECHAL grumbling: *If I'd looked back, I might not be able to leave. . . .*

Cut back to ELSA and LOTTE still at the door (*Still*). ELSA makes up her mind, closes the door and takes her daughter over to the table, putting her in front of a bowl. She starts moving about busily, removing plates and glasses, then leaves the room. Stay on the little girl.

Pan to reveal the mountains, covered with snow, then show above MARECHAL and ROSENTHAL on the look out, in hiding behind some pine-trees (*Still*). They have been walking for two

148

nights and have reached the Swiss border. Their only problem now is to avoid the German patrols guarding the frontier. So the two men have been hiding at the edge of a wood, as they examine the deserted landscape, all covered in snow.

ROSENTHAL: *Well, aren't we going to wait till night?*

MARECHAL: *Not a chance. We'd lose our way. Besides, the wood is so thick, when we get to the valley, we can go on our hands and knees.* A pause. *Are you sure, at least, that that's Switzerland over there?*

ROSENTHAL looking at his map: *Absolutely sure.*

Quick pan over the valley and come back to the two men.

MARECHAL: *It's just that German snow and Swiss snow look pretty much the same!*

ROSENTHAL: *Don't worry, there's a genuine man-made frontier right there, even though nature doesn't give a damn.*

MARECHAL: *I don't give a damn either. . . .* A pause. *And when the war's over I'll come and get Elsa.*

ROSENTHAL: *Do you love her?*

MARECHAL sighing: *I guess I must!*

ROSENTHAL his hand on his friend's shoulder: *Remember, if we get across, you'll be going back to a squadron, and I back to a battery. We've got to fight again. . . .*

MARECHAL swearing: *We've got to finish this bloody war . . . let's hope it's the last.*

ROSENTHAL: *That's all an illusion! Come on, back to business. If we're seen by a patrol, what'll we do?*

MARECHAL: *Well, you run for it in one direction, and I in another . . . and it's each man for himself.*

They are standing face to face now, seen from below.

ROSENTHAL: *In case that happens, it might be safer to say our good-byes now . . . and see you soon.*

They warmly embrace.

MARECHAL: *So long, you bloody yid!*

ROSENTHAL: *Bye bye, old cheese!*

Then side by side, they start running across the snow-covered fields towards the frontier. Pan to another area of the mountain to show in a long shot from above, a German patrol following the tracks of the two men. Suddenly, a German soldier sees two black shapes in the valley, about one hundred yards away. He makes a gesture to the others, who aim their rifles and fire (*Still*). Cut to the two black shapes running. Medium close-up of a German soldier starting to raise his rifle again. The sergeant goes over to him and pushes the muzzle of the rifle down. Both are seen from below as they speak in German.

THE SERGEANT: *Don't shoot. They're in Switzerland!*

The soldier puts the rifle in its sling on his shoulder.

THE SOLDIER: *Lucky for them.*

Pan across the valley. Right at the bottom of the valley, the two small shapes strain forward, sinking knee-deep in the snow at every step. Cut to them walking away up the snowy hillside.

CREDITS:

Produced by	Sacha Gordine
Directed by	Max Ophuls
Scenario by	Jacques Natanson and Max Ophuls, from the play *Der Reigen* by Arthur Schnitzler
Dialogue by	Jacques Natanson
Music by	Oscar Strauss
Songs by	Louis Ducreux
Assistant directors	Tony Aboyantz, Paul Feyder
Camera operators	Alain Douarinou, Ernest Bourreaud
Director of photography	Christian Matras
Sound	Pierre Calvet
Sets	Jean d'Eaubonne
Costumes	Georges Annenkov
Editor	Léonide Azar
Shooting date	1950

CAST (in order of appearance):

The Leader	Anton Walbrook
Léocadie, the prostitute	Simone Signoret
Franz, the soldier	Serge Reggiani
Marie, the chambermaid	Simone Simon
The Brigadier	Jean Clarieux
Alfred, the young man	Daniel Gelin
Professor Schüller	Robert Vattier
Emma Breitkopf, the married woman	Danielle Darrieux
Charles, her husband	Fernand Gravey
The girl	Odette Joyeux
Toni	Marcel Merovée
Robert Kuhlenkampf	Jean-Louis Barrault
The actress	Isa Miranda
Theatre caretaker	Charles Vissière
The Count	Gérard Philipe

LA RONDE

The credits appear in roundhand on a black ground, framed by a rococo-style border.[1]

It is almost night and a light fog envelopes an unusual setting of a street which appears to be overlooked by a theatre stage. A man, his back to us, appears; he is wearing a raincoat with the collar turned up. We move with him as he walks slowly forward, hands in pockets. He climbs up a number of steps and finds himself on the scaffolding which looks like a theatre stage. Part of the curtain and footlights become visible. The man walks up and down in front of them, then begins to speak, almost as though to himself.

LEADER OF LA RONDE: *La Ronde? You're probably wondering what my part in the story is. Author? . . . Compère? . . . A passer-by? . . .* He stops for a moment and seems to be at a loss for words. *. . . I am. . . .Well, I could be anyone among you. . . .* He carries on walking again. *. . . I am the answer to your wish . . . to know everything. People never know more than a part of reality. Why? . . . Because they only see a single aspect of things. But I see them all, because I see . . . in the round, as it were. . . .* He makes a sweeping movement with his hand *. . . and that allows me to be everywhere at the same time . . . everywhere.* He continues walking, examining his surroundings carefully. *But where are we? . . . In a theatre? (Still).* He comes down and passes in front of some floodlights. *In a studio?* He turns his head. The setting of a street appears; in the background is the Augarten bridge. *We don't know any more. . . . In a street. . . .* As if he had noticed the setting for the first time. *Ah! . . . We are in Vienna . . . 1900. . . . Let's change our costume.*

He goes to a coat-rack, removes his raincoat and takes a cloak, a top hat and a cane. Still talking, he resumes his casual walk towards a roundabout.

LEADER OF LA RONDE: *Nineteen hundred. We are in the past. I adore the past; it's so much more peaceful than the present and so much more certain than the future. There's the sun. Spring. You can tell from the way the air smells that love is around. . . . Can't you?*

What's still missing, for love to start La Ronde? ... The music ...
and here it comes!

The man is now standing near the motionless roundabout. He pushes one of the seats with his cane ... the roundabout starts to turn and the organ starts to play a waltz tune.

LEADER OF LA RONDE *humming: The waltz. ... The roundabout turns ... and La Ronde of love can now begin too. ...*

LEADER, *singing: My characters turn and turn,/The earth turns day and night./Rainwater is transformed into clouds,/And the clouds fall again as rain./Honest women, and others less virtuous,/Aristocrats, and even soldiers,/Revolve and dance to the same tune,/When love takes them by surprise./Now La Ronde is beginning./It's the peaceful time of twilight. . . ./Look, the girl comes forward. . . ./This is La Ronde of love. . . ./Ti, la li la, li la, La Ronde ... of love.*[2]

A GIRL is standing on the empty roundabout, which gradually comes to a standstill; the GIRL stands facing us near the LEADER.

GIRL: *Are you coming, handsome blond?*

LEADER OF LA RONDE: *Ah! no ... no ... there must be some mistake, madame.*

GIRL, *almost insulted: Madame? ... You must be joking! ...*

LEADER: *Me ...? I don't joke about anyone.*

GIRL: *Are you coming or not, then?*

LEADER, *gallantly helping her down: I'm not part of the game.*

GIRL: *What game?*

LEADER: *I lead La Ronde. You understand? And it's going to start with you. ...* Leading her into the street. *Now, put yourself there, on the corner of the street. . . . Please!* A pause, then the call of a bugle is heard in the distance. *Do you hear that?*

GIRL: *Yes ... it's the soldiers. ... More soldiers.* Sound of boots approaching.

LEADER: *More and more soldiers. But yours is the sixth.*

GIRL, *shrugging her shoulders: He'll be like all the others.*

LEADER: *Yes ... but he'll be with you in a moment.* Bowing to the GIRL. *Good night, madame.*

GIRL: *Good night.*

The GIRL shrugs her shoulders again and goes to lean on the wall at the corner of the dark street. The LEADER slips away,

154

then turns round. He glances towards the roundabout as the bell begins to chime.

LEADER, announcing: *THE GIRL AND THE SOLDIER.*

Immediately after this announcement the sound of a bugle call is heard. Several soldiers pass by the waiting GIRL. In the background are a caravan and a circus tent.

GIRL, counting softly: *One, two, three, four, five. . . .*

A sixth soldier appears, alone . . . he is smoking a pipe as he walks.

GIRL: *Are you coming, handsome blond?*

The SOLDIER turns round, surprised, and looks at her, then carries on walking without replying. The GIRL rushes after him. We follow them as they walk away together.

GIRL: *Don't you want to come with me?*

SOLDIER: *It's me you were calling handsome blond?*

GIRL: *Who did you think it was? . . . I live very near. . . . Come and warm yourself. . . . It's a bit chilly, even though it's spring.*

SOLDIER: *I haven't the time. . . . Must get back to my billet.*

GIRL: *It's still too early to go back to your billet! Come to my place . . . it's warmer.*

SOLDIER, smiling: *Ah! I'm sure it is. . . .*

GIRL, stopping him: *Hush! . . . not so loud . . . there's often a policeman around here.*

SOLDIER, preening himself: *Don't worry. . . .* He pats his sword. *I'll cut his throat.* He carries on walking, still followed by the GIRL.

GIRL: *You fight a lot?*

SOLDIER: *A bit.*

GIRL, fascinated: *Come on, then. . . . I'm inviting you.*

They climb a staircase which runs up from the pavement, the SOLDIER going first.

SOLDIER, shrugging his shoulders: *Forget it. . . . I've got no money.*

GIRL, very proud: *But I don't need the money.*

SOLDIER, surprised: *You don't need the money? Who are you, Rothschild's kid?*

GIRL: *No. . . . I make the men in the town pay. It's free for soldiers like you.*

Interested now, the SOLDIER stops and turns towards the GIRL. They are face to face, very close to each other.

SOLDIER: *Free?*

155

GIRL: *Yes.*

SOLDIER: *It must be you Michel told me about.*

GIRL: *I don't know anyone called Michel.*

SOLDIER: *Yes . . . remember . . . at the bar in the Schiffsgasse. . . . You took him home.*

GIRL, sighing: *Well . . . I have picked up quite a few at the bar in the Schiffsgasse.*

SOLDIER, making his mind up: *Well! . . . let's go . . . but let's hurry.*

GIRL, following him with difficulty: *Ah! . . . you're in a hurry now you know it's free. . . . Taking his arm. Kiss me all the same. . . . It's nicer when you really like somebody.*

SOLDIER, smoking his pipe nervously: *Come on, come on. . . .*

They carry on walking.

GIRL: *Have you been in the forces long?*

SOLDIER: *You don't want me to tell you the story of my life now, do you? . . . Annoyed. Where is it you live?*

GIRL: *Oh! . . . it's about ten minutes' good walk.*

SOLDIER: *You said it was very near.*

GIRL: *It's not far when you really like somebody.*

SOLDIER: *I like you, but it's a long way all the same.*

A very short pause. . . . They take the opposite direction again.

SOLDIER: *That's it . . . yes . . . give me your address.*

GIRL: *Oh! . . . no then . . . you won't come.*

SOLDIER: *Of course I will!*

GIRL: *Listen. . . . If my place is too far, let's go down there . . . we'll be quiet there. Nobody ever goes that way.*

SOLDIER: *You know some pretty odd things.*

The GIRL leads the SOLDIER to a dark corner of the wharf.

SOLDIER: *Where are we?*

GIRL: *Don't worry.*

SOLDIER: *I don't like it here.*

GIRL: *I like it anywhere. She approaches the wall. Don't fall in the water. . . . You can't touch the bottom here. . . . This is suicide corner.*

The SOLDIER bends down to pick up his pipe which he had dropped, then he presses himself against the GIRL.

SOLDIER: *You're a funny one . . . you really are!*

GIRL: *We'll find a bench down there.*

SOLDIER, holding her very tightly: *We don't need a bench. We don't*

have to bother about appearances.
GIRL: *Oh! Get off, you.*
SOLDIER: *Well, need we?*
GIRL: *I've always wanted somebody like you.*
SOLDIER: *You reckon. . . . I'm the jealous type.*

We are in the courtyard of the local barracks: a bugle call and
the clatter of boots. In the foreground, first from behind, then
turning towards us, we see a soldier sounding the call to
parade. As he turns round, he plays a false note and we can see
that he is in fact the LEADER in a new disguise.
LEADER OF LA RONDE, facing us: *Oh sorry. . . .* Noticing his soldier's
uniform. *This is my first disguise.*
The LEADER puts his bugle to his mouth again and starts to
play. Soldiers jump over the wall, pass near him and hurry to
their quarters.
FIRST SOLDIER: *Oh! all right. . . . Eh! we've had enough of your
music. . . . That's the twentieth time he's played it. . . .*
SECOND SOLDIER: *Who is he, anyway?*
THIRD SOLDIER: *I've never seen him. . . . He must be a new recruit.*
FOURTH SOLDIER: *Have you seen Franz? . . . He's got my spurs.*
FIFTH SOLDIER: *Franz isn't there yet. . . . Think he must be busy
somewhere. . . .*
We come back to the LEADER.
LEADER, sighing: *Yes, busy. . . . But it's going on a little too long.*
He sounds a call on the bugle again, as if for the SOLDIER.

Dissolve to the wharf: the SOLDIER is running, while buttoning
his tunic. Faraway we hear arms fire, which then stops. He
climbs the steps from the wharf. The GIRL looks on reproach-
fully.
GIRL: *Don't run off like that!*
SOLDIER: *Can't you hear? . . . I shall get four days inside for this.*
GIRL: *Tell me what your name is, anyway.*
SOLDIER: *What difference would that make?*
GIRL: *Mine's Léocadie.*
SOLDIER, turning: *That's a funny name!*
GIRL: *You must have a cigarette, anyway . . . to say good-bye!*
SOLDIER: *No, I haven't any left and anyway I've got to clear off.*

157

Good night.

The GIRL remains standing where she is. In the distance, the SOLDIER can be seen running away.

GIRL, shouting and becoming angry: *Good night!* . . . *Well, how about that!* . . . *I'd have a lot of fun if everybody was as mean as you.* Shouting. *Clear off.* . . *Filthy swine.* . . . . *Look at him running off.* . . . *Just look at him clearing off.* . . . *What a bastard!* . . . *Not even a cigarette!* Shrugging her shoulders. *That's men for you!*

The SOLDIER jumps over the wall of the barracks and arrives breathless, holding his sword. He passes near the LEADER, who is sitting next to the sentry-box, without paying any attention to him.

LEADER OF LA RONDE: *A minute later* . . . *and the dance would have stopped.* . . . *Hurry, man* . . . *you're in trouble.*

SOLDIER, stopping a moment: *And what the hell's that to you?*

LEADER, maliciously: *You don't want to miss your Saturday off.* . . . *Get a move on, friend.* . . .

SOLDIER: *Shut up, will you!*

LEADER: *And get a move on.* . . .

The SOLDIER goes off and we move closer to the LEADER, who is now facing us. He removes his cap and sings to music.

LEADER: *The soldier goes back to the barracks,/but he'll be out again on Saturday.* . . ./*He'll go dancing beneath the bright lights/ and there he'll meet Miss Marie.*

LEADER, announcing: *THE SOLDIER AND THE CHAMBERMAID.*

Long shot of an illuminated pavilion in pleasure-garden style. Numerous dancers are visible through the windows. We move towards the windows; one couple becomes more distinct: the SOLDIER and the CHAMBERMAID. As he dances, the SOLDIER holds his partner very tightly against him and edges her towards the door. They go out and walk towards a path in a public park. The SOLDIER, without his great coat, as though dressed for spring, and the CHAMBERMAID walk side by side and gradually move away from the lighted pavilion. Below them, in the distance, are the lights of Vienna.

A couple passes, moves away and disappears behind the statue of a faun playing the flute. We hear them talking as they disappear from view. Another statue, Venus-style.

SHE, off: *And when you think I didn't want to the first time. . . .*
Do you remember? . . .
HE, off: *It's not my fault if you look so attractive.*
    We return to the SOLDIER and the CHAMBERMAID. They walk
towards us, talking all the time. *(Still)*
SOLDIER: *Oh! . . . Miss Marie. . . . You were by far the prettiest girl
there tonight.*
CHAMBERMAID: *You've tried them all, then?*
SOLDIER: *When you dance, you can always tell. You can compare
people.*
CHAMBERMAID: *Yes, I think you like making comparisons. You asked
her more often than me, that ugly blonde.*
SOLDIER: *You think so?*
CHAMBERMAID: *Five times. Oh! I counted. I even thought that. . . .*
SOLDIER: *What?*
CHAMBERMAID: *I even thought: it's funny he likes dancing so much
with a girl with an ugly face.*
SOLDIER: *Oh! she's the friend of a friend.*
CHAMBERMAID: *The brigadier with the curled-up moustache.*
SOLDIER: *No, the civilian with the husky voice.*
CHAMBERMAID: *That's nothing . . .!*
SOLDIER: *Yes it is! It means a lot to me. You don't know me. Let's
sit on this bench, Marie. . . .*
    The SOLDIER espies a bench in the dark and pushes the
CHAMBERMAID towards it by her arm.
CHAMBERMAID: *Oh! . . . no, Franz . . . it's too dark here.*
SOLDIER: *Don't be afraid. . . . I'm with you.*
CHAMBERMAID: *That's just it. . . .*
    They carry on walking, the SOLDIER keeping very close to the
CHAMBERMAID.
SOLDIER: *We should get to know each other a bit better . . . give
you more confidence.*
CHAMBERMAID: *We haven't known each other very long.*
SOLDIER: *Some married people think they've known each other well
for the whole of their lives and don't really know each other better
than we do.* He sees another bench. *There, there's a bench.*
    But before the girl has time to reply, another couple rushes
towards it . . . and a young woman sits down, very pleased with
herself.

Young Woman: *Got it!* . . .

Her Companion: *I'm sorry!*

The Soldier: *No, no . . . after you!*

The young woman holds out her arms towards her companion who, laughing, pulls her to him.

The Soldier pulls the Chambermaid after him. They run along another path towards a little mound.

Soldier: *Don't be afraid.*

Chambermaid: *No, no, I don't want to!*

Soldier, not listening: *There's another bench! We can sit down a bit. . . .*

Chambermaid, with a last effort at modesty: *But you'll behave yourself, Franz. . . . You promise, you promise?*

As she says these last words, they fall on the bench, she on top of him.

Quick shot of the fawn. Music (muted) of *La Ronde*.

The Leader, dressed as a park attendant, watches them.[3]

Leader: *Oh!* . . .

Then he moves away. . . . For a moment we follow him along the paths of the park; he is carrying a lantern.

The Soldier and the Chambermaid are now on their feet and start running towards the pavilion. In the bend of a path the Soldier feels at his belt and stops, worried . . . and then turns back suddenly. We follow him back to the bench where another couple already sits entwined in each other's arms.

Soldier: *Say, mate.* The man turns his head. *Oh! sorry . . . brigadier.*

Brigadier, embarrassed: *What's the matter?*

The Soldier, even more embarrassed, stands to attention and salutes, then mutters something while pointing to the bench. (*Still*)

Soldier: *Well . . . hum. . . . I think I forgot my sword . . . on the bench.*

Brigadier, picking up the sword and giving it to him: *Is this your sword? . . . There it is. Try to remember in future that a soldier must never be parted from his sword.*

Soldier, fastening his sword, with a knowing smile: *I was only parted from it for a few minutes.*

Brigadier: *Even a few minutes. . . . Your sword is your sword. Get off, now . . . and don't let me catch you at it again, eh?* . . .

160

The SOLDIER salutes and runs away, leaving the BRIGADIER and his girl.

YOUNG GIRL, admiring: *You have a lot of authority!*

BRIGADIER: *It's the only way to handle men.* He looks at her. *But as far as beautiful women go. . . .*

He takes her in his arms again, but his movement is hampered by his sword which gets caught in the slats of the bench. He unfastens it impatiently. . . .

BRIGADIER: *Oh! . . . this sword! . . .* And he places it on the ground. Then he embraces his partner again.

The SOLDIER and the CHAMBERMAID are walking in another part of the park. The CHAMBERMAID wants to take the SOLDIER's arm; he frees himself to buckle his belt.

CHAMBERMAID: *What's the matter?*

SOLDIER: *Nothing . . . I'm fastening my sword.*

CHAMBERMAID: *Franz! . . .*

SOLDIER: *What's he done, Franz?*

CHAMBERMAID: *You're a naughty boy. . . .*

SOLDIER: *Am I?*

CHAMBERMAID: *Do you love me?*

SOLDIER: *Yes, of course.* He quickens his pace, annoyed.

CHAMBERMAID: *Where are you running like that?*

SOLDIER: *Well . . . we're going back.*

CHAMBERMAID: *Where?*

SOLDIER: *Back there. . . . There's no reason for staying in the park now.*

CHAMBERMAID: *It's true you love me, Franz?*

SOLDIER, dancing about: *You can hear the music.*

CHAMBERMAID: *There you are . . . you still want to dance!*

SOLDIER: *Why not?*

They pause for a moment; they are facing each other near the pavilion, from which comes the sound of more music.

CHAMBERMAID: *But I can't! I've got to get back! I'll get told off already. The lady I work for is like that, she never likes people going out.*

SOLDIER: *If you've got to, you'd better go back.*

CHAMBERMAID: *I thought you'd take me home.*

SOLDIER: *You want me to?*

161

CHAMBERMAID: *It's so miserable going back alone.*

SOLDIER: *Oh! . . . yes, of course. Where do they live, the people you work for?*

CHAMBERMAID: *In the Porzellengasse.*

SOLDIER: *Oh, it's on my way! But I'm not going back immediately. I feel like enjoying myself a bit more. I've got a midnight pass, you see.*

CHAMBERMAID: *I understand very well; it's the turn of the blonde with the ugly face.*

SOLDIER: *I don't think she's got such a bad face.*

They approach the terrace of the pavilion.

CHAMBERMAID: *Men are disgusting. . . . Franz . . . please. . . . Don't dance any more tonight.* She insists and suddenly tears appear in her eyes. *Franz . . . stay a bit longer with me.*

SOLDIER, taking her by the arm: *Listen, if you want to wait for me, sit down, there. . . . I'll fetch you later.* She sits down. *Are you thirsty? . . .* She doesn't reply. *Waiter, a half for the lady.* He turns and repeats his demand to the waiter. *Boy . . . a half for the lady.*

The SOLDIER moves away, leaving the CHAMBERMAID alone; she sadly watches him go. Through the windows, we see the SOLDIER asking a blonde girl to dance and then waltzing away with her among the dancing couples.

The CHAMBERMAID is still alone, sitting at a table; she suddenly looks bothered, as though she feels that someone is approaching from behind. A SOLDIER greets her.

SOLDIER: *Dance?*

CHAMBERMAID, turning round: *No thanks. I'm not dancing any more this evening.*

The cane carried by the LEADER is tapping against her chair. We move back to see the LEADER wearing a cape and top hat, as at the beginning of the film. He has a flower in his buttonhole. He gallantly invites the CHAMBERMAID to rise from her seat.

LEADER: *Allow me!*

CHAMBERMAID: *I don't know you. Who are you?*

LEADER: *Nobody. . . . That is, anybody.*

CHAMBERMAID: *What do you want?*

LEADER, smiling: *To ask you to come for a little walk.*

CHAMBERMAID, already half getting up: *But I must get back.*

162

LEADER: *I know.* He takes her by the elbow and she follows him. *Unfortunately, you're going to be sacked for going out this evening without permission.*

CHAMBERMAID: *Then I'll have to find another job, won't I?*

LEADER: *You'll find one. . . .*

They leave the setting of the public park and pass through an indefinite and diffused landscape, half film studio, half setting with trees, netting and projectors.

LEADER, continuing: *. . . Trust me . . . a job like any other, neither better, nor worse. . . . And I know that, in two months, fate will be very kind to you.*

CHAMBERMAID, looking around her, as if just waking up: *Where have you brought me? Where are we?*

LEADER: *We're having a short walk in time.*

CHAMBERMAID, sighing: *Two months! July is a long way away.*

They stop. He spreads his arms to display the sun and fine weather.

LEADER: *No, you're already there. Look for yourself.*

The astonished CHAMBERMAID sees that her dress is different. She is wearing the apron of a maidservant.

CHAMBERMAID, astonished: *Oh! . . . Oh! . . . it's true. . . .*

LEADER: *Of course it is. . . .*

With his cane, the LEADER points out a spiral staircase in the courtyard of a private town house.

LEADER, leading her: *There . . . there's the house . . . climb the stairs . . . go on. It's a new job.* Insisting and almost pushing her towards the staircase. *Go on.*

CHAMBERMAID: *But sir, are you sure?*

LEADER, smiling: *Of course. . . .*

CHAMBERMAID, getting ready to go up, but turning round again: *Really?*

LEADER: *Of course I'm sure . . . go on, be brave.*

CHAMBERMAID: *You're not going to leave me alone.*

LEADER: *I have to, miss . . . but don't be afraid. Your soldier is going to be much nicer to you.*

The CHAMBERMAID climbs a few stairs and waves to the LEADER.

CHAMBERMAID: *Good-bye.*

The LEADER turns round towards us. He sighs.

LEADER: *Let's hope it won't be too late. . . .*

163

He comes down a few steps of the staircase. The bell of the roundabout is heard and the LEADER starts to hum.

LEADER: *My characters turn and turn./He's the one who loves you now,/but your inconstant heart/will prefer another lover. . . ./ . . . La, la, la. . . . Another lover. . . .*

At the foot of the staircase, the LEADER unearths a clapperboard. Humming, he writes on it with a piece of chalk. (*Still*) He opens and shuts the clapper, with its usual sharp noise, then turns to face the audience to show what he has written.

LEADER, announcing: *THE CHAMBERMAID AND THE YOUNG MAN.*

It is a hot summer's afternoon; we are in the kitchen of the house. The CHAMBERMAID is sitting at the table, on which lie writing paper, a pen and an ink bottle. We see that she is holding a letter from the SOLDIER, and we hear the voice of the SOLDIER reading the text of the letter.

SOLDIER, off: *Dear Miss Marie. Thank you for sending your new address. I'm glad the people you work for are nice people. But how old is the son of the house?* Quick shot of the son of the house reading on a sofa. *I saw you yesterday on the way back from the parade ground. I waved to you, but you didn't reply. Was it on purpose, or didn't you see me?*

The CHAMBERMAID puts the letter on the table, takes her pen and dips it into the ink bottle and starts to write. The text is not visible, but we hear it read in her own voice.

CHAMBERMAID'S VOICE: *Dear Franz. . . . I have plenty of time to write to you this afternoon, because my master and mistress have gone to the country. I was very pleased to get your letter.*

SOLDIER, off: *But how old is the son of the house?*

In the drawing-room the YOUNG MAN, casually dressed because of the heat, is stretched out on the sofa, reading.[4]
Bored with his book, the YOUNG MAN rings, then continues reading.
The bell rings in the kitchen. The CHAMBERMAID, slightly disturbed, puts the pen down and gets up.
The YOUNG MAN is reading in the drawing-room. We look towards the door as a light knock is heard.

YOUNG MAN: *Come in.*

The CHAMBERMAID sidles through the half-open door.

CHAMBERMAID: *Mr. Alfred rang?*

The YOUNG MAN pretends to read.

YOUNG MAN, timid: *Yes, Marie. . . . Yes, I did ring . . . yes. What did I want to ask you? Oh! . . . yes . . . would you pull the blinds down, please. . . .* The CHAMBERMAID goes to the windows and pulls the blinds down. . . . *Yes. . . . Like that, it won't be so hot.*

CHAMBERMAID: *Mr. Alfred is very brave, working in such nice weather!*

YOUNG MAN, who has been gazing after her: *Marie!*

CHAMBERMAID, approaching: *Yes, sir.*

YOUNG MAN, feverishly: *Ma . . . Marie . . . bring me a large glass of water.*

CHAMBERMAID: *Yes, Mr. Alfred.*

She is getting ready to go, when he raises himself slightly and looks in her direction.

YOUNG MAN: *Marie?*

CHAMBERMAID, looking back flirtatiously: *Mr. Alfred! . . .*

YOUNG MAN, hesitant and embarrassed: *. . . Let it run so that it'll be cool, won't you?*

She goes out, leaving the YOUNG MAN gazing after her.

The CHAMBERMAID comes into the kitchen and passes in front of the table.

SOLDIER, off: *You haven't answered my question. . . .*[5]

She takes a glass, places it under the tap and allows the water to run.

The YOUNG MAN continues reading nervously in the drawing-room.

In the kitchen, the CHAMBERMAID goes to the sink and turns the tap off, takes the glass and a saucer and passes again in front of the table.

SOLDIER, off: *Was it on purpose, or didn't you see me?*[6]

She leaves the kitchen.

In the drawing-room: the YOUNG MAN holds his book closed in his hand. He turns his head on hearing the noise at the door. The CHAMBERMAID enters the room, goes up to him and offers him the glass, which he takes. He looks nervously at the girl, thinking about his next move.

165

YOUNG MAN: *Ah! thank you. Ah! very good. . . .*

Their fingers have touched as he has taken the glass. Still timid, but wanting to hide his embarrassment, the YOUNG MAN looks at her with a certain boldness. She lowers her eyes. He drinks . . . then, almost trembling, replaces the glass on the saucer. Their fingers brush again, their hands tremble and the glass almost falls.

YOUNG MAN: *Why are you trembling? . . .* Encouraged by the evident timidity of the CHAMBERMAID, he goes on, very sure of himself. *Careful with the glass! . . .* A pause while he stretches his limbs. *What on earth is the time?*

CHAMBERMAID: *Nearly five o'clock, Mr. Alfred.*

YOUNG MAN, stretching himself again: *Oh! . . . already. . . .* A pause. *All right, thank you.*

She goes towards the door, but she turns round on the threshold. The YOUNG MAN has been gazing after her. She smiles and goes out, while the YOUNG MAN remains lying where he is for a moment. Then he gets up and goes to the door, comes back and sits down again on the sofa and sighs. He opens the book at random and starts reading.

The CHAMBERMAID is sitting down in the kitchen and holding the SOLDIER's letter.[7]

SOLDIER, off: *I'm writing on my bed and thinking a lot about you.*

A bell rings. The CHAMBERMAID gets up, throwing the letter on the table . . . then smiles as she goes into . . .

Her bedroom, which we glimpse very briefly. She straightens her hair and arranges her bodice. The bell rings again and she goes out smiling.

She passes quickly through the kitchen, glancing ironically at the SOLDIER's letter on the table.

SOLDIER, off: *How old is the son of the house?*

The YOUNG MAN is smoking nervously. He rings again. The CHAMBERMAID appears in the doorway.

CHAMBERMAID, coming in: *Mr. Alfred?*

YOUNG MAN: *Oh! yes. . . . Has anyone rung at the door?*

CHAMBERMAID: *No, sir.* Hesitating. *Is Mr. Alfred waiting for someone?*

YOUNG MAN: *Professor Schüller, yes. . . . You know him?*

CHAMBERMAID: *The little man who came the day before yesterday?*

YOUNG MAN: *He comes twice a week, at five o'clock; he's giving me French lessons for the exams. . . . What time is it?*

CHAMBERMAID: *Quarter to five, sir.*

YOUNG MAN: *Mind you, he's always late.* A pause. *Marie.*

CHAMBERMAID, coming a little nearer: *Mr. Alfred?*

YOUNG MAN, feverish: *Come. . . . Nearer. . . . I thought . . . .*

CHAMBERMAID: *What did Mr. Alfred think?*

YOUNG MAN: *Nothing, it's your bodice.*

CHAMBERMAID: *What's wrong with my bodice? Doesn't Mr. Alfred like it?*

YOUNG MAN: *Oh! yes . . . yes, it's. . . .* Correcting himself, wonderingly. *. . . it's blue . . . eh?*

CHAMBERMAID: *Yes. . . .* Very softly. *It's a blue bodice.*

He takes her in his arms and slips off her apron. She makes a half gesture of modesty.

YOUNG MAN: *In fact . . . you dress very . . . very nicely.* Holding her tightly. *Aren't you hot?*

CHAMBERMAID: *It's too light. . . .*

YOUNG MAN: *You're right, Marie. It's too light.*

He rushes to the open windows and closes the shutters.

YOUNG MAN, while pulling the shutters to: *Mind you. . . . You mustn't be embarrassed by me. In fact, you shouldn't be embarrassed by anyone . . . you're so pretty. Oh! Marie! how nice your hair smells!*

CHAMBERMAID: *Yes, sir.*

YOUNG MAN, nervous: *You know, I've already seen you, one evening. . . . I came home late. Then I . . . I passed the kitchen to get some water . . . the . . . the door of your room was open. Then . . . I saw all sorts of things. . . . Oh! . . . you have such a white skin.*

CHAMBERMAID: *What if someone rang?*

YOUNG MAN, smiling: *We wouldn't open . . . we wouldn't open. . . .*

He closes the last shutter.

We move to the staircase in the courtyard of the house, as a clock strikes five somewhere and the theme music of *La Ronde* becomes audible.

PROFESSOR SCHULLER crosses the inner court and prepares to climb the staircase. We move towards the open window of the PORTER's lodge; the PORTER (who is in fact the LEADER) is quietly smoking and watching the court.

The PROFESSOR goes up to the lodge window. (*Still*)

167

PORTER (LEADER): *Where are you going, sir?*
PROFESSOR: *Third floor, my man.*
PORTER: *I'm sorry, sir. Those people have gone to the country.*
PROFESSOR: *I know, but I came to see the son.*
PORTER: *He isn't there, sir.*
PROFESSOR: *No, you must be wrong. The young man told me that he was not going to the country with his parents.*
PORTER: *He must have changed his mind, sir.*
PROFESSOR: *Certainly not! He's waiting for me to give him his French lesson.*
PORTER: *Do you think so?*
PROFESSOR: *Wait a minute, who are you?*
PORTER: *You wouldn't know me. I'm quite new.*
PROFESSOR: *Quite new!*
PORTER: *Yes . . . and I can tell you, sir, that there's no one up there.*
PROFESSOR: *How very odd!*
PORTER, with a movement of his head: *Anyway you can see that the shutters are closed as you go by.*
PROFESSOR, convinced: *Well, thank you. . . . You've saved me climbing three flights for nothing.*
PORTER: *Don't thank me, professor, it's to keep it going round.*
PROFESSOR, moving away: *Going round . . . what?*
PORTER: *La Ronde, professor.*
PROFESSOR, trying to understand: *Ah! yes, La Ronde.* A pause. . .
La Ronde?
PORTER: *Yes, professor.*
The PROFESSOR walks swiftly away, still puzzled.
The CHAMBERMAID is seen opening the windows of the drawing-room. (*Still*)
YOUNG MAN, off: *Someone rang . . . ah! I'm sure someone rang. Go and see . . . will you?*
She crosses the room and goes out.
Long shot of the drawing-room as she comes back.
The YOUNG MAN is on his feet, still in his shirtsleeves. A clock chimes.
YOUNG MAN: *Well?*
CHAMBERMAID:, *No nothing. . . . He almost certainly didn't come.*
YOUNG MAN: *Ah! Well, that's luck for you!* He takes his coat and hat from the coat-rack. *I'm going out. I feel like walking . . .*

breathing . . . I . . . I feel ten years older.
CHAMBERMAID: *Have a nice walk, Mr. Alfred.*
YOUNG MAN: *You're not annoyed?*
> He goes to the front door.
CHAMBERMAID, smiling: *Oh! no. . . . I'm sure of seeing you again.*
YOUNG MAN, astonished: *Obviously! Why did you say that?*
CHAMBERMAID: *No reason.*
YOUNG MAN: *Till tonight, then.*
CHAMBERMAID: *Till tonight, Mr. Alfred.*
> The YOUNG MAN goes out triumphantly.
> The kitchen is deserted.[8]
SOLDIER, off: *How old is the son of the house?*
> The CHAMBERMAID, cigarette in her mouth, takes the letter she
> has been writing and slowly tears it up.
SOLDIER, off: *Was it on purpose or didn't you see me?*
> The CHAMBERMAID casually takes the SOLDIER's letter, lights it
> at the stove and lights her cigarette with it.
SOLDIER, off: *Was it on purpose or didn't you . . .?*
> The letter goes up in flames.

We move in towards the roundabout, on which the LEADER is
standing. He is wearing a cloak, top hat and carrying a cane.
He turns the crank which works the roundabout and sings.
LEADER, singing: *Some time after/that red-letter day/love went to
his head,/beautiful love,/everlasting love/for/an honest woman.*
> He pauses.
LEADER, continuing: *My characters turn and turn. . . ./He follows
her with his love./But, alas! She won't let herself go./When he
speaks to her, she runs away.*
> The roundabout turns more quickly.
> The YOUNG MAN is seen feverishly buying flowers in a flower
> shop while, off, the LEADER continues his song.
LEADER, singing off: *If she needs flowers to change her mind,/Then
here are the roses of summer./But even that's not enough to over-
come/all her modesty. . . .*
> The YOUNG MAN bursts into another shop and comes out again
> almost immediately, carrying bottles. The song continues.
LEADER, singing off: *Just a drop to make her drunk/and she'd have
given herself . . ./but such a charming woman/doesn't drink on*

street corners.

We are looking up the staircase of an elegant town house. The lift is going up. The LEADER's song continues.

A hand opens a door with a key.

LEADER, singing off: *Go and find the caretaker/of this discreet apartment./For a few coins/it's yours . . . here's the key. . . .*

The YOUNG MAN appears on a bicycle; he rides along the street, stops and enters the building.

LEADER, off: *One fine day, burning with impatience. . . .*

The YOUNG MAN is walking round and round his bachelor apartment; he arranges a vase and flowers, looks at himself in the mirror, and then surveys the whole effect.

LEADER, singing off: *At the time arranged. . . ./He's all dressed up/ and full of confidence. . . ./He's happy,/she has promised. . . . She has promised!*

A cab arrives in front of the house and comes to a halt.

The window of the cab: the blind is lifted, showing the face of a YOUNG WOMAN. She climbs out and addresses the CABBY who turns round and shows himself to be really the LEADER.

YOUNG WOMAN: *Wait for me, five minutes. . . .*

The CABBY-LEADER nods his head, then smiles as the YOUNG WOMAN runs quickly into the house.

LEADER, announcing: *THE YOUNG MAN AND THE MARRIED WOMAN.*

The YOUNG MAN leaves the window of his apartment quickly, straightens his tie and waits, very disturbed and nervous. He rushes to the door.

The YOUNG WOMAN appears on the threshold, her face hidden by veils.

YOUNG MAN, beside himself: *Ah! . . . Emma. . . . You've come! Oh! thank you!*

The YOUNG MAN seizes the hand of the YOUNG WOMAN and kisses it.

YOUNG WOMAN, worried: *Close the door quickly.*

YOUNG MAN, closing the door: *Were you followed?*

YOUNG WOMAN: *Ah! . . . I hope not. . . . I changed cab three times. . . . A pause as she sighs. Ah! . . . Alfred! . . . Alfred! . . . What madness! I can hear my heart beating.*

170

Young Man, eager: *Come and sit down.*

Young Woman: *What time is it?*

> She stretches her hand towards the Young Man's jacket and pulls out his watch from his pocket with a graceful movement.

Young Man, surprised, looks at the time: *Well! . . . Quarter to six . . . . You're not late. . . .*

> The Young Woman goes to sit down, though only on the arm of an armchair, then she goes to the fireplace and turns round to inspect the room.

Young Woman: *It's nice, your place.*

Young Man, very softly: *Yes . . . isn't it? . . .*

Young Woman: *Yes, it's cosy. . . . A pause. Is it really your place?*

Young Man, embarrassed: *Mm! . . . Yes . . . well . . . for the time being.*

Young Woman: *Ah! since when?*

Young Man: *For some time now.* He pauses. *Don't you want to sit down?*

Young Woman: *Yes . . . my legs are trembling. . . . It must be emotion.*

> She sits down; the Young Man approaches her.
>
> He kneels down to speak to her.

Young Man: *Take your stole off. You'll feel better.*

> He tries to help her. She offers no resistance.

Young Woman: *You think so?*

Young Man: *Yes. . . . And your veil.*

Young Woman: *Two.*

> He takes one veil off.

Young Man: *Two? . . . A pause. . . . One.*

Young Woman: *One. . . .*

Young Man: *Two. . . .*

Young Woman, her smiling face becoming visible: *Two. . . .*

Young Man: *Take your hat off, you'll feel better.*

Young Woman, pretending to be surprised: *You think so?*

> The Young Man removes her hat.

Young Woman: *Don't disturb my hair.*[9]

Young Man: *I've got a comb.*

Young Woman: *You've got a comb here?*

Young Man: *Of course. . . .*

Young Woman, pretending to be confused: *Oh! Alfred!*

YOUNG MAN, excusing himself: *It's practical. . . .*

YOUNG WOMAN: *It's practical, but it's. . . . Alfred, don't look at me like that. . . .*[10]

YOUNG MAN, standing near the fireplace: *How beautiful you are! . . . I don't know what you do. . . . You get more beautiful all the time. . . .*

YOUNG WOMAN: *You're sweet. . . . Do you love me?*

YOUNG MAN: *I hope you don't doubt it?*

YOUNG WOMAN: *Then you're going to prove it. . . . You're going to let me go.*

YOUNG MAN: *Oh! Emma!*

YOUNG WOMAN: *I did what you asked me to. I came.*

YOUNG MAN, dropping down on his knees: *Emma, don't be cruel. . . .*

YOUNG WOMAN: *You promised to be reasonable.*

YOUNG MAN: *I swear I'll be reasonable. . . .*

They remain silent for a while. . . . Finally the YOUNG WOMAN begins to be impatient, tries to hide it, but. . . .

She is still sitting down, the YOUNG MAN at her feet.

YOUNG WOMAN: *Well, now . . . good-bye.*

YOUNG MAN: *Emma . . . don't torture me.*

YOUNG WOMAN: *The five minutes are over.*

YOUNG MAN: *Not five minutes, it's hardly five seconds.*

YOUNG WOMAN: *What time is it?*

YOUNG MAN: *I don't know.*

Again, the YOUNG WOMAN pulls on the YOUNG MAN's watch-chain and looks at the time. She reads it out.

YOUNG WOMAN: *Five to six. I should have been at . . . at . . . my sister's a long time ago.*

YOUNG MAN: *Your sister can wait. You see her every day.*

YOUNG WOMAN: *Oh! Alfred, Alfred. . . . Why did I listen to you?*

The YOUNG MAN is still at her feet; he kisses her hand at regular intervals.

YOUNG MAN: *Emma, Emma, I've thought a lot about you and I know you're unhappy.*

YOUNG WOMAN: *Ah! Yes!*

YOUNG MAN: *Yes. . . .* A lengthy pause. *Oh! . . . life is so disappointing.*

YOUNG WOMAN: *Ah yes!*

YOUNG MAN: *So empty and then . . . so short, so terribly short. . . .*

The only real happiness is meeting someone you love.
  Series of shots and reverse shots in close-up following whoever
  is speaking.
YOUNG WOMAN: *Whoever could have told me that a week ago. . . .*
Even yesterday!
YOUNG MAN: *You promised the day before yesterday.*
YOUNG WOMAN: *The day before yesterday you'd managed to get
round me. Yesterday, I thought about it. I've decided not to see
you any more. I've written you a long letter.*
YOUNG MAN: *I haven't received it, you know.*
YOUNG WOMAN: *I tore it up. I should have sent it.* A pause. *Oh!
Alfred, good-bye. . . . We mustn't see each other again. . . . What's
behind that door?*
YOUNG MAN: *Well . . . it's a room.*
YOUNG WOMAN: *Yes, but what sort of room?*
YOUNG MAN, embarrassed: *Well, a drawing-room, another drawing-
room.*
YOUNG WOMAN: *You have two drawing-rooms?*
YOUNG MAN: *Yes . . . it's a big apartment you know.*
YOUNG WOMAN: *Alfred. . . . I'm going to ask you a question.*
YOUNG MAN: *Yes?*
YOUNG WOMAN: *You swear to tell the truth?*
YOUNG MAN: *Yes.*
YOUNG WOMAN: *Have other women already been here before?*
YOUNG MAN: *Really, Emma, this house has been built for more than
fifty years . . . really. . . .*
YOUNG WOMAN: *That's not what I'm asking you. You understand
me very well.*
YOUNG MAN: *Oh! never, Emma, never. I explained to you that. . . .*
YOUNG WOMAN: *Yes, in fact, it's to receive me that you. . . .*
YOUNG MAN: *Yes. . . . What's wrong with that?*
YOUNG WOMAN, pretending to be annoyed: *Nothing. . . . Nothing. . . .*
She gets up and takes her coat. *My violets? . . .* She looks around.
  He rushes towards her and takes her in his arms just as she
  reaches the door. He kisses her face, her neck and tries to kiss
  her lips, but she prevents him. Finally, she gives in . . . with a
  long sigh.
YOUNG WOMAN: *Alfred . . . Alfred . . . Oh! . . . What are you doing
to me? . . . No. . . . No. . . .* A pause. She falls back again in an

armchair. *Oh! . . . What time is it?*

YOUNG MAN, firmly: *I don't know.*

YOUNG WOMAN: *I thought it was later. . . Oh! . . . Oh! . . . Alfred! . . .*

YOUNG MAN, pressing: *Emma. . . .*

YOUNG WOMAN, breathless: *Give me something to drink. . . . Give me a glass of water.*

YOUNG MAN: *You want a glass of water?*

YOUNG WOMAN, passionately: *I'm thirsty!*

YOUNG MAN, a little gauche: *You don't prefer . . . what I bought . . . that would be more. . . .*

YOUNG WOMAN: *Anything. . . .*

> The YOUNG MAN stands up and goes to the kitchen casting a slightly anxious glance towards the YOUNG WOMAN, who is now standing up.

YOUNG MAN: *Euh! . . . Mind you, the cork was ruined. . . . I bit. . . .*

YOUNG WOMAN: *Go on . . . go on. . . .*

> He walks quickly away from her, then turns round at the door to show the other door, that of the bedroom.

YOUNG MAN, embarrassed: *. . . I wanted to tell you . . . the room next door . . . is . . . is. . . .*

YOUNG WOMAN, cutting him short: *Go on . . . go on. . . .*

> He goes out. Left alone, the YOUNG WOMAN gets up and goes softly to the front door, then changes her mind and goes to the bedroom door.

> The YOUNG WOMAN enters, as we look towards the bed. She comes out again. Noise of crockery breaking in the kitchen.

> In the tiny kitchen, the YOUNG MAN is struggling with the bottle with the spoilt cork; he is trying to get the contents into a decanter. There is the sound of a door closing. Terrified, he whirls round holding the bottle and the corkscrew. He goes out into the corridor still holding them.

> On the landing, still with the bottle and corkscrew, he leans over the banisters.

YOUNG MAN, calling: *Emma. . . .*

> No reply, no sound of footsteps on the staircase. Taken aback and upset, he goes back. . . .

> In the drawing-room, the YOUNG WOMAN's coat and hat are there. The YOUNG MAN leaps to the bedroom door. On the

threshold, he stops, overcome with happiness.

YOUNG MAN: *Emma. . . . You do frighten me! Oh! . . . Emma! . . .* Rapid dissolve to the LEADER on the roundabout: he is standing at the crank which he is turning. (*Still*) Suddenly the roundabout stops, the engine giving off a lot of smoke. The man opens the casing and tries to examine the mechanism inside; he looks very surprised.

LEADER: *Well . . . well . . . that's curious! . . . What's happening?* Slow dissolve back to the bedroom in the bachelor apartment. The YOUNG MAN is in the foreground, wearing pyjamas, sitting on the bed near the YOUNG WOMAN, who is lying down. He holds his head with one hand and frowns. The YOUNG WOMAN turns her head on the pillow towards him. He turns his back to her. (*Still*)

YOUNG WOMAN, in a kind tone: *Don't be upset, darling.*

YOUNG MAN, irritated and crestfallen: *I was sure of it. . . . I've been like a madman all day. . . . Have you read Stendhal?*

YOUNG WOMAN: *Stendhal?*

YOUNG MAN: *Yes, the book by Stendhal: love. . . ." On Love "!*

YOUNG WOMAN: *No.*

YOUNG MAN, turning his head: *Well, there's something very characteristic there.*

YOUNG WOMAN: *Oh, yes?*

YOUNG MAN: *Yes, it's . . . cavalry officers . . . who tell the stories of their love affairs . . . and do you follow me?* He turns round for a moment.

YOUNG WOMAN: *Yes, yes . . . their love affairs; and then?*

YOUNG MAN: *And then . . . they tell how it is with the woman they have wanted most . . . that the same thing happened to them . . . finally . . . the same thing as to me . . . It's very . . . very . . . typical, isn't it?*

YOUNG WOMAN, in quick close-up: *Very . . . very.*

   The YOUNG WOMAN must not look as though she is making fun of him. She is very attentive, but hardly convinced.[11]

YOUNG MAN: *And better than that!* He gives a forced smile. *Better than that: there is one of them who claims that it has never happened to him.*

YOUNG WOMAN, critical: *Who claims . . .? Perhaps it was true?*

YOUNG MAN, peremptory: *Exactly! Stendhal says he was a braggart.*

175

YOUNG WOMAN: *I see.* . . . A pause. . . . *All the same, I don't see why there shouldn't have been one.* . . .

YOUNG MAN: *Wait!* . . . *You haven't heard the best of the story yet.* Articulating carefully. *What if one of the officers.* . . . He emphasises his words deliberately . . . *of cavalry.* . . . He continues more naturally . . . *says that he has spent, with the woman he really wanted . . . three nights . . . or even six . . . I can't remember very well.*

Here follows a series of rapid close-ups, following whoever is speaking.

YOUNG WOMAN: *It must be three.* . . .

YOUNG MAN, turning again towards her: *Why do you say that? You don't know what I'm going to say.*

YOUNG WOMAN: *No, but . . . all the same . . . it must be three.*

YOUNG MAN: *Let me finish, will you? This officer spent . . . three nights . . . with the woman he loved . . . and all they did was weep.*

YOUNG WOMAN, looking up for a moment: *They wept? . . . both of them?*

YOUNG MAN: *Yes . . . for joy . . . for . . . for the joy of being together.* . . . *Can't you understand that? I think it's only natural when you're in love.*

YOUNG WOMAN: *But there must certainly be some who don't weep?*

YOUNG MAN, irritated: *Yes, yes . . . of course!*

YOUNG WOMAN: *I see.* . . . *No. Because I thought . . . that Stendhal said . . . that all.* . . . She stresses the word . . . *cavalry officers wept at such times.*

YOUNG MAN, turning round, angry: *Ah! You're making fun of me.*

YOUNG WOMAN: *Not at all.*

YOUNG MAN, excited: *Yes, yes, you're making fun of me.*

The YOUNG MAN becomes more and more annoyed by the replies of the YOUNG WOMAN, who has unwittingly touched a soft spot. He claps his hands together and turns his back towards her.

The YOUNG WOMAN stares in consternation at his back.

YOUNG WOMAN: *Oh, darling, don't be upset.*

YOUNG MAN: *I get even more upset when you say that.*

YOUNG WOMAN: *You'll make yourself ill.*

YOUNG MAN, sighing: *That's even better!*

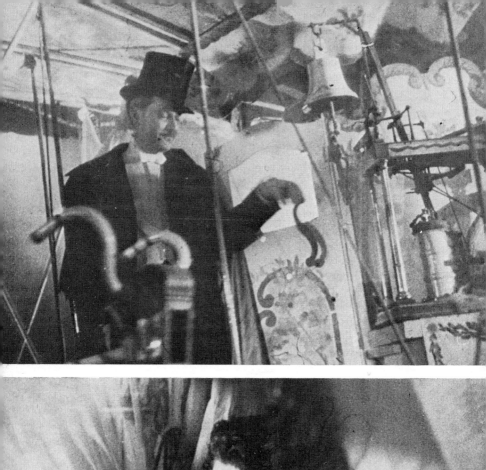

YOUNG WOMAN: *I find it very sweet, on the contrary, to remain good friends.*

YOUNG MAN: *Well, that's that, I suppose.*

YOUNG WOMAN: *I don't know what to say any more.*

YOUNG MAN, sulkily: *Well! Let's keep quiet. It'll be symbolic.*

YOUNG WOMAN: *Alfred. . . .*

YOUNG MAN: *Yes. . . .*

YOUNG WOMAN: *Darling Alfred. . . . What time is it?*

YOUNG MAN: *Oh! that, it's a long time. . . .*

YOUNG WOMAN, insisting: *Where's your watch?*

YOUNG MAN: *In my waistcoat.*

YOUNG WOMAN: *Where's your waistcoat?*

YOUNG MAN: *I don't know. . . . There.* Indicates with his head.

The waistcoat is lying on a chair near the YOUNG MAN. The YOUNG WOMAN stretches her arm over the YOUNG MAN to take the watch. The YOUNG MAN cannot resist any longer, and he kisses the pretty arm.

Shot of the waistcoat and the YOUNG WOMAN's hand moving towards the watch. But the hand remains suspended; suddenly we hear the YOUNG WOMAN.

YOUNG WOMAN, off: *Ah! . . . no . . . Alfred! . . . Alfred! . . . I must go. . . . It must be terribly late . . . Oh! Alfred! It was so nice to be friends!*

Close shot of the waistcoat on the chair.

The LEADER, sleeves rolled up like a mechanic, looks very pleased with himself as he closes the casing of the repaired engine. He shrugs, smiles and takes the crank-handle again and begins to turn. The roundabout starts its circular movement again.

LEADER, to himself: *Ouf! . . . That's better. . . .*

LEADER, singing: *The young man was at a period/when accidents tend to happen./But since his passions have been aroused again,/ Let's forget it . . . and turn over the page.*[12]

In front of the house: the YOUNG MAN comes out first, looks right and left, then hurriedly tells the YOUNG WOMAN to come out.

YOUNG WOMAN: *Eight o'clock. . . . It's dreadful. . . . Luckily the cabby waited for me.*

She smiles at the CABBY-LEADER, and goes quickly to the cab,

185

as the Young Man is talking.

Young Man: *Well, you told him to!*

Young Woman: *I told him five minutes, didn't I? . . .*

Young Man, proudly: *He knows his way around!*

He smiles at the Leader.

Leader, softly to the Young Man: *I know the house!*

The Young Woman has climbed into the cab. She sticks her head out of the window.

The Young Man stands by the cab to kiss her good-bye.

Young Man, kissing her hand: *Well . . . tomorrow evening . . . at the Lobheimer's reception? . . . We'll dance the first waltz.*

Young Woman: *I wouldn't dare.*

Young Man: *Well, the day after tomorrow, here. . . .*

Young Woman: *You're mad, darling.*

Young Man, tenderly: *You don't want to come again?*

Young Woman: *We'll talk about it tomorrow. . . . When we have the first waltz together.*

He kisses her hand again, as the cab moves off.

The cab drives away into the distance.

Camera resumes on the Young Man, who looks very pleased with himself.

Young Man: *Ah! . . . I'm the lover of a married woman now!*

We go back to the roundabout which seems to have changed its appearance. It is now hung with silk curtains and lit with elaborate candelabra, giving the impression of a ballroom. The roundabout turns to the strains of a waltz.

The Young Man and the Young Woman are waltzing near the roundabout, holding each other very tightly and talking softly.[18]

Young Man: *My darling! It's wonderful to feel you in my arms. . . .*[14]

Young Woman: *Be quiet. . . . Everyone's looking at us. . . .*

Young Man: *You're imagining it. Will you come again? . . .*

Young Woman: *You're asking me, darling?*

Young Man: *I love you. Tomorrow? . . .*

Young Woman: *No . . . not tomorrow. It's Sunday.*

Young Man: *So what?*

Young Woman: *My husband stays at home.*[15]

We see a number of figures in groups on the platform of the

186

roundabout; they are in evening dress, drinking champagne and gossiping and looking at the dancers. Finally, we see the LEADER who is looking after the roundabout.

LEADER, announcing: *THE YOUNG WOMAN AND HER HUSBAND.*

The music changes, becoming calmer, suggestive of family life; we are in the conjugal bedroom.

The conjugal bedroom with twin beds: in the background, a chest of drawers and on it a small clock.

The YOUNG WOMAN is reading in bed.

We draw back to see the YOUNG WOMAN and her HUSBAND lying in the twin beds. (*Still*) Bedside tables: a glass of water on the HUSBAND's and a plate with apple sauce.[16] Above each bed there is a gas reading lamp.

Everything in the room is neatly arranged, even the two pairs of slippers and the two dressing-gowns. The HUSBAND's pocket-watch is on its stand on the bedside table; his clothes hang tidily on a clothes-stand.

As more of the room becomes visible, the regular ticking of the small clock on the chest opposite the beds becomes very audible. We look at the two beds from behind the clock, of which the pendulum is visible.

The HUSBAND has files of various sizes strewn on the bed as he does his accounts. He is wearing spectacles.

The HUSBAND in profile; in the background, his wife.[17]

HUSBAND, nose in his books: *Eight hundred more. . . . What are you doing? . . . Eight hundred and fifty plus thirty. . . .*

YOUNG WOMAN: *I'm reading Stendhal.*

HUSBAND: *Is it a good book? Nine hundred. . . . A thousand. . . .*

YOUNG WOMAN: *Very instructive. . . .*

The HUSBAND gravely nods approval and starts studying his accounts again.

HUSBAND: *Nine hundred payable the fifteenth . . . plus a credit of four thousand one hundred due in September.*

Then, doing a belated double-take, he looks at his wife more closely. She feels he is looking at her and looks up.

We move closer to the couple.

YOUNG WOMAN: *What's the matter?*

HUSBAND: *I should be asking you.*

187

YOUNG WOMAN: *What have I done?*

HUSBAND: *You're very pretty today. . . . My dear, you look quite different.*

YOUNG WOMAN: *Was I ugly before?*

HUSBAND: *You were young . . . and now you're really beginning to bloom.* He looks in his books again and starts counting.

YOUNG WOMAN: *You're very gallant tonight!*

HUSBAND: *Business is going well. . . . Four thousand one hundred at six per cent, multiplied by six. . . .*

YOUNG WOMAN: *Ah! yes, of course!*

HUSBAND: *Four thousand three hundred and forty-six. . . .* A pause. *You know, husbands. . . .* He searches for the right expression . . . *do have worries. . . . Their minds aren't always free . . . and five hundred and sixty-four.*

YOUNG WOMAN: *Are you working or talking?*

HUSBAND: *I'm working . . . of course. . . . I'm working.*

The YOUNG WOMAN draws herself up slightly to put the light out, after closing her book.

YOUNG WOMAN: *I'm going to sleep.*

HUSBAND: *Good. . . . Good night, then, darling.*

The YOUNG WOMAN puts her book away, then presents her forehead for her HUSBAND to kiss.

YOUNG WOMAN: *Good night, Charles.*

He kisses her on the forehead. She gets down in bed. The HUSBAND starts work again.

HUSBAND: *Four thousand, three hundred and forty-six net income, plus general expenses . . . let's say at fifteen per cent . . . in one month.* A pause while he turns round towards his wife. . . . *Emma!*

Short series of alternating close-ups following the speaker.

YOUNG WOMAN, from the depths of the sheets: *Eh!*

HUSBAND, looking up in despair: *You remember Venice?*

YOUNG WOMAN: *Venice?*

HUSBAND: *Yes, our honeymoon. . . .*

A little confused, the HUSBAND glances furtively at the other bed. His businessman's mind is beginning to be more and more troubled.

YOUNG WOMAN: *Yes . . . it was nice. . . .*

Quick shot of both of them.

HUSBAND: *Put the light on. . . .* His wife does so. *Were you sleep-*

ing? . . . Thanks. Close-up of him, then a series of close-up shots and reverse shots, following the speaker. *There, I'd like to explain something to you. . . . There . . . you know, husbands. . . . No, it's not that. . . . Husbands can't always be lovers.*

YOUNG WOMAN: *Ah! . . .*

HUSBAND: *Yes, there's a time for everything. There are calm periods when you live . . . like close friends. And then . . . other times . . . less calm, huh! . . . We've already had several periods . . . of both sorts. And it's very good like that . . . in fact . . . huh! . . . huh! . . .*

He takes his spectacles off and places them on the bedside table.

YOUNG WOMAN: *Fine.*

HUSBAND: *No?*

YOUNG WOMAN: *I didn't say: no. I said: fine.*

HUSBAND: *Ah! . . . fine.* A pause. The HUSBAND clears his files from the bed, places them to one side, as his wife puts her light out. Next he puts his light out. Musing in the dark. *Mind you . . . yes . . . I've already told you. . . . Yes, it's very good isn't it. . . . Because if there were no calm periods, there wouldn't be any periods . . . ha! . . . less calm. . . . You see.*

YOUNG WOMAN: *That's very clear.*

HUSBAND: *The principle of life, you see, is variation. Marital love, you see, is, how shall I put it, is. . . . A pause. . . . Marriage. . . . Marriage is a disturbing mystery. You young middle class girls come to us still pure and ignorant. You haven't lived, you couldn't know. We, we know. But at what a price! It would be so easy to become disgusted with love, knowing the women you have to go with at the beginning. But . . . there's no choice!*

YOUNG WOMAN, turning towards him: *Tell me. Tell me about those creatures; I find it so interesting.*

HUSBAND: *You're joking, I hope.*

YOUNG WOMAN: *No, I've always asked you to tell me about your youth with . . . with those creatures. . . .*

HUSBAND: *No, Emma, no. You don't realise, that would be . . . how shall I put it, that would be a sort of profanity.*

YOUNG WOMAN: *Oh! It was such a long time ago.* A pause. *Have you ever been the lover of a married woman?*

HUSBAND, embarrassed: *What do you mean?*

YOUNG WOMAN: *My question seems quite clear.*

HUSBAND: *Yes. . . . Yes. . . . But why do you think of such ques-*

tions? Do you know one of those women . . . who. . . .

YOUNG WOMAN: *Married?*

HUSBAND: *Yes, well . . . guilty?*

YOUNG WOMAN: *I don't know. How could I know?*

HUSBAND: *Among your friends, perhaps?*

YOUNG WOMAN: *I don't know, Charles!*

HUSBAND: *Has one of them told you anything?*

YOUNG WOMAN: *No, no! Nothing!*

HUSBAND: *Do you suspect one of them, perhaps?*

YOUNG WOMAN: *Ah! no, no, not even trying hard. . . . I can't think of anyone.*

HUSBAND: *Are you sure?*

YOUNG WOMAN: *Yes, Charles.*

The HUSBAND puts his light on again and looks towards his wife.

HUSBAND, angered: *Emma, you must swear to one thing: that you will never be connected with women you suspect of . . . not being irreproachable in their conduct. I know very well that you're not the sort of person to look for that sort of acquaintanceship. . . . But it's just those women . . . those with dubious reputations . . . who look for the society of honest women . . . because of a sort of . . . longing for virtue. They suffer from their own unworthiness.*

YOUNG WOMAN: *You think so?*

HUSBAND: *What do you mean, you think so? But I'm certain of it, my dear. Just imagine that dreadful life, of trickery, lies, constant danger. Ah! They pay a high price for the little . . . happiness . . . not even happiness . . . of. . . .*

YOUNG WOMAN: *Of pleasure.*

HUSBAND: *Of pl. . . . How can you call that pleasure?*

YOUNG WOMAN: *Well, I suppose . . . otherwise, they wouldn't. . . .*

HUSBAND: *But they've lost their heads.*

YOUNG WOMAN: *Lost their heads . . . ?*

HUSBAND: *Yes, lost their heads. . . .*

YOUNG WOMAN: *Well, have you taken advantage of it?*

HUSBAND, after hesitating: *Yes, once.*

YOUNG WOMAN: *Who was it. . . . Was it a long time ago?*

HUSBAND: *A very long time ago. She's dead.*

The YOUNG WOMAN switches her light on and sits up.

YOUNG WOMAN, frightened: *Dead?*

HUSBAND: *Yes, yes . . . anyway all those women die young.*

YOUNG WOMAN: *You're sure they die young?*

HUSBAND: *It's a fact . . . a sort of justice!*

YOUNG WOMAN: *Did you love her?*

HUSBAND: *My dear, you don't love that sort of woman.* A pause. *You can only love where there is truth and purity.*

YOUNG WOMAN: *That's right!*

HUSBAND: *That's right!*

> We draw away from the couple, as she raises her arm towards the lamp. (*Still*)

YOUNG WOMAN: *What time is it?*

HUSBAND, coming nearer: *What does it matter, we have our whole life in front of us.*

YOUNG WOMAN: *What peace!*

> She puts her light out. He does the same. Darkness. We draw back . . . and see them with the pendulum of the clock in the foreground. The monotonous ticking can be heard.

HUSBAND: *Think of Venice!*

YOUNG WOMAN: *Venice! . . .*

HUSBAND, very tender: *Give me your hand. . . .*

> We look down from behind the two beds.[18]

> The LEADER, dressed as a head waiter, is in the main hall of a Viennese restaurant.

LEADER, announcing: *THE HUSBAND AND THE GIRL. . . . Ah! How shall I put it . . .? How shall I put it . . .?*

> The head waiter (LEADER) goes towards TONI, a commis; through the window they watch the HUSBAND getting out of a cab with a young woman.

TONI: *The little working girl?*

LEADER: *No, no . . . she's not a working girl . . . she doesn't work. . . .*

TONI: *The little tart, then?*

LEADER: *No, that girl's no tart. She's very nice.* Dismissing him. *You don't understand anything.*

TONI, excusing himself: *I'm just a beginner, sir. . . . I haven't got your experience of the job.*

LEADER: *. . . Oh! you know. . . . A bit of experience in life is enough.*

> While saying these last words, the LEADER goes towards the

couple who have come in by the entrance to the private rooms. The GIRL starts to climb the first steps of an important-looking staircase. The LEADER approaches the HUSBAND, who has signalled to him.

LEADER, bowing: *Certainly, Mr. Breitkopf!*

HUSBAND: *Ah! tell me. . . . How do you know my name?*

LEADER: *Me. . . . Ah! I often had the honour of serving you in the past at Wachtl's, in Mayerling.*

HUSBAND: *Ah! Mayerling! Then, in that case, you also know my tastes . . . in food?*

LEADER: *Certainly, Mr. Breitkopf . . . and to drink?*

HUSBAND: *Champagne, of course.*

LEADER: *Certainly, Mr. Breitkopf.*

He turns on his heels; the HUSBAND follows the GIRL.

The HUSBAND closes the door and climbs the stairs behind the GIRL, of whom only the legs are visible.[19]

We return on LEADER and TONI.

TONI, enlightened: *His girl friend, then!*

LEADER: *Not yet. But it could happen.*

He puts a coin in the pianola.

LEADER: *I'll look after the order.* He announces the following in the direction of the kitchen: *Two hors-d'oeuvres, a dry " Veuve Cliquot " 'ninety-eight.*

The pianola starts playing a waltz.

LEADER, continuing: *Toni, see to the music. When it stops, put another coin in.*

TONI: *Till when?*

LEADER: *Till the bill!*

TONI, pointing to a list stuck on the pianola: *There are twelve pieces.*

LEADER: *Prepare eleven coins.*

TONI: *That's enough for two hours.*

LEADER: *That depends. . . . You've got to take into account the part played by pleasure, as well as the part played by feeling. . . . The psychology of love is a sort of job, too. . . . How old are you, Toni?*

TONI: *Thirteen.*

LEADER: *You've got plenty of time to learn.*

Another waiter comes from the buffet and brings the tray and the champagne.

The LEADER hands the tray to TONI and opens the glass-panelled door for him.

LEADER: *Go on. Don't look at the lady's eyes, nor the gentleman's hands. Nor the feet.*

TONI, going out: *Which ones?*

LEADER: *None.*

TONI, climbing the stairs: *What do I look at, then?*

LEADER: *The table. It's big, it's white, it's clean. And close your ears.*

TONI is half way up the stairs.

TONI: *How?*

LEADER, shouting to him: *Without letting go of the tray, of course!*

TONI climbs the stairs.

He knocks at the door at the top of the stairs.

The sound of knocking is heard inside the private room.

The HUSBAND and the GIRL, still wearing hat and coat, separate suddenly, as if they have just been kissing.

HUSBAND: *Come in!*

He takes his cigar from the ashtray and starts smoking.

The GIRL goes to a mirror and tidies herself up.

TONI enters with his tray. He walks straight ahead, looking at the table. He puts the tray on the table.

TONI: *There. . . . Sir. . . . M'am.*

He starts to leave the room.

HUSBAND: *Thank you, boy.*

The LEADER is sitting in the restaurant next to the pianola. He marks the words " hors-d'oeuvres " and " shell-fish " with a pencil on the menu.

He breaks into song.

LEADER, singing: *Getting to work/during the hors-d'oeuvres,/but interrupted immediately./Thanks to this pile of prawns,/the easy young woman/keeps her virtue intact!*[20]

The LEADER leans on the bar in the hall and goes over the menu.

LEADER: *Prawns . . . sliced . . . pineapple! Why not? She's young!*

The HUSBAND and the GIRL sitting at the table in their private room.

HUSBAND: *You're thirsty.*

GIRL: *Oh! yes. . . .* A pause. *Whatever must you think of me?*

HUSBAND, insisting: *Why must you always be so distant when you speak to me?*

GIRL: *Whether I'm distant or not, it won't change anything. . . . Whatever must you think of me?*

HUSBAND: *Why?*

GIRL: *Coming with you like that, straightaway, to a private room.*

HUSBAND: *What? . . . To a private room? It's a restaurant here. You don't think anything out of the ordinary could happen? The waiter could come in from one minute to the next.*

The GIRL sits down and takes the plate of prawns.

GIRL: *I love prawns!*

The HUSBAND fills the glasses.

HUSBAND: *Well! . . . help yourself, my dear, eat.*

GIRL, eating: *Hum . . . it's good.* She drinks. *It prickles, doesn't it!*

HUSBAND, satisfied and looking around him: *It's very nice here. . . .*

GIRL, with admiring eyes: *It's posh! . . .*[21]

Close-up of the menu as it is opened.[22] It reads: " Sliced venison with chestnut purée." The LEADER starts to sing.

LEADER, singing off: *As entrée/I've chosen/sliced/venison./The husband/is surprised,/hindered in his/approaches/by the waiter/who is serving/a spoonful/of chestnut/purée.*

The hors-d'oeuvres have been replaced by the entrée.

We move back to see the HUSBAND facing the GIRL. The two wait for the WAITER to leave. Then they begin to talk.

GIRL, while eating: *I like to have you opposite me.*

HUSBAND: *Why?*

GIRL: *Because I can see you like that. You're the sort of person people notice immediately, you know.*

HUSBAND, flattered: *Had you noticed me?*

GIRL: *In the Singerstrasse . . . yes.*

HUSBAND: *No! I'm not talking about today. I've been following you for three days!*

GIRL, bothered: *Ah! I get followed so much, you know! The other evening, my cousin's husband! He hadn't recognised me in the dark.*

HUSBAND: *And then? What do you do when that happens?*

GIRL: *Nothing. I don't react.*

HUSBAND: *Hum! . . . But you did with me!*

GIRL: *Because it was you! I hope you're not complaining about it?*

The HUSBAND, delighted, kisses her hand.

HUSBAND: *You have pretty hands.*

In the restaurant: the LEADER changes the cylinder of the pianola. A young peasant bride is visible on the illuminated glass.

We see the title of the piece. ' *The Bartered Bride*,' beside the coin slot.[23]

The private room: the HUSBAND is no longer sitting opposite the GIRL, but next to her.

HUSBAND: *Tell me. . . . Have you ever been in a private room before?*

GIRL: *Do you really want to know?* A pause. *Well! Yes.*

HUSBAND: *Ah! . . .*

GIRL: *Oh! but not how you think. With a friend and her fiancé.*

HUSBAND: *You know, I wouldn't have thought any the worse of you if you'd been with your boy-friend.*

GIRL: *Oh! I have no boy-friend. None at all.*

    She drinks.

HUSBAND: *No?*

GIRL: *I swear.*

HUSBAND: *Listen, you're not going to get me to believe that. . . .*

GIRL: *What. . . . It's six months since I had one. . . .* She drinks again.

HUSBAND: *And who was that?* He pours some champagne out for her.

GIRL: *He looked like you. Ah! If it hadn't have been for that . . .!*

HUSBAND: *What? If it hadn't have been for that. . . . Ah! You mean that's why you didn't ignore me in the Singerstrasse?*

GIRL, eating all the time, absent-mindedly: *He was so charming! And you speak the same way as he did, and have the same look too. . . .*

HUSBAND: *Oh! yes. And what did he do in life?*

GIRL, turning towards him: *In life!*

    He leans towards her.

HUSBAND, removing his monocle: *Ah! What eyes you have!*[24]

    Close-up of the menu.[25] The hand of the LEADER marks with a pencil: " Filet de boeuf charolais aux pommes soufflées." He starts to sing.

LEADER, singing: *Gradually time is passing/and the meal will soon be over. . . ./After the main course,/she pretends to resist.*

    In the private-room: the dishes are almost empty. We see the hands of the GIRL putting down the cutlery and the napkin.

Then she gets up and prepares to take her coat and hat.

GIRL: *It's time I got back. What'll my mother say?*

HUSBAND: *You live with your mother?*

GIRL: *Of course I live with my mother. Does that surprise you?*

HUSBAND: *You live alone, with her?*

GIRL: *Alone? Oh! dear, dear! There's five of us; two boys and three girls.*

Close-up of the menu. The hand of the LEADER marks the word " dessert ". We hear him singing.

LEADER, singing off: *This is the fatal time/when a " no " is no longer possible./Pineapple à l'orientale/excuses all excess*

TONI leaves the private room with the empty dessert tray. He goes down the stairs, humming.

TONI, humming: *This is the fatal time/when a " no " is no longer possible./Pineapple à l'orientale/excuses all excess.*[26]

We return to the private room.

HUSBAND, emotionally: *You too, you remind me of someone.*

GIRL: *Ah! Yes?*

HUSBAND: *My youth. . . .* He coughs.

The GIRL, looking slightly tipsy, has just finished her glass. She gets up . . . smiles . . . looks at her glass again.

GIRL: *It's empty, my glass.*

HUSBAND goes to the bottle.

HUSBAND: *Wait . . . wait . . . there should be a drop left.* He pours.

GIRL: *A drop.*

HUSBAND, emptying the bottle: *Yes . . . a drop!*

GIRL, turning towards him after drinking: *How old are you? (Still)*

HUSBAND, with a vague gesture: *That's not important. . . . But what about you? Eighteen?*

GIRL: *No! Nineteen.*

HUSBAND: *Ah! . . . that's something.*

GIRL: *And you? Thirty?*

HUSBAND: *Yes . . . well . . . more or less!*

The HUSBAND, delighted with his ambiguous reply, approaches her and tries to take her by the waist. She laughs and escapes, reeling slightly. He follows her.

GIRL: *There must be something in that champagne. . . . My head's going round and round.* She staggers and lies down on the sofa. *I wonder what's going to happen if I can't get up.*

196

He looks at her, stretched out on the sofa. . . . Then goes to put out the light.

HUSBAND: *I adore you.*

GIRL: *You adore me?*

HUSBAND: *I adore you.*

Dissolve to a close-up of the pianola in the restaurant.[27]

A pot-pourri of music and pictures on all the titles from no. 6 to no. 12 passes and dissolves, finishing with a picture of waves. (Music: ' *The Blue Danube* '.)

The room is empty. TONI puts out the gaslights. The music comes to an end.

HUSBAND, off: *The bill!*

The LEADER comes from the buffet, checking the bill.

LEADER: *The voice is good. . . . That'll be fifteen per cent.*

TONI: *Shall I go?*

LEADER: *No. At your age, you work to learn.*

He takes a small plate and puts the bill upon it.[28]

The LEADER climbs the staircase leading to the private room. The HUSBAND is waiting in front of the half-open door of the private room. The LEADER offers him the plate.

LEADER: *Here's the bill, sir.*

HUSBAND, absent-minded: *What?. . . Ah, yes! the bill.*

He approaches the LEADER and speaks to him in a low voice.

HUSBAND, whispering: *Tell me . . . you saw her, the girl?*

LEADER: *Yes, I noticed the lady when you arrived, Mr. Breitkopf.*

HUSBAND: *You know her?*

LEADER: *No, it's the first time I've seen her.*

HUSBAND: *Really. . . . I wonder what it is. . . . After all, I don't know anything. . . . I got carried away. . . . It's ridiculous.*

LEADER: *You shouldn't regret it, sir.*

HUSBAND: *Yes, do you think so?*

LEADER: *I'm used to it. . . . Thank you, sir.*

HUSBAND: *Good night.*

Return to the private room: The GIRL is wearing her hat and coat and is eating the rest of the pineapple, so as not to waste anything. The HUSBAND comes in discreetly.

HUSBAND: *Can I?*

GIRL: *Yes.*

197

HUSBAND: *Are you ready?*

GIRL: *Ah! that naughty champagne, what it made me do. Whatever must you think of me?*

HUSBAND: *I think you like me, that's all.*

GIRL: *Yes, but that champagne, all the same.*

HUSBAND: *When two . . . young people like each other . . . they don't need any drug in their champagne to. . . . I can tell you that. . . .*

GIRL: *You know. . . . I was only saying that. Everyone has some dignity. . . . Really, I feel a bit ashamed.*

She goes to the sofa and searches among the cushions.

HUSBAND: *And why? Since I remind you of your first lover.*

GIRL: *Yes. . . . Of course. . . .*

HUSBAND: *And you still haven't told me what he did. Was he a lieutenant?*

GIRL: *No, he's out of the army. His father runs a café. . . .* She takes her belongings. . . . *My bag, my gloves. . . .*

HUSBAND, looking at the time on his watch: *Oh! my dear, do you know what time it is? Half-past eleven.*

GIRL: *So what?*

HUSBAND: *What about your mother?*

GIRL: *Ah! good . . . are you fed up with me?*

HUSBAND: *It's you who said a while ago. . . .*

GIRL: *I don't even know your name.*

HUSBAND: *Charles.*

GIRL: *Charles.* A pause. *Charles, you're not the same any more.*
He leaves the room.

HUSBAND, absent-minded: *Yes.*
She turns back.

GIRL: *Wait. My umbrella . . . .*
They go out . . . but she returns to take a biscuit. She bites it. The couple walk down the staircase, through the hall and into the street.

GIRL: *Shall I see you soon?*

HUSBAND: *I don't live in Vienna. . . . I just spend a few days here from time to time.*

GIRL: *I bet you're married!*

HUSBAND: *Why?*

GIRL: *When a man says that he doesn't live in Vienna, he's usually married!*

HUSBAND: *And you wouldn't feel guilty about going off with a married man?*

GIRL: *I don't care. I suppose his wife's doing just the same, while he's at it.*

HUSBAND, shocked: *I forbid you to say that! I don't like that.*

GIRL: *Ah! You see you have a wife! . . .*

HUSBAND: *Yes, well. . . . Whether I have one or not, I find that joke in very bad taste.* A pause. *Are you coming? Are you coming?*

She goes down more quickly and catches up with him.

GIRL: *Yes.*

The couple have left the main restaurant hall.[29] The LEADER of LA RONDE and TONI, ready to leave themselves, watch them go out.

LEADER: *Perhaps you'll be right. She makes him angry. Perhaps she will become his girl-friend.*[30]

Slow dissolve to a motor car.[31] We see the HUSBAND at the steering handle of his cabriolet. The GIRL is beside him. Bumping, then silence. The HUSBAND begins to speak, but without looking at the GIRL, because he is keeping his eyes on the road.

HUSBAND: *I'd like to see you again, often.*

GIRL: *Is that true?*

HUSBAND: *Of course. But I'd have to be sure of you, because I couldn't keep a watch on you.*

GIRL: *You know, you don't meet men like you every day.*

HUSBAND: *Yes . . . of course . . . but, well, it doesn't stop you from being . . . how shall I put it, not innocent, but very young. There are people without scruples and for young girls like you, temptations. . . . Anyway, even though I don't live in Vienna, we could work something out. . . . So, if you want to love me, to love no one but me. . . .*

GIRL: *Love no one but you?*

HUSBAND: *Well, we could find some little corner where I could come to see you every time I come here. . . . I can manage that . . . renting, of course?* Then, *I can imagine that in a nice area* (off) *a beautiful house, a beautiful entrance, floors well-waxed, shining brass and an immaculate staircase.*

199

While the HUSBAND is talking, the picture dissolves to a lift going up in a luxurious-looking building. Pause. Coming out of the lift, a man gives way to the GIRL. . . . On the landing, we look towards a door and down to the mat on which the word " WELCOME " can be read.

Off, the LEADER can be heard.

LEADER, singing: *Welcome! It's for that young thing/that this word is written on the mat!/Because she has followed a poet,/more exciting than the husband.*

LEADER, off: . . . *More complicated too, because with him, those blasé people who are incapable of loving someone else take their place in* La Ronde.

Books, manuscripts, statuettes, paintings with and without frames and exotic masks furnish the living room of the POET's studio flat. A fire is burning in the grate.[32] The curtains are drawn back and we can see the roofs of the sleeping town. In a corner is a piano, at which the POET goes to sit, with his overcoat half undone. The GIRL is on the floor at his feet.

GIRL, on the floor: *Is that yours?*[33]

POET: *Almost.*

GIRL: *What do you mean, almost?*

POET, stopping playing: *If I'd have been a composer, I'd certainly have composed that tune. It's my sort of music.*

GIRL: *What sort?*

POET: *The sort that goes with my inspiration.*

GIRL: *Ah yes! . . .*

POET: *Do you understand what I'm trying to say?*

GIRL: *No. Not often.*

POET: *It's marvellous.*

We follow him as he takes his hat and coat off. He starts again, delighted.

POET: *You don't understand anything! . . . How restful!*

GIRL: *I'm not stupid, you know!*

POET, charmed: *What freshness, on my burning brow!*[34]

The GIRL is sitting on the floor on a soft carpet, while the POET sits on the piano stool, smoking a cigarette. During the whole scene the POET waves his arms about in the air and moves about, going up to his loggia to write down what he says, then coming down to sit down again.

GIRL: *Are all poets like you?*

POET: *All the great ones, yes, but there aren't many of us.*

GIRL: *I'm a bit frightened.*

POET: *Do I impress you?*

GIRL: *Yes. You . . . you wouldn't like to light all the other candles?*

POET: *It would be too early, my angel. We have lived in an ocean of light all day and we come out of the depths and throw a gown of shadow over our shoulders . . . no, not a gown, that's prosaic . . . what do you think? (Still)*

GIRL: *Me?*

Resume on the POET.

POET: *Hum!*

GIRL: *Nothing. . . .*

High and low angle shots and reverse shots of the POET shrugging his shoulders and sighing.

POET: *It's marvellous! Sublime incomprehension! Nothing? Nothing? . . . like a gown . . . like a gown, like a dressing gown . . . like a coat of stars. There, that's it!*

He rushes to the loggia and takes a goose quill to put down what he says or recites.

GIRL: *Why of stars?*

POET, writing: *Shut up. . . . Shut up, shut up! . . . Please shut up.*

GIRL: *But can you write like that in the dark?*

POET: *By the light of my thoughts . . . yes. Let's see, ocean, light, water, yes. . . .*

GIRL: *Are you putting all that down?*

POET: *Yes, inspiration is a long memory. . . . Unfortunately I have no memory.* He walks round his writing desk, thoughtful. *Our real drama is the continual marriage of frenzy . . . and organisation. Yes, yes, that's it. Yes, that's it, frenzy and organisation. Aren't you thirsty?*

He looks down at the GIRL from the staircase.

We look down on the GIRL from the POET's viewpoint.

GIRL: *No, I'm hungry.*

POET: *I'd prefer you to be thirsty.*

GIRL: *Why? Since I tell you I'm hungry.*

POET: *I've got something to drink, but nothing to eat. Do you want me to go and get some cooked meats?*

201

GIRL: *Oh no! not cooked meats. No.*

POET: *Then, would you prefer us to eat in a private room?*

GIRL: *Again! . . . It must be a mania with men.*

POET: *You've already dined in a private room, then?*

GIRL: *Yes.*

POET: *With a seducer?*

GIRL: *As it happens, no. With a friend and her fiancé, you see.*

POET: *No, I can't see. I can't even see if you're blushing. All the same, I think you're lying. In fact, I can't see at all.*

GIRL: *But you ought to have noted in your note-book how I was!*

POET: *But that's a very great insight you've just uttered. You've summed up the tragedy of desire in a single word.*

GIRL: *Oh! Come off it! . . . Why can't you talk like everybody else.*

POET: *I've never tried. Tell me first if you love me.*

GIRL: *Yes, I love you.*

POET: *Why?*

GIRL: *Because you're not like the others.*

POET: *Can you see that?*

GIRL: *I can hear it more than anything! I think loving you must be a thing. . . .*

POET: *Well?*

GIRL: *A thing. . . .*

POET: *Intangible! Off with your dress!*

He begins to come down the stairs.

GIRL: *Robert!*

POET, on the stairs: *I told you: off with your dress! . . . Night is there with its veil, its stars . . . it has spread all the Milky Way at our feet. A thousand golden points glitter beneath our eyes, come on, take your dress off, take everything off. . . .*

GIRL, off: *But I'm cold!*

POET: *The night gives us back twenty, thirty, fifty suns, which the light of the day hid from us! Imagine we are in the Indies, in a mysterious palace, come on, take your blouse off . . . the nights are warm in the Indies. Ah! . . . A heavy burning humidity hangs about us. Take your blouse off. . . .*

He takes his jacket off. A pause.

GIRL, off: *Do you love me?*

He snuffs out the candle flames with his fingers.

POET, off: *Hush. . . .*

202

He bends down towards the GIRL.

The LEADER, still dressed as the head-waiter, has remained in the restaurant.[35] He and TONI begin to turn out the last remaining lights of the restaurant. The strains of ' *The Blue Danube* ' issue from the pianola.

TONI: *I put another coin in.*

HUSBAND, off, very bitter: *The bill!*

TONI, shaking his head: *That's only three per cent.*

LEADER, getting up: *You're making progress.*[36]

The LEADER climbs the staircase to the private room, carrying the bill.

Inside the room we see that the table has been set for two. Facing us the HUSBAND is sitting at the table alone. He has already put his hat on. There is a discreet knock at the door.

HUSBAND: *Come in.*

The LEADER comes in and holds out the bill.

LEADER: *There, sir . . . the bill.*

HUSBAND, taking the paper: *Yes.*

He looks at the total and pays.

LEADER: *Thank you, sir.*

HUSBAND: *What time is it?*

LEADER: *Just after eleven, sir.*

HUSBAND, with a slight hope: *Ah?*

He puts some more change on the little plate . . . and looks at his watch.

HUSBAND: *I make it five to twelve.*

LEADER, bowing: *So do I.*

HUSBAND: *Something must have prevented her from coming.*

LEADER: *Yes, sir. . . . But I'm sure it's nothing serious.*

HUSBAND, getting up: *You think so?*

LEADER: *Certain of it.*

As the LEADER follows the HUSBAND towards the door, he glances at the bottle of champagne.

LEADER: *Aren't you thirsty, sir?*

HUSBAND, downcast: *No! . . .*

The HUSBAND makes a gesture of annoyance and goes out followed by the LEADER. Still shot of the bottle and dinner.

The POET's apartment: The POET is standing writing at his work table (in the loggia).

We look down on the GIRL, who is enveloped in a fur coverlet. She is sitting on the floor, near the fireplace, drinking brandy.

GIRL: *It's funny, but I prefer brandy to champagne.*[37]

We resume on the POET, who is looking very pleased with himself. Very theatrically, he comes down into the room, leaning from time to time on the banisters, then walks round the room around the GIRL.

POET, declaiming: *Whether the wind be gentle or tempestuous,/ whether its breath be warm or cool,/what does it matter! Since our heads rest/in the feast/of the white/branches/of snow in the woods!*

He is now at the foot of the stairs and he approaches her with great ceremony.

POET: *And now, my child. I'm going to give you something which will dazzle you. I am going to reveal my name to you! A pause. I'm called Kuhlenkampf! . . . You're astounded, aren't you?*

GIRL: *No, no, why, it's just an ordinary name!*

POET: *What, you don't know who Kuhlenkampf is?*

GIRL: *Is it true that you write plays? Plays that get put on in theatres?*

POET: *Oh! my child, you are beauty, you are simplicity, you are life. Then you really would have loved me, even if I'd been a grocer's assistant.*

GIRL: *Of course I'd have loved you.*

The POET kneels down and prostrates himself theatrically.

POET: *Ah! Swear to me. . . . I want you to swear to me that you didn't know I was Kuhlenkampf.*

GIRL: *I've already told you I didn't!*

POET: *Ah! I've got tears in my eyes. . . . Well forget it all. No, I'm not Kuhlenkampf. No, I'm Robert, and nothing more. I'm not a writer. I'm a lawyer's clerk. And I play the piano in the evening in a bar. Ah! my angel, we'll never leave each other, we'll love each other with grandiose . . . simplicity.*

GIRL: *Is it true you play in a bar in the evening? Which one?*

The POET lies on his back in the centre of the room. He is in the foreground, and the GIRL in the background.

POET: *Hush. Don't ask any more questions. Shall we go away? Do you want to?*

204

GIRL: *Go away?*

POET: *For three months . . . or for three weeks.*

GIRL: *What about your boss, the lawyer? And my mother?*

POET, getting up and approaching her: *They'll console each other. . . . We'll live in the middle of a forest . . . completely naked . . . we'll drink water from the murmuring streams. We'll eat the golden fruits provided by mother nature. . . . And then . . . we'll say good-bye.*

GIRL: *But why good-bye? I thought. . . .*

POET: *There is no true love which isn't followed by a good-bye. Kiss me . . . and next Sunday you'll go and see Kuhlenkampf's play.*

GIRL: *Kuhlenkampf again?*

POET: *Yes, he's a friend. You will be solemnly present at the fiftieth performance. I'll wait for you at the exit and you'll tell me what you think of that admirable work.*

We cut to the theatre.

Sounds of applause and of scenery being moved.

VOICES: *Bravo. . . . Great success! . . .*

Quick shot of the ACTRESS leaving the stage. Close by in the wings, is the POET in evening dress, who approaches her.

We look almost vertically upwards to see the LEADER on the light bridge of the theatre, working on a spot-light. (*Still*)

We move towards him, looking down slightly.

LEADER, announcing: *THE POET AND THE ACTRESS.*

In the wings: very sure of herself, the ACTRESS rushes towards her dressing-room, followed by the POET, the wardrobe-mistress and admirers.

POET: *Tell me, why did you cut the last cue?*

ACTRESS: *What cue?*

POET: *Always the same.*

ACTRESS: *Because I don't feel it.* Declaiming. *". . . My angel, we'll never leave each other and we'll love each other with grandiose simplicity."* A pause. *You never say that in real life! . . .*

POET, hardly convinced: *Ah! . . . You don't think so?*

She goes into the dressing-room, as does the POET.

In the ACTRESS's dressing-room.

POET, to the wardrobe-mistress: *A moment. Charlotte!*

The POET makes a sign to CHARLOTTE not to go in and closes

205

the door.

CHARLOTTE: *Certainly, sir.*

We move towards the ACTRESS, who is now opposite the POET.

ACTRESS: *I'd like to know why you've sent Carlotta away?*

POET: *Because I want to kiss you, if you'd believe it.* He blows her a kiss. *Anyway, we've got all night, haven't we?*

The ACTRESS is sitting at her make-up table, doing her eyes. He walks up and down the room.

ACTRESS: *Yes.* A pause. *You really want to go there?* She turns her head towards him. *Two hours of sleigh in the night. . . . If only there was no performance tomorrow! . . .*

POET: *Oh! that . . . but you wanted it. You made me reserve the rooms, didn't you? Two rooms, what's more. . . . I don't know why. . . .*

ACTRESS: *Does one ever know how things turn out?*

POET: *Turn out?*

Music: the theme, " My characters turn and turn."

The theme music continues, while we see the GIRL waiting at the exit to the theatre.[38]

The POET is now sitting down in the ACTRESS's dressing-room, rather crushed. The ACTRESS would like to take her make-up off, but the conversation prevents her. She looks in her mirror. (*Still*)

POET: *Let's go to my place, then.*

ACTRESS: *Your place? It'll be cold if you've let the fire out.*

POET: *All right, let's go to your place.*

ACTRESS: *My place? You must be joking! What about my mother?*

POET: *Let's go away then. . . .*

Noise of people coming out of the theatre, accompanied by the theme music of *La Ronde*.

The GIRL is pacing up and down by the stage door. After a short time, tired of waiting, she knocks on the window of the CARETAKER's lodge. We move closer to see the GIRL's face and the window opening. The CARETAKER's face.

GIRL: *Excuse me, sir, what time is it, please?*

CARETAKER: *Just past eleven, miss.*

GIRL: *Thank you.* She hands some money to him.

CARETAKER: *Thank you very much.*

GIRL, looking at her watch: *. . . But I make it five to twelve.*

206

CARETAKER: *So do I, miss.*

The GIRL knocks again at the window of the CARETAKER'S lodge, as the theme music of *La Ronde* is heard again.[39]

GIRL: *Excuse me . . . but perhaps something has prevented him from coming?*

CARETAKER: *Yes, miss, but it isn't serious.*

GIRL: *You don't think so?*

CARETAKER: *I'm certain.*

In the dressing-room: the ACTRESS pulls the bell-rope.

ACTRESS: *Are you going to let me take my make-up off?*

POET: *You must decide something, all the same.*

ACTRESS: *Later.*

POET: *What do you mean, later? The sleigh is coming.*

ACTRESS: *Oh well, let it come.*

CHARLOTTE enters the room.

DRESSER: *Did you call me, miss?*

ACTRESS: *Yes, Charlotte, I'm in a hurry.*

POET, smiling: *Are we going, then?*

ACTRESS: *Leave me alone a moment. When I'm dressed, I shall be able to see more clearly.*

POET: *More clearly.*

He leaves the room, shaking his head.

DRESSER, smiling: *Mr. Kuhlenkampf looks annoyed.*

ACTRESS, tenderly: *He's adorable.*[40]

In the dressing-room, the POET sits down near the ACTRESS; he asks her a number of questions, softly. Series of shots and reverse shots.

POET: *Why are you playing with me? You are talent itself, beauty, life. . . .*

ACTRESS: *Because I'm an actress. . . .*

POET: *Can't you forget acting for a single moment?*

ACTRESS: *Why forget it? You write plays. I act them. If we didn't act, what would we be?*

He stands up.

POET: *A man and a woman.*

ACTRESS: *You don't really believe that a man and woman would have decided to go away, as we are going to do, if they hadn't been involved in acting?*

POET: *Yes. . . . A pause. . . . Anyway, you don't love me any more!*

ACTRESS: *And you?*

He sits down on a step near the door, facing her.

POET, laughing: *You're right. Ah! The theatre is an incredible thing! We know in advance everything we are going to say to each other. You've chosen this inn because it reminds you of a past love, haven't you?*

ACTRESS: *Yes.*

POET: *Yes, you find it funny to compare the past and the present. You'll be stirring up old memories all evening. Do you think it's pleasant for me? You'll send me back to my room twenty times.*

He gets up and approaches her.

ACTRESS: *Yes, but you also know that the twenty-first time I won't send you back. You know that, don't you?*

POET: *Yes, I know.*

ACTRESS: *That's why I love you.*

POET, coming closer: *And those who don't know, do you love them too?*

ACTRESS, in close-up: *All of them.*

Furious, the POET slaps her. Still more furious, she slaps him in turn . . . then they embrace passionately.

Outside the stage door: the POET, carrying two suitcases, walks up and down in front of the CARETAKER's lodge, waiting for the ACTRESS.[41] The theme music of *La Ronde* becomes audible.

He is wearing a fur-lined overcoat, and a fur-lined, Russian-style hat.

Sleigh bells can be heard and two horses are seen arriving outside the ice-covered window.

CARETAKER, opening the little window of his lodge: *Sir. . . .*

POET: *Thank you.*

CARETAKER, embarrassed: *Sir . . . when the girl left, she even. . . .*

POET: *Good. . . . Did you tell her I was ill?*

CARETAKER: *Yes, sir, but. . . .*

POET: *What?*

CARETAKER: *Then, the girl told me to tell you . . . that she understood.*

POET: *Ah!*

CARETAKER, taking out a little bouquet: *She asked me to give you. . . .*

208

POET, taking the bouquet: *Thank you. . . .*

CARETAKER: *. . . And then to tell you that she likes your play very much.*

POET: *Poor child. . . . And you say she's gone?*

CARETAKER: *Just this moment. . . . She can't be far. . . . Do you want me to look?*

POET, with a certain sadness: *No . . . thank you. . . .*

The CARETAKER closes his window.

The POET sniffs the bouquet.

The ACTRESS is heard suddenly.

ACTRESS: *Is the sleigh there, then?*

The POET stuffs the bouquet in his pocket and turns round.

The ACTRESS walks up the spiral staircase.

ACTRESS: *What are you looking at me like that for? Have you changed your mind?*

POET, going to meet her: *I'd like. . . . I'd like you to be a little more sincere.*

They walk towards the exit.

POET: *I'd like you to promise not to send me back to my room twenty times.*

ACTRESS: *Oh well! Let's say eighteen times. It's a bargain.*

POET: *I could strangle you, you know!*

ACTRESS, laughing: *Strangle me if you want.*

POET, furious: *You're quite capable of letting me walk beneath your window, in the snow, waiting for your light to go out.*

ACTRESS, laughing: *I hadn't thought of that, but it's a good idea.*

The POET stops and puts the cases down.

POET: *I'm not going.*

ACTRESS, playing the same game: *You're quite right. Better not.*

POET: *I'll take you home.*

ACTRESS: *Thanks, that's very kind of you.*

They take their cases and climb into the sleigh. The theme music of *La Ronde* is taken up by the bells. In front of the door they turn towards the CARETAKER.

POET and ACTRESS, to the CARETAKER: *Good night, Mr. Steineggl.*

CARETAKER: *Good night, Gentlemen. . . . Ladies. . . . Good night. . . . Till tomorrow. . . .*

It is night, and we are in front of a hotel. A single window is lit up. The POET, crossing and recrossing his arms, like a coachman, and stamping his feet to keep them warm, paces to and fro in the snow, looking towards the window.

The LEADER appears, also enveloped in his fur coat.

LEADER: *Good evening.*

POET, politely: *Yes?*

LEADER: *You came all the same?*

POET: *But. . . . Who are you?*

LEADER: *A neighbour. I knew you had reserved rooms.*

POET: *But how did you know that we almost didn't come?*

LEADER: *It was fate.*

POET: *Ah?*

LEADER: *I knew that you would end up by coming and that I would meet you, alone, beneath this window.*

POET: *But that's not normal.*

LEADER: *It's the least of things.*

POET: *You're clairvoyant.* He puts his hands in his pockets.

LEADER: *No, but I've seen a lot.*

POET, absent-minded: *What on earth's this?* He takes the little bouquet out of his pocket.

LEADER: *Violets.*

The POET looks at him, amazed. The LEADER excuses himself, smiling.

LEADER: *I could see it! Even without being clairvoyant!* He looks up. *The light's out.*

POET, looking: *You're right.*

LEADER: *Someone's waiting for you. . . .* The POET looks at him. Same exchange as above. *It's easy to guess: you look happy!*

POET, starting to go towards the inn: *Yes. . . .*

LEADER, softly: *What success . . . !*

POET: *What?*

LEADER, smiling kindly: *I wish you a good night.*

The POET doesn't know what to do with his bouquet. He is going to put it back in his pocket.

LEADER: *No. . . . Give it to me. That'll help you.*

POET, surprised: *But. . . .*

LEADER: *It's bad for the heart, to get all that mixed up.*

The POET gives him the bouquet and, intrigued, he hesitates before going away.

LEADER: *Go on . . . go, quick. . . . Look, she's put the light on again!*

As he says, the light is on again.

POET, alarmed: *What does that mean?*

LEADER: *It means that they like to make people wait for them, but they don't like others to make them wait as long.*

The POET runs away and goes into the inn. The LEADER sniffs the bouquet of violets.[42]

The COUNT, in full dress uniform, crosses the ante-room.[43]

LEADER, singing off: *My characters turn round and round./The earth turns day and night./Rain water is transformed into clouds/And the clouds become rain again.*

LEADER, announcing off: *THE ACTRESS AND THE COUNT.*

A photographic portrait of the POET with the following dedication: *To my unforgettable interpreter, in memory of a marvellous artistic partnership. Kuhlenkampf.*[44]

We move very slowly across the room to a magnificent four-poster bed.

LEADER, off: *THE ACTRESS. . . .*

We turn towards the far end of the room to see the glass-panelled door of the bathroom, from which comes the sound of splashing.

LEADER, off: *. . . AND . . .*

A MAIDSERVANT comes in by another door and goes towards the door of the bathroom which she half-opens to announce the COUNT's arrival to the ACTRESS, who is still invisible.

MAIDSERVANT: *. . . THE COUNT.*

ACTRESS, off: *Show him into my bedroom.*

The MAIDSERVANT goes away and enters the ante-room. There, surrounded by laurel crowns, photographs of the ACTRESS, trophies from her successes, the COUNT, accompanied by his greyhound Harras, waits very stiffly, dressed in the full dress uniform of a captain of cavalry.

The door opens.

MAIDSERVANT: *If the Count would be good enough. . . .*

COUNT, to his dog: *Harras, wait for me and lie down!*[45]

The COUNT comes into the bedroom.

ACTRESS, off: *Is that you, Count? Will you excuse me a moment?*

COUNT, looking at a basket of flowers: *Oh, yes certainly, miss. . . . It was your gracious mother who gave me permission to. . . . Other-*

211

wise I would never have permitted myself. . . .

ACTRESS: *Sit down, my dear Count.*

COUNT: *Thank you.*

He sits down, keeping his helmet on his head and his sabre straight up in front of him. He remains very stiff, monocle in eye.

COUNT: *I have come to pay my respects to you.*

ACTRESS, off: *Thank you for your lovely flowers.*[46]

COUNT, looking at a basket of flowers: *Oh, that was nothing at all.*

ACTRESS, off: *They are there. Have you seen them?*

COUNT: *Yes, I can see them.*

ACTRESS, off: *And what other interesting things can you see in my bedroom?*

COUNT: *Everything in your bedroom interests me.* He looks at the bed.

ACTRESS, off: *And what else?*

COUNT: *Well! I can see a photograph.*

ACTRESS, off: *Ah! yes. . . .*

COUNT: *A friend?*

ACTRESS, off: *Yes. . . . Well . . . something like that.*

COUNT: *More than a friend?*

ACTRESS, off: *A writer. . . . That doesn't count.*

COUNT: *That doesn't count? Do you mean to say that, in your profession, a writer is a friend, whose mistress you would never dream of becoming? Or, on the contrary, that such a thing is so natural that. . . .*

ACTRESS, off, after a long rippling laugh: *You're adorable.*

COUNT: *Thank you. I am pleased that your opinion of me is a favourable one.*

ACTRESS, off: *It doesn't bother you to wait for me?*

COUNT: *When one is a soldier, one gets used to waiting.*

ACTRESS, off: *I find it delicious, myself. We talk to each other, we can't see each other, but we are so sure. . . . It's marvellous to wait for another when you are certain the other person will be there.*

We hear the ACTRESS getting out of the bath.

COUNT: *You are an extraordinary person. I would even go as far as to say: enigmatic.*

ACTRESS, off: *Does Elfriede Birken seem less mysterious to you?*

COUNT: *Obviously, little Elfriede Birken doesn't seem complicated.*

But, you know, I don't know her very well.

ACTRESS, off: *Ah! really?*

COUNT: *Oh yes, not well at all. . . . You are an enigma become woman. I have always been attracted by mystery. Ah! what wasted time and pleasure!*[47]

COUNT: *When I think that I saw you act for the first time yesterday evening!*

ACTRESS, off: *Only yesterday?*

COUNT: *Yes, we were still dining when you began to act.* Very low, as though to himself. *Then, the theatre . . . you know. . . .*

> The ACTRESS appears in extraordinary dishabille. She holds out her hand for the COUNT to kiss.

COUNT: *Oh! . . . You are even more beautiful close to, if that's possible.*

ACTRESS: *Would you mind if I lie down again?*

COUNT: *Oh, please do!* Seeing that he is facing her as she lies down, he turns his head away, embarrassed and stiff. *Excuse me! (Still)*

ACTRESS: *Sit down, my dear Count. . . . What were we saying?*

> Series of shots and reverse shots. The ACTRESS is smoking a cigarette.

COUNT: *That I was dining late.*

ACTRESS: *Ah! yes. . . . Well, in future, you will dine earlier.*

COUNT: *I'd already thought of that. I could also not dine at all. Dining is not a pleasure.*

ACTRESS: *And what exactly are the pleasures that you like at your age.*

COUNT: *I've often discussed that with my friend, Count Bobby.*

ACTRESS: *And love?*

COUNT: *Those who believe in love always find a woman to love them.*

COUNT: *I wonder sometimes.*[48] *My friend Bobby often tells me that I'm a philosopher. He means that I think too much.*

ACTRESS: *Yes. . . . Thinking, that's a big mistake.*

COUNT: *I thought that in Vienna all that would change, that I would be amused and entertained! Not at all! It's the same as the other place.*

ACTRESS: *Where, the other place?*

COUNT: *Well! Down there in Hungary, in the little garrisons.*

ACTRESS: *Ah! yes. . . . And what were you doing there?*

COUNT: *Well! active service.*

213

ACTRESS: *But why did you stay there so long?*

COUNT: *Because it's usual for young officers.*

ACTRESS, dreamily: *Young officers. . . . That's delicious. . . . I can imagine. . . . But doesn't it drive people mad?*

COUNT: *Why? there's more to do than here. There's the training of recruits, the breaking of young horses. And then, the country has its charm. There are magnificent sunsets. More than once I've regretted not being a painter. But I'm boring you with my story.*

ACTRESS: *Not a bit of it! I'm enjoying it immensely.*

COUNT: *You see, you are the sort of woman it's possible to talk to. Count Bobby told me. It's rare, you know!*

ACTRESS: *Certainly, in Hungary.*

COUNT: *In Vienna too. Tell me, do you like people?*

ACTRESS: *I never see anyone. My door is always closed.*

COUNT: *I was sure you were a misanthropist. An artist like you. . . . You aspire to higher things. I do envy you, having an aim in life.*

ACTRESS: *Me? I wonder what I'm doing on earth!*

COUNT: *What? You? Famous! Celebrated! Acclaimed!*[49]

ACTRESS: *Do you think that's happiness?*

COUNT, making vague gestures: *Happiness? Excuse me, but happiness doesn't exist. Anyway it's the things which are most talked about which have the least reality. (Take love, for example. Love doesn't exist.)*[50]

ACTRESS: *That's so true!*

COUNT: *Drunkenness, enjoyment exist.*

ACTRESS: *Yes.*

COUNT: *Let's say that if I felt enjoyment. . . . Good, I know what I'm feeling. Or else I'm. . . . Anyway! That's a fact. And when it's gone, then it's gone. . . .*

Rapid close shot of the ACTRESS.

ACTRESS, with authority: *It's past.*

COUNT: *The future is unknown, and the past is so sad. . . . There's only the present left for us. . . . We don't really know where we are. . . . You see what I mean . . . ?*[51]

ACTRESS, seriously: *You're a sage.*[52]

COUNT: *Well, once you've understood all that, it doesn't matter much whether you live in Vienna or the Pusta, or in the provinces. Well, for instance. . . . Where can I put my helmet? There? Thank*

214

you. What was I saying?
ACTRESS: *In the provinces.*
COUNT: *Ah! yes. . . . There's no difference. Whether I spend the evening at the Club or at the Casino, it's the same nothingness.*
ACTRESS: *And love? What do you make of that?*
COUNT, in close-up: *I told you. . . .*
    Series of shots and reverse shots.
ACTRESS: *Yes, yes, it doesn't exist, that's understood. It's all right in conversation, but. . . .*
COUNT: *Those who believe in love always find a woman to love them.*
ACTRESS: *Elfriede Birken, for instance.*
COUNT: *Why on earth do you talk all the time about little Miss Birken?*
ACTRESS: *Because she's your mistress.*
COUNT: *That girl? . . . Well, I never!*
ACTRESS: *Everyone knows.*
COUNT: *Really? Well, I didn't know! That's very strange!*
ACTRESS: *You fought a duel over her.*
COUNT: *Me?*
ACTRESS: *My dear Count, you are a gallant man. . . . Come and sit next to me.*
ACTRESS: *Yes . . . sit next to me.*[53]
    The COUNT gets up, still with great dignity, and takes off his
    helmet.
COUNT: *Where can I put my helmet?* The ACTRESS shows him with a gesture. *Thank you.*
    The COUNT goes to stand close to the ACTRESS.
ACTRESS: *I knew that you would come today. I knew yesterday evening at the theatre.*
COUNT: *Yesterday evening?*
ACTRESS: *Didn't you understand that I only acted for you?*
COUNT: *You saw me in the auditorium?*
ACTRESS: *Take your sabre off.*
COUNT: *Certainly.*
ACTRESS: *No . . . give it to me.*
COUNT: *Certainly. . . .*
    The COUNT takes off his sabre and lays it on the bed. The
    ACTRESS, smiling, plays with it.
ACTRESS: *It would have been better if I'd never met you.*[54]

215

COUNT: *Permit me to hold a different opinion.*

ACTRESS: *How affected you are, Count. A lot of men, in your place, would be very happy.*

COUNT: *But I am very happy.*

ACTRESS: *You and your philosophy!* . . . *Come close to me.* . . . *You are too handsome.* . . . *Ask me something.* . . .

ACTRESS: *Well . . . ask me something.*[55]

The COUNT gets up, hand raised to his monocle, turns towards the ACTRESS and kisses her hand.

COUNT, even stiffer: *I ask your permission to come this evening.*

Series of shots and reverse shots following the speaker.

ACTRESS: *No.* . . . *Why put off to the evening what can be done in the morning?*

COUNT: *It's that . . . love, the morning.* . . . *No, I see things differently!*

ACTRESS: *How do you see it?*

COUNT: *I will wait for you with my carriage at the stage door.*

ACTRESS: *Yes.* . . .

COUNT: *We will have supper together.*[56]

ACTRESS: *And then?* . . .

COUNT: *We'll come back.* . . .

ACTRESS: *And then?*

COUNT: *And then matters will follow their usual course.*

ACTRESS: *You're so sweet! Come closer to me.* . . . *Don't you find that it's warm in here?*

The COUNT kisses her on the neck, then straightens himself again.

COUNT, with some irony: *Yes, it is.*

ACTRESS: *Unfasten that . . . quickly.*

He begins to unfasten the first buttons . . .; she pulls him on the bed against her.

COUNT: *But.* . . .

ACTRESS: *It's almost as dark as evening. You could almost imagine it was night. And no one can see us.* . . . A pause. *Except ourselves.*

We look down on them clasped together, then up to the top of the four-poster, which is, in fact, a mirror reflecting the couple.

We are suddenly removed to a film editing room: the LEADER

216

unrolls a length of film, looks at it in the light, smiles and cuts it. He whistles the theme tune of *La Ronde*.

LEADER: *Censored!*

Back in the bedroom of the ACTRESS, the COUNT is standing up and fastening the collar of his jacket.

The ACTRESS gets ready to lie down again.

ACTRESS: *You don't mind if I lie down again?*

COUNT: *Please do.* A pause. *Then let's say the day after tomorrow? Hmm?*

ACTRESS: *Why after tomorrow? You wanted today.*

COUNT: *Oh! that wouldn't mean anything any more. I mean . . . morally speaking. . . .*

ACTRESS: *Well, morally speaking, I absolutely have to see you this evening. I've one or two things to say to you about our souls.*

COUNT: *Ah! good, well, I'll wait for you when you come out of the theatre.*

ACTRESS: *Not at all, you'll wait for me here.*

COUNT: *In your home?*

ACTRESS: *In my bedroom.*

COUNT: *We won't have supper at the Imperial?*

ACTRESS, ironically: *No. That would have no philosophical meaning.*

COUNT: *That's understood, then.* He coughs and takes his helmet. *I must have a day or two off. . . . I think that for a visit to pay my respects, I have abused . . . a little.*

He kisses her hand . . . then takes his sabre.

ACTRESS: *Charmed, my dear Count, to have made your acquaintance.*

COUNT: *Would you be good enough to present my compliments to your most gracious mother.*

The COUNT walks over to the door. He turns round, nods and goes out, as we hear the theme music of *La Ronde*.

The COUNT passes through the ante-room. He turns towards the kitchen door, passing the MAIDSERVANT and CHARLOTTE.

COUNT, calling: *Harras. . . .*

But the dog lingers near the LEADER, who is disguised as a valet.

COUNT, nervous: *Come on! . . .* The dog approaches. *Good.*

The COUNT passes the LEADER on his way out.

COUNT: *I seem to have seen you somewhere before?*

LEADER: *It's possible, Count, I move around a lot.*

COUNT: *Have you worked here for long?*
LEADER: *I don't work here, Count, I'm here for the love of art.*
COUNT: *Ah! and what art?*
LEADER: *Love.*
COUNT: *I beg your pardon?*
LEADER: *For love of the art . . . of love!*
COUNT: *Very strange. . . . Good-bye.*
    The COUNT moves away.
LEADER: *Towards what love are you going now, Count?*

We are in the bedroom of the GIRL who figures in the first
sketch of the film.[57] The COUNT's head is seen as he lies on her
bed.
LEADER, announcing off: *THE COUNT AND THE YOUNG GIRL.*
We look around the room where the COUNT is lying: it is, in
fact, a poorly furnished attic room, with a smoking oil lamp on
the table. It seems to be about six o'clock in the morning. We
move over to look into a mirror, in which can be seen, very
indistinctly, the face of the drunken COUNT. . . .
COUNT: *There's no doubt about it. . . . I've had a few too many. . . .*
In the mirror another officer can now be seen with the COUNT.
COUNT: *Bobby was drunk too.*[58]
The COUNT comes unsteadily through the revolving door of a
café, followed by his friend Bobby, who appears to be as drunk
as the COUNT. They lean on each other for support.
    Shot of the COUNT in a restaurant eating opposite his dog
Harras.
    Very sketchy décor: a motor car passes in the street. Since it
is a convertible, it is possible to see the COUNT sitting inside
in a pitiable state. Harras follows.[59]
COUNT, off: *Where did I go yesterday evening? I didn't go to her
place. I was alone . . . no . . . I was with Count Bobby. I was in a
terrible state. And I didn't go to the stage door. I must have had
supper alone with Harras. A very disturbed dinner, I think. And a
very jolly group followed me. Katie, Doudou and Harras for certain.
And where is that woman? No, I didn't follow that woman, no, I
wanted to be alone. . . . Absolutely not followed. . . . No . . . what
has happened has happened, . . .*
    The COUNT walks past the GIRL of the first sequence: she makes

advances to him, but he shrugs his shoulders and moves away. The theme music of *La Ronde* can be heard again.

COUNT: *One just doesn't know where one is any longer.*

We move now to the GIRL's bedroom; the COUNT is searching for his cloak, while the GIRL lies naked beneath the coverlet, sleeping peacefully. There are bank notes on the bedside table. The COUNT, who has assumed his helmet and his monocle, turns towards the GIRL, who stretches herself in her bed and smiles. He greets her with a nod of his head, very militarily.

GIRL: *Slept well?*

COUNT: *Hum! Tell me.*

GIRL: *Hum!* . . .

COUNT: *Does it matter to you whether a person is young or old . . . or a gentleman?* . . .

GIRL: *I'm sleepy.*

GIRL: *Kiss me.*[60]

The COUNT looks as if he is about to kiss her, but he changes his mind.

COUNT: *I was just going to go.*

GIRL: *You want to leave me like that?*

COUNT: *What d'you mean, like that?* He thinks he understands. *Ah!*

He takes his wallet out again.

GIRL, seeing his movement: *I didn't mean that.*

COUNT: *But.* . . .

Slightly embarrassed, he puts his wallet away for the second time.

GIRL: *Fine, fine, good-bye, until next time.*

COUNT: *That's right, good-bye.* . . . *Give me your hand.* The GIRL brings out her arm from beneath the blanket. *What an arm! What purity of line!* He kisses her hand. *You see.* . . . *Like a princess's!* . . . *Anyway, when one sees that.* . . .

GIRL: *Why are you looking at me?*

COUNT: *When they wake up, they all have the same virginal look.* . . . *By Jove, you could even imagine yourself.* . . . *If it didn't smell so much of oil.* . . .

GIRL: *They're filthy, those lamps!*

COUNT: *How old are you?*

GIRL: *What do you think?*

Series of shots and reverse shots.

COUNT: *Twenty-four?*

GIRL: *Come off it!*

COUNT: *More?*

GIRL: *I'm not even twenty. But it's the job that makes you look older.*

COUNT: *Is it a long time?*

GIRL: *A year.*

COUNT: *You started early.*

GIRL: *Better early than too late.*

COUNT, sitting down on the edge of the bed: *And you wouldn't prefer to have a lover?*

GIRL: *Don't you think I haven't any?*

COUNT: *Just one, who would keep you. Instead of going with the first comer.*

GIRL: *But I don't go with the first comer; I choose.*

The COUNT looks around him.

GIRL: *Next month we're moving, we're going to live in a posh district.*

COUNT: *Who, we?*

GIRL: *Well, the boss and the other girls.*

COUNT: *Ah! there are others?*

GIRL: *Can't you hear, next door?*

COUNT: *I can hear someone snoring.*

GIRL: *That's Mélie. She sleeps till the evening. And then she goes to the bar.*

COUNT: *It's horrible.*

GIRL: *Me, at lunch time, I'm already in the street.*

COUNT: *To do what?*

GIRL: *Well . . . my job, you know!*

COUNT: *Yes. . . . Absolutely. . . .*

He gets up, takes his wallet out again and pulls out a note which he places on the bedside table.

COUNT: *Good-bye.*

GIRL: *See you soon.*

COUNT, stopping at the door: *Tell me. . . . Don't you care?*

GIRL, yawning: *About what? I'm sleepy.*

COUNT: *Don't you care whether a person is young or old, or a gentleman . . . ?*[61]

220

COUNT: *That's it, I know who you remind me of.*

GIRL: *Ah! I remind you of someone!*

COUNT: *It's fantastic. . . . The same eyes, ah! It's incredible! Let me kiss your eyes before I go.*

> He bends over towards her, kisses her, then gets up. . . . Shot of the GIRL.

GIRL: *Cheers!*

COUNT, turning: *Tell me. . . .*

GIRL: *Hum! . . .*

COUNT, embarrassed: *It doesn't annoy you.*

GIRL: *What?*

COUNT: *That . . . that we didn't, euh. . . .*

GIRL: *That we . . . oh! there are plenty of men like that. . . . It just wasn't your day, that's all. . . . And anyway, I know you like me! Good-bye, soldier!*

COUNT: *Good-bye! . . . A pause. How do you know I like you?*

GIRL: *Well, last night. . . .*

COUNT: *Last night. . . . I didn't fall on the sofa?*

GIRL: *Yes, yes, you fell on the sofa. But with me.*

COUNT: *No. . . .*

> We see both of them together in medium shot.

GIRL, in close-up: *You don't remember?*

COUNT, in close-up: *Good gracious. . . .*

> The COUNT and the GIRL together again.

GIRL, seeing that he is looking at her curiously: *Do I look more like her than earlier?*

COUNT: *Less, less than earlier. You just don't know where you are any longer. Do you understand me?*

GIRL: *Ah, yes.*

COUNT: *Good-bye!*

> He goes out.
>
> He crosses the corridor of the poor, small apartment where everyone is sleeping. The kitchen is empty. A cat sleeps on an armchair, in front of which lies the COUNT's dog, Harras. The COUNT calls him.
>
> The COUNT goes out with his dog.
>
> The COUNT crosses the courtyard, passes in front of the CARE-TAKER's lodge where the curtains are still drawn. He opens the door and disappears with his dog into the dawn.

The Count walks dreamily along a street.

A clock is heard striking six. The Count crosses the décor of the first sketch of the film. He passes a lamp-lighter, then walks along a street overlooking the town, which is coming to life.

He passes into another street, where we see, a few feet away, the Soldier of the first sketch of the film.

The Count does not see the Soldier, and the Soldier pretends not to see the Count.

A furious voice makes them both jump.

Leader, who has appeared mysteriously, dressed as an adjutant: *So, we don't salute officers any more?*

The Count notices the Soldier, who salutes. Then both look round to look at the Leader, who salutes the Count. The Count replies and goes on his way. Then the Soldier salutes the Leader, who replies. The Soldier goes on his way. (*Still*)

Leader, to the audience: *It would have been a pity for those two not to have saluted each other!*

The Leader goes towards the coat-stand which we have seen at the beginning of the film. He hums as he changes his coat.

Leader: *La Ronde is over.*

As at the beginning of the film, the Leader, dressed in his rain-coat, goes towards the roundabout, now quite still. Once again he passes the Count and his dog.

Leader, singing: *That's the way La Ronde finishes./Just like me, you have seen/That it's the story of the whole world./And there's nothing more left to say.*

These last four lines are repeated at length by the chorus.

Still shot of the roundabout which has been switched off before the last word " End ".[62]

NOTES

1 The credits were scripted as follows by Max Ophuls, but not filmed: the titles are written on the barrel-organ of a turning roundabout. On each seat is a character of *La Ronde*. Each time a character passes, the bell of the roundabout chimes and the name of the actor and his role appears on the screen. Finally, the roundabout is enveloped in a thick fog and disappears from sight.

2 The lines sung by the LEADER are taken up by an invisible choir.

3 Shot cut during editing.

4 Max Ophuls specifies in the script that the YOUNG MAN is reading *Mademoiselle de Maupin* by Theophile Gautier, and smoking Turkish cigarettes. In fact, the YOUNG MAN is not smoking at the beginning of the scene.

5 Lines cut during editing.

6 Lines cut during editing.

7 The following scene, concerning the SOLDIER's letter, was cut during editing.

8 This scene, again concerning the SOLDIER's letter, was cut during editing.

9 These lines were cut during editing.

10 End of cut.

11 Note in the script.

12 These lines were not heard in the prints used to establish this text.

13 The actual position of the couple is difficult to define. They appear to be dancing on a small whirligig which is apart from the main roundabout, thus creating an impression of seperateness from the rest of the guests. In addition, the movement of the whirligig is in the opposite direction to that of the roundabout.

14 These lines were cut during editing.

15 End of cut.

16 Specified in the original script.

17 During the whole of the scene in the bedroom there are a high number of shot changes. In the interests of fluency, therefore, it seems sufficient to note that the scene is made up almost entirely of series of shots and reverse shots, with occasional long shots behind the small clock.

18 The beds look vaguely like gondolas in the darkness.

19 This scene was cut during editing. It should be noted that this particular sketch suffered heavily at the editing stage. All the cuts, however, are given in full.

20 End of cut. At this point a mount passes on to the screen bearing the words " Hors d'oeuvres ".

21 A mount appears at this point bearing the word "Entrée".
22 This scene was cut during editing.
23 End of cut.
24 A mount passes on the screen bearing the word "Desserts".
25 This scene was cut during editing.
26 End of cut.
27 This scene was cut during editing.
28 End of cut.
29 This scene was cut during editing.
30 End of cut.
31 Still shot with wind and bumping effects.
32 During the opening shots of this scene there is nothing to indicate that this is not the "love nest" proposed to the GIRL by the HUSBAND.
33 The first part of this scene was cut during editing.
34 End of cut.
35 The first part of this scene was cut during editing.
36 End of cut.
37 Line cut during editing.
38 Ophuls notes in his script that she has a small bunch of violets in her hand.
39 The end of this scene and the beginning of the next were cut partly before filming and partly during editing.
40 End of cut.
41 The following scenes were filmed but cut during editing; the ninth sketch starts at this point.
42 End of cut.
43 This is a long corridor in the form of a foot-bridge, with cable-moulded columns painted white.
44 This scene was cut during editing.
45 End of cut.
46 This scene appears in the script but was not filmed.
47 End of scripted-only material.
48 Scene cut during editing.
49 End of cut.
50 Line cut in film version.
51 The script gives an alternative version of this reply: *But when. . . . How shall I put it? . . . When you don't enjoy the present. . . . When you think of the future. . . . Or you try to remember things. . . . That's fatal. The past is sad. The future remains unknown. In fact, we don't know any more where we are.*
52 This part of the scene appears in the script but was not filmed.

53 Dialogue of the filmed version resumes here.
54 These lines do not appear in the filmed version.
55 Resumption of dialogue of the filmed version.
56 An alternative version of the lines to the end of this scene appeared in the script:

COUNT: *Well, then! . . . There. . . . I wait for you in my carriage, at the stage door . . . we'll have supper somewhere. . . .*

ACTRESS: *I'm not Miss Birken.*

COUNT: *I'm perfectly aware of that. But we must try to create the right atmosphere. I need a certain ambiance at supper. And then after . . . when we come back, both of us. . . .*

ACTRESS: *And?*

COUNT: *Well, and . . . matters will take their usual course.*

57 The first part of this scene does not appear in the filmed version.
58 End of cut.
59 These shots are accompanied by the following monologue.
60 This part of the scene was not in the filmed version.
61 End of cut.
62 A more elaborate ending was envisaged by Ophuls, but not filmed: camera leaves the LEADER and approaches the empty roundabout on which now appear all the actors, as in the credits sequence.

ACTORS, singing: *And it's the chorus that leads La Ronde of Vienna,/ And it's the chorus that leads La Ronde of love.*

CREDITS:

Produced by	Charles Borderie and Louis Wipf
Production companies	C.I.C.C., Filmsonov, Vera Films and Fono Roma
Directed by	Henri-Georges Clouzot
Scenario and dialogue by	H.-G. Clouzot and J. Géronimi
Director of photography	A. Thirard
Assistant cameraman	R. Juillard
Assistant directors	R. Savarese, M. Romanoff
Sound	W. R. Sivel
Design	R. Renoux
Editors	H. Rust, M. Gug, E. Muse
Script-girl	L. Hargous
Music by	G. Auric
Production assistants	H. Jaquillard, L. Lippens

Grand Prix International at the Cannes Film Festival 1953

CAST:

Mario	Yves Montand
Jo	Charles Vanel
Luigi	Folco Lulli
Bimba	Peter van Eyck
Linda	Véra Clouzot
O'Brien	William Tubbs
Hernandez	Dario Moreno
Smerloff	Jo Dest
Camp chief	P. Centa

with: Pat Hurst, Luis de Lima, J. Mitchell, Gromoff, Faustini, Miss Darling, R. Baranger, F. Valorbe, R. Zermeno, J. Palau-Fabre, E. Larenagas.

The credits come up on a black background, then the film opens on a close-up of some insects running to and fro across a patch of earth, which is cracked and scorched by the sun. A hand holding a straw plays with the insects. The camera tilts up to show a small black CHILD wearing only a patched vest and a shapeless sombrero. He gets up as an ICE CREAM SELLER passes by.

Long shot: We are in the main and only street of a South American village, Las Piedras. The ICE CREAM SELLER passes, pushing his cart and shouting.

ICE CREAM SELLER, in Spanish[1]: *Nice soft drinks — lemon, vanilla, coffee, barley water . . . Nice creamy ices!*

Ragged children crowd around him. A NEGRO dressed in white comes up and buys an ice cream, then goes away again, passing a crippled beggar, who holds out his hand.

BEGGAR, in Spanish: *Alms, señor, alms . . .*

As the NEGRO gives the BEGGAR a coin, the camera pans to follow a woman carrying a basket of laundry on her head. She crosses the street, sidestepping the puddles. Suddenly a motorcycle appears, followed by a jeep, which splashes the passers-by. The jeep nearly runs down a herd of black pigs wandering down the street. The camera moves on to a trough, where a group of negro women are washing clothes.

ONE WOMAN, to another in Spanish: *What you need is a good bleaching, you've been burnt black by the sun.*

OTHER WOMAN, in Spanish: *See this bit of soap? I'm going to use it to bleach your tongue.*

Resume on the main street. The motorcycle and the jeep go off into the distance. Two horsemen gallop past, then the camera tracks in on the verandah of a café — *El Corsario Negro*. Several men are sitting on the steps outside. As the track ends, the ICE CREAM SELLER crosses the shot and stops in front of

---

[1] All dialogue in the original film is in French unless otherwise stated.

the café. A MAN picks up a stone and throws it viciously at the dog which is tied to the ICE CREAM SELLER's cart. The dog barks.

We see another MAN, looking on, then resume on the first MAN, who throws another stone, then gets up and goes up onto the verandah, where he sits down in a rocking chair, near another MAN who is reading a newspaper.

SMERLOFF: *Son-of-a-bitch. I can't stand 'em.*

MARIO: *Who wants to know?*

The camera shows a number of other men, also sprawled on the verandah. One of them, the eldest, is formally dressed, and wearing a pith helmet. He is the DOCTOR.

DICK, in English: *What a sizzler!*

DOC, in English: *Lucky for you. The hotter it is, the less you've got to eat!*

SMERLOFF, in German: *No one asked you for a diagnosis, Doc!*

Shot of the street, seen from the café. The camera pans with a horse drawing a water cart, which is spraying the roadway. Two naked CHILDREN are following it, taking a bath in the shower of water. We see the DRIVER, a Negro, who is dozing, letting the horse guide the cart.

Back on the verandah, DICK gets up, mopping the sweat from his forehead.

Close shot of MARIO and SMERLOFF. The latter picks a bottle of mineral water from the table and pours it over his face.

BERNARDO, in Spanish, looking at the DRIVER of the water cart: *Lucky bastard!*

SMERLOFF: *I wouldn't mind a job like that.*

MARIO: *Reserved for electors. Got your card?*

BERNARDO, in Spanish: *If anybody had ever told me that one day I'd be dying for work!*

The café's owner, HERNANDEZ, appears, dressed in pyjamas.

HERNANDEZ, in Spanish[1]: *There's never any work for layabouts like you.*

HERNANDEZ grabs the bottle of mineral water from SMERLOFF and looks furiously round at the men, seated or sprawled on the verandah.

---

[1] The following conversation between HERNANDEZ and the men takes place in Spanish.

HERNANDEZ: *Well, what are you going to drink?*

The camera pans across the men. MARIO looks indifferent. DICK yawns beside him.

HERNANDEZ: *Well, make up your minds. What's it going to be?*

A series of close shots follows the dialogue.

DOC: *A lemonade, please.*

HERNANDEZ: *Just one, for the lot of you?*

DICK: *Serve it and shut up.*

HERNANDEZ: *What charming manners!*

HERNANDEZ goes over to a rocking chair.

HERNANDEZ, shouting: *Linda, a lemonade for the Doctor!*

Then he sits down and rocks to and fro, fanning himself.

Resume on the men looking at him. SMERLOFF in particular is wearing an ironic smile. Annoyed, HERNANDEZ gets up and addresses SMERLOFF.

HERNANDEZ: *Are you getting at me?*

SMERLOFF: *There's nothing else to do.*

HERNANDEZ: *If it wasn't so goddam hot!*

He makes as if to sit down again, then changes his mind; he turns towards the men and shouts at them furiously.

HERNANDEZ: *Get out of here. Out, or I'll call the police. What about that, eh? They can ask to see your identification papers, and then we'll see what happens.*

BERNARDO, in French: *You sneaking bastard!*

SMERLOFF: *You mean you'd turn us in?*

All the men except MARIO are now in the street. HERNANDEZ continues to shout at them from the verandah.

HERNANDEZ: *I belong here, I'm a native. I'm not some goddam foreigner!*

JORNET: *You're a real credit to the white race.*

Having chased them away, HERNANDEZ comes back to the centre of the empty verandah. Only the DOCTOR remains, calmly drinking his lemonade. We follow HERNANDEZ as he goes into the interior of the café.

Inside the café MARIO is standing in the middle of the room near LINDA, who is on all fours, washing the tiled floor.[1]

HERNANDEZ, to MARIO: *What are you doing here?*

MARIO turns round and looks him up and down, then glances

---

[1] The conversation continues in Spanish.

229

at LINDA. Shot of her backside as she continues to clean the floor.

HERNANDEZ, to MARIO: *Are you deaf?*

He moves threateningly towards MARIO.

Shot of the two of them.

HERNANDEZ: *Get out!*

MARIO: *If I ever find you've laid a finger on her . . .!*

HERNANDEZ looks amazed and glances down at LINDA's buttocks.

HERNANDEZ: *Me? I don't want to do her any harm!*

He looks intensely towards LINDA.

HERNANDEZ: *On the contrary . . . what I'm going to do to her now will do her a lot of good . . .*

HERNANDEZ jerks his head at LINDA, who has turned round.

HERNANDEZ: *Right, honey? . . .* A pause. *Go up to my room.*

Seen from above, LINDA gets up, wipes her hands on her apron and starts to move away.

HERNANDEZ: *I'll be with you in a moment.*

LINDA: *Si, señor,*

The camera follows LINDA to the door of the café. She starts to climb an outside staircase.

Resume on the two men, face to face. MARIO lights a match and flips it in HERNANDEZ's face.

HERNANDEZ: *You think you're really smart, don't you?*

Very coolly, MARIO passes in front of HERNANDEZ, crosses the room and starts to go out of the door. HERNANDEZ follows in a fury, hurling insults after him.

HERNANDEZ: *Get out of here you son-of-a-bitch. You make me vomit . . . Filthy stinking rat!*

At these words MARIO turns round and stands over HERNANDEZ. They are both now on the verandah.

MARIO: *Hey! . . . Take it easy!*

He walks calmly down the steps from the verandah and into the street, still followed by HERNANDEZ, hurling insults.

Long shot of the street, taking in the two men and LINDA, who has stopped half way up the outside staircase, then resume on the two men.

HERNANDEZ: *Get out of here!*

MARIO: *The street doesn't belong to you.*

HERNANDEZ: *Well stay there! . . .*

As he speaks we suddenly hear the noise of an aircraft, off. The street is seen from above.

HERNANDEZ: *And tomorrow I'm going to fix an appointment for you with the immigration authorities.*

MARIO: *You dirty rat!*

The noise of the aircraft gets louder, and its shadow swoops across the street.

Rapid shot of LINDA's face. From the staircase, she watches the aircraft off-screen, following it down with her eyes as it lands nearby.

Seen from above, MARIO walks away, while HERNANDEZ notices LINDA and calls up to her.

HERNANDEZ: *Are you going up or not?*

LINDA goes up several steps, while HERNANDEZ suddenly remembers something and rushes into the café.

Cut to a shot of HERNANDEZ running into the patio of the café, apparently looking for someone. He stops in the foreground, near a hammock.

HERNANDEZ[1]: *Where's that lazy son-of-a-bitch got to now?*

A head emerges from the hammock. It is BIMBA.

BIMBA: *Here!*

HERNANDEZ turns round and starts to berate him. BIMBA gets out of the hammock.

HERNANDEZ: *What about the post? Didn't you hear the aeroplane?*

BIMBA rushes towards the van belonging to the café, followed by HERNANDEZ.

HERNANDEZ: *You should already be at the airport. Get a move on, goddamit!*

BIMBA is by the van. HERNANDEZ has stopped . . . He continues to address BIMBA from off-screen.

HERNANDEZ, off: *You're ruining me, the lot of you! I'll go bust and it'll be all your fault!*

Close shot of BIMBA as he opens the door of the van. A man is lying down on the seat, hiding. It is BERNARDO.

BIMBA, in an undertone[2]: *What are you doing here?*

BERNARDO: *Take me with you.*

BIMBA gets into the driving seat.

---

[1] HERNANDEZ's conversation with BIMBA also takes place in Spanish.
[2] In talking to BERNARDO, BIMBA switches to French.

The van moves off and passes in front of HERNANDEZ, who is looking satisfied. The camera holds on him. He comes back towards the café, looks up at the bedroom, takes a small mirror out of his pocket and combs his hair, then goes towards the outside staircase. In passing he picks up an apple, which he crunches as he climbs the first few steps.

Resume on the van in the street, as it passes MARIO, who is signalling to LINDA.

We see her standing at the window of HERNANDEZ's bedroom, smiling down at MARIO. MARIO smiles back.

Resume on the window. LINDA suddenly disappears from view, and HERNANDEZ appears in her place, crunching his apple. He sees MARIO and spits down at him.

MARIO shrugs his shoulders and nonchalantly lights a cigarette, still looking up at the window.

At the window, HERNANDEZ draws the curtain.

MARIO is seen from above as he walks slowly off down the street. Dissolve to BERNARDO and BIMBA, seen through the windscreen of the van. BIMBA is driving.

BERNARDO: *One day I'll find a pilot who's a good guy.* A pause. *He'll take me with him, or let me stow away in the baggage. I'll show him my visa for the States.*

The two of them are seen in profile. BIMBA, in the foreground, drives on imperturbably.

BERNARDO, insistently: *It's a real visa, you know!* He brandishes a passport . . . *It's real! Have I shown it to you?*

BIMBA: *You've shown it to everyone . . . and you shouldn't. Some people might be interested.* A pause. *Go on, put your papers away.*

Seen in long shot, the van arrives at the almost deserted airport. The plane is standing in the middle of the field. A group of natives stand looking at the aircraft and at the van, which has just come to a halt. Near them is a building with the words SAN MIGUEL AIRPORT — LAS PIEDRAS painted in large black letters on the white wall.

The airport staff wheel a gangway up to the aircraft. The PILOT emerges first and comes rapidly down the steps.

PILOT, to one of the ground staff, in Spanish: *Hi, Pepiot, what's new?*

232

The Employee mumbles something in reply and the Pilot moves away, pursued by Bernardo, who runs after him brandishing his passport.

Bernardo: *One moment, please . . . I've got a passport . . . One moment, please!*

Cut to show the passengers coming down the gangway from the aircraft. A Man appears in the doorway at the top, immaculately dressed in a white suit, a black shirt and a straw hat. He looks haughtily around, mops his forehead, waves his fly whisk and finally starts to descend. We follow him for a moment.

Resume on the gangway, where a Native is dragging a goat down the steps and onto the ground.

Dissolve to the interior of the police office at the airport, which is in a bamboo hut. A Policeman is sprawled in an armchair, his feet on his desk. Beside him, a black Servant hands him a bottle of beer. The Policeman gulps it down, mops his face, and then starts to check the passengers' papers. The first is a Negro, followed by a Woman carrying a child.

Resume on exterior shot of the airfield. The Man dressed in white is walking towards the hut, looking very sure of himself. He stops for a moment, takes out his passport, looks at it and smiles.

Close-up of the passport as he slips a banknote between the papers. He shuts the passport, puts it back in his pocket and walks on towards the hut.

Resume on the interior of the hut. We see the Man in white, whose name is Jo, and the Policeman. Their conversation takes place in Spanish.

Policeman, to Jo: *Luggage?*

Jo: *I haven't got any.*

Policeman: *No passport either?*

Jo: *Yes . . . yes . . . I've got a passport.*

Jo takes the passport out of his pocket and hands it to the Policeman. Close-up of the passport in the Policeman's hands.

Policeman: *Got a job?*

Jo, off: *I don't know yet.*

We see the Policeman's hands as he opens the passport. Very slowly, one of the hands slips the banknote under some papers on the desk. Resume on the two of them, the Policeman

233

sprawled in his chair, and Jo standing beside him.

POLICEMAN: *Okay, we'll put 'tourist'.*

The POLICEMAN stamps the passport and gives it back to Jo.

Dissolve to a shot of the main street in Las Piedras, almost deserted, as a taxi arrives and suddenly stops.

At the crossroads, a policeman stands under a huge umbrella. Shot of a NATIVE trying in vain to drag along an overloaded donkey.

Jo, as he opens the door of the taxi, looks at his surroundings and addresses the negro DRIVER.

Jo, in Spanish: *What is it?*

DRIVER, philosophically, in Spanish: *A traffic jam.*

Resume on the NATIVE dragging at his donkey. The camera pans to a corner of the crossroads, where a photographer — it is SMERLOFF — is taking a photograph of a group of natives as they pose in front of the camera. MARIO watches the scene with an ironic expression. The taxi has moved off again, and the camera follows it in a circle round the square. The taxi stops right in front of a large, dirty puddle. Jo gets out, leaving the door open, and looks around, while a gang of small children in rags watch him in astonishment and then come up to beg from him.

TAXI DRIVER, in Spanish: *Hey! . . . Wait a moment . . . that's a dollar.*

Jo, in Spanish: *Wait . . . maybe we're not there yet!*

The children crowd round him, followed by boot-blacks and beggars. Jo looks scornfully down at them.

MARIO comes up, passes the front of the taxi, whistling to himself, and drums nonchalantly on the bonnet with his fingers.

He senses Jo's eyes, which are now fixed on him, and comes up to him with a defiant and threatening expression. (*Still*)

MARIO, in Spanish: *D'you want my picture?*

Then MARIO walks round Jo, starting to whistle again. He whistles the tune *Valentine*, made famous by Maurice Chevalier. Then he stops and stares at Jo.

Shot of Jo, who picks up the tune, whistling in his turn.

The camera cuts rapidly from one to the other, ending on MARIO, who looks astonished.

234

Mario: *No kidding! . . . You too?*

We see the two of them as they both laugh and greet each other warmly. Jo slaps his compatriot heartily on the shoulder.

Jo: *Hey! It's good to find one, I can tell you, because . . .*

Mario: *Where are you from?*

A crippled beggar watches the scene.

Resume on Jo and Mario. Jo takes out a cigarette, puts it in his mouth and offers another to Mario.

Jo: *Number 20 . . . rue des Pyrénées.*

Mario: *I'm from Propriano.*

Mario gives Jo a light.

Jo: *Ah, so you're a Corsican!*

Mario: *Yes, but I worked in the rue de Douai, so I'm from the old place just the same.*

Jo and Mario move a few yards away from the taxi. Jo looks around the square.

Rapid shot of the ragged natives.

Jo: *Things are looking up. It won't be as bad as I thought.*

Mario: *You've come from Tegucigalpa?*

Jo: *Where else?*

Shot of the two of them. Jo shakes off an importunate native.

Jo: *Hey, keep your hands off.* He leads Mario away, taking him by the arm. *I don't have a cent . . . not even for a meal.* A pause. *Is there somewhere you can get it on the slate?*

Mario: *You could try Hernandez. He owns the café. A big mouth . . . but not a bad type.*

Jo: *Is it far?*

A new shot shows the café, *El Corsario*, just opposite on the other side of the square. Mario, followed by Jo, comes back towards the taxi which is still waiting.

Mario: *Let's take the taxi. It's a dollar in any case . . . and we'll make a better entrance that way.*

Mario gets in beside the driver and Jo in the back.

Seen from above, the taxi moves off, drives round the square and stops in front of the café. Mario gets out immediately and goes up to Hernandez, who is on the verandah in conversation with the Doctor.

Mario, in Spanish: *Hi, patron. I've brought you a pal of mine!*

Hernandez, who has not noticed the taxi, shrugs his shoulders and replies, furiously.

HERNANDEZ, in Spanish: *Aren't there enough of you fleecing me as it is?*

HERNANDEZ turns round, and notices the taxi with surprise. Jo is getting out of it with an important air. HERNANDEZ immediately rushes forward, bowing.

HERNANDEZ, in Spanish: *Hey now! This is a sight for sore eyes!*

HERNANDEZ has gone up to Jo and is bowing and scraping in front of him, brushing off his jacket. Jo looks him up and down haughtily without saying anything, then advances towards the café, still looking very important. He addresses HERNANDEZ curtly.

Jo: *Pay the taxi!*

MARIO, in Spanish: *Just who is this guy?*

HERNANDEZ, in Spanish: *I thought he was a pal of yours.*

MARIO to DOC: *You know what they're like . . .*

DOC, emphatically and slightly mysterious: *I've heard!*

HERNANDEZ has already gone into the café and MARIO follows him. We move inside the café which is seen from the door. Jo sits down at a table, while HERNANDEZ bustles obsequiously round him and wipes the table top. MARIO comes through the doorway, in the foreground and advances towards Jo, the camera tracking after him.

Jo, to MARIO: *Come on, come over here.*

MARIO has arrived at the table. HERNANDEZ is serving Jo with a drink.

Jo: *The same again for my friend here.*

Shot of three of them.

Jo, in Spanish: *Take a seat.*

MARIO sits down opposite Jo, and we cut to a shot of the two of them as HERNANDEZ comes back and serves MARIO.

MARIO: *Thank you, you're very kind.*

Jo: *You can cut out the formality. I'm Jo . . . to you.* A pause. He looks at HERNANDEZ who finishes serving them, and continues in Spanish: *But I'm Señor Jo to everyone else.*

HERNANDEZ goes away. The two men raise their glasses and look one another in the eye.

MARIO: *Here's to you . . . Jo!*

We see some fruit hanging from the banisters of the staircase.

LINDA's legs appear and she comes down the stairs, buttoning up her blouse. As she arrives at the bottom of the steps she looks across at MARIO and Jo. Her expression freezes. Zoom in on Jo and MARIO seated at the table.

MARIO: *Everything'll work out fine, don't worry.*

Jo: *It's not so bad here.*

MARIO: *One soon gets tired of it.* A pause. *It's none of my business, but what made you pick this hole?*

Jo has taken a pack of cards out of a nearby cupboard and is playing patience.

Jo: *Sometimes one doesn't have the choice. This time I had to run for it . . . didn't even have time to go to the bank. I made straight for the airport . . . I emptied out my wallet . . .*

Close-up of Jo as he continues his game of patience.

Jo: *. . . Then I said to them: ' Where can I go for fifty dollars?'*

LINDA's hand appears as she places it on MARIO's shoulder.

Jo, continuing: *And that's how I ended up here.*

As he speaks he raises his head.

Close shot of LINDA. The camera shows the three of them, in turn, then ends on a shot of all three.

MARIO: *This is Linda . . . She's a nice kid.*

Jo: *So I see!*

MARIO, in Spanish to LINDA, who is standing dumbly by: *Come on, say something! Be nice to the gentleman! . . .*

Shot of MARIO as he takes off his jacket and holds it out to LINDA. He is wearing only a vest underneath.

MARIO, to Jo: *She's nice . . . but not educated. She's half savage.* A pause. He addresses LINDA in Spanish: *I've lost a button. Go and fix it!*

LINDA goes off. The camera pans after her and holds on a group of negro women seated on the ground, eating. They laugh.

Resume on MARIO and Jo.

MARIO: *You know the type?*

Jo: *They come straight off the coconut tree.*

MARIO: *Have you eaten?*

Jo: *Oh . . . yes . . . in the plane . . . It's included in the fare.*

MARIO, getting up: *In that case you'll excuse me — I must go and have a bite.*

Standing up, MARIO gives Jo a friendly wave of the hand and

walks towards the centre of the café while LINDA comes towards him and holds out his jacket. She helps him on with it. MARIO thanks her with a friendly grimace.

Jo, off: *Don't you eat here?*

MARIO: *Oh no, I've got a room in town . . . You've got to be independent, after all.*

Jo: *Of course.*

MARIO: *OK . . . I'm off, but I won't be long.*

MARIO is now standing in the doorway of the café. He pauses, searches in his pocket and pulls out a coin, then turns back towards Jo, tossing the coin in his hand.

MARIO: *You see! . . . I wasn't looking for it.*

Jo: *Of course.*

Dissolve to show MARIO walking down the village street. Seen in a close shot he stops in front of the window of the tobacconist's. He looks at the boxes of cigars for a moment, smiling and tossing his coin.

Dissolve to LUIGI and MARIO's room. In the foreground, LUIGI is making pasta beside a pastry mould. MARIO appears in the doorway opposite him and approaches.[1]

MARIO: *Have you been playing in the cement again this morning?*

LUIGI: *I've finished the shuttering. And they've brought an enormous, brand new concrete-mixer.*

LUIGI leaves the table on which he is making pasta and approaches MARIO.

LUIGI: *We may be getting a vibrato, too.*

MARIO listens with half an ear as he searches around in the cupboard and takes something out of it. LUIGI meanwhile drinks from a glass and then, facing MARIO again, notices two cigars in the pocket of his jacket.

LUIGI: *Hey! . . . Have you just robbed a bank, or is it your birthday?*

MARIO: *It's for a present.*

Embarrassed by the question, MARIO turns towards the stove, lifts the lids of the saucepans and turns up his nose.

MARIO: *Not pasta again?*

LUIGI: *Don't worry . . . keep calm. I'll make you a sauce.*

As LUIGI speaks MARIO goes up to a mirror and starts to lather

---

[1] MARIO's conversation with LUIGI takes place in Italian.

his face with a shaving brush.

MARIO: *There's no time. I'll eat your pasta by itself.*

LUIGI starts. He looks at MARIO, bewildered and rather jealous.

MARIO: *I've got a date.*

LUIGI: *A date? With a woman?*

MARIO: *Some woman . . . no, a man, a real man . . .*

With these words MARIO dabs LUIGI's nose with the shaving brush.

LUIGI in close up looks at him in amazement.

Dissolve to the interior of the café, where Jo, having taken off his jacket, is still seated at the same table. LINDA is serving him a coffee.

LINDA, in Spanish: *Here!*

Jo, in Spanish: *Thanks a lot.*

LINDA, in Spanish: *You're welcome.*

Then she moves away, looking at him ironically and banging rhythmically on her tray. Music. She dances across to the bar, where BIMBA is standing. He looks both vacant and alert at the same time.

BIMBA, in Spanish: *I'm thirsty.*

LINDA, in Spanish: *Do you have any money?*

BIMBA, in Spanish: *What about what I'm owed?*

LINDA, in Spanish: *Let's see.*

LINDA goes and fetches a slate from behind the bar and looks at it, while HERNANDEZ appears, carrying a bottle of whisky.

LINDA, to BIMBA in Spanish: *Poor boy!*

HERNANDEZ, to LINDA in Spanish: *Two beers outside.*

LINDA leaves the bar and goes to serve the customers outside, while HERNANDEZ stands looking at BIMBA's slate.

HERNANDEZ, in English: *You've got two bucks left till the end of the month.*

As he speaks, BIMBA grabs the bottle of whisky and takes a large gulp from it while HERNANDEZ watches him in astonishment.

BIMBA, putting the bottle down, in English: *This will make us about even.*

HERNANDEZ, in English: *Hey! Hey! . . . What the hell are you going to drink till the First?*

Close shot of BIMBA, who leans on the bar with both hands

239

and thrusts his face at HERNANDEZ.

BIMBA, in English: *You'll give me a raise.*

HERNANDEZ, in English: *Why?*

BIMBA, in English: *Because its getting real hot.*

Dissolve to show MARIO, freshly shaved, crossing the verandah and going to sit at Jo's table inside the café.

Jo: *That was quick work.*

MARIO, sitting down: *I can't eat much when I'm feeling good.*

Having sat down, MARIO proudly offers Jo a cigar.

Jo: *Ah! Thanks, my boy . . . Have a drop of this.* Pointing at his glass. *It's cognac . . . the real stuff.*

MARIO: *He gave you a fair measure.*

Jo: *Oh . . . I served myself.*

As they talk, MARIO gives Jo a light, then lights his own cigar. The café is silent, all eyes fixed on the two men.

We see BIMBA, sitting on top of the bar watching them, smoking.

Then the table next to MARIO and Jo, which is occupied by the men whom HERNANDEZ chased off the verandah previously. DICK gets up and goes towards MARIO, his unlit pipe in his mouth.

DICK, in English, leaning towards MARIO: *Permit me, my lord!*

He tries to take MARIO's cigar to light his pipe, but MARIO snatches it away from him.

MARIO: *Hey! . . . Hold it, chum!*

He snatches back his cigar and tosses a box of matches at DICK. Then after a while he turns round and puts on the radio beside him. Interference and music from the radio.

Jo: *Cut that out! . . . I can't stand music.*

MARIO turns it off immediately.

At the next table, the men are eyeing MARIO suspiciously. One of them, SMERLOFF, gets up and goes over to the radio.

Close-up of his hand turning the knob. Music. SMERLOFF comes back to his table, performing a grotesque little dance. MARIO starts up to turn the radio off, but Jo stops him with a gesture and calls HERNANDEZ.

Jo, in Spanish: *Hey!*

HERNANDEZ approaches.

Shot of the three men. MARIO, Jo and HERNANDEZ.

240

Jo, in Spanish: *Turn it off.* A pause. He continues in French. *You're driving us crazy with that racket.*

Ingratiatingly, HERNANDEZ obeys and turns off the radio.

Shot of the next table, where the men are sitting in silence. After a moment the DOCTOR bangs on the table with both hands and gets up. The others do likewise.

DOC, in English: *Well boys, I think we've understood!*

They all start to leave, accompanied by HERNANDEZ, who is delighted to have a pretext for getting rid of them.

BERNARDO, in Spanish: *You won't see us again!*

SMERLOFF, in Spanish: *We won't set foot in this joint again!*

BERNARDO, in Spanish: *Yeah ... let's go to the Palmera.*

HERNANDEZ, in Spanish: *Good riddance!*

Having followed them to the door, HERNANDEZ comes back to the table where MARIO and Jo are sitting, and passes in front of them, shrugging his shoulders.

HERNANDEZ, in Spanish: *Sour grapes ...*

He disappears.

Shot of MARIO and Jo; the camera cuts between the two of them, following the dialogue.

MARIO: *The trouble is, no one here's got a job.* A pause. *We make out ... get enough to eat and a lay now and then.*

Jo: *Why don't you get out?*

MARIO: *It's not for lack of wanting ... you'll see.*

Shot of the deserted street, the sun blazing down.

MARIO, off: *There's no bars ... just open space ...*

The two men are now standing on the verandah, looking out over the village, the sun beating down on the empty street in front of them. Jo leans on the balustrade. MARIO stands beside him, talking without looking at him.

MARIO, off at first: *That's the killer ... it's too big. You've got to make one hell of a big leap to get out.*

Jo: *Can't you jump a train?*

MARIO: *There's no railway.*

Jo: *The road?*

MARIO: *There's only one — it stops at the oil-well.*

Jo: *By air?*

MARIO: *Look at the fares.*

The camera shows the window of a travel agency advertising

air fares.

MARIO, off: *Caracas is too close. We're bad news round them parts.*
The two men are now standing by the window. They stop for
a moment.

MARIO: *After that it's two or three hundred bucks straight off. A*
pause. *You got them?* Silence. *Me neither!*
They walk down the street.

MARIO: *And a visa. You need a visa over there.*

Jo: *You can always get a visa.*
They stop, facing each other, near a half-constructed building.

MARIO: *Yes, but a real one.*

Jo: *A real one too.*

MARIO: *If you've got the dough. And to get the dough you've got*
to earn it . . . and to earn it you need work . . . and that's the one
thing there isn't any of. A pause. *Take that building, for instance.*
He points towards it. *They started it two years ago . . . and they've*
let everything drop . . . with this sun it's understandable. A pause.
No, I tell you, this place is like a prison. Getting in is easy . . . come
right on in . . . But if you want to get out . . . no dice! And if you
don't get out, you die.

Jo: *Well I don't want to die.*

MARIO: *Nobody wants to . . . But they die all the same.*
On these last words, the camera tilts rapidly upwards to show
the top of the half-finished building, then dissolves to a high
angle shot of the two men, carrying flowers, followed by BIMBA
and three or four other men. The camera tracks ahead of them.
Reverse shot of the group from behind. We now see that they
form part of a very meagre procession following a hearse.

MARIO: *There's your proof.*

Jo: *Okay, but he wasn't even on his feet.*

MARIO: *Sure, he had a fever . . . But there's more to it than mos-*
quitoes . . . we have spiders and little things that eat your liver
from the inside . . . We even have leprosy.
Close shot of the two of them, still walking forwards, following
the hearse.

MARIO, continuing: *There's only one bad disease, and that's chronic.*
It's called hunger. Most of the guys round here have died of it. Not
over there.
The camera follows Jo's glance to show a side of the cemetery

very neatly kept, with elaborate crosses on the graves.

MARIO, off: *That bit belongs to Uncle Sam.*

Jo: *There are Yanks in Las Piedras?*

MARIO: *You bet! When there's oil . . . they're not far off.* A pause. *S.O.C. — that's the name of the company. They've got a camp not far from here. They're well organised. They've got their huts, their canteen, a completely prefabricated cemetery. O'Brien drops in once a week to see if everything's in order.*

Jo: *O'Brien? Bill O'Brien . . . a big guy?*

MARIO: *Yes, do you know him?*

Jo: *You bet I do . . . We did the traffic together in Guayaguil in '32.* MARIO and Jo hurry towards the grave, quickly throw in their flowers and leave the cemetery.

Jo: *That changes everything . . .*

Dissolve to interior shot of O'BRIEN's office in the Southern Oil Company. Jo is seated in the foreground, O'BRIEN standing beside his desk, his hands in his pockets.[1]

O'BRIEN: *Sorry, but it doesn't, pal . . . Not with you. I can't. They've got their records at headquarters.*

O'BRIEN comes up to Jo.

O'BRIEN: *They'd throw you out three days later and me with you.*

Jo, in English: *Listen my friend . . . I need money.*

Close-up of Jo, who talks in a mixture of French and English.

Jo: *And when I need dough . . . you know what I'm like, I don't know what I'm doing. So be careful.*

O'BRIEN: *I am.*

Jo has got up and gone over to a map of the S.O.C. oil-wells. He examines the map and smiles, passing his hand over his hair.

Jo, in French: *You've got 1,500 kilometres of pipeline there . . . A pipeline is fragile.* Looking fixedly at O'BRIEN. *A couple of fireworks in that would make quite a mess . . . and if the cops want to pin it on me . . .* A pause. *They will not have a chance.* He bangs his fist in his palm. In English: *In the baba!*

As Jo speaks, O'BRIEN comes to him. They stand facing each other for a moment. O'BRIEN is smiling unconcernedly.

O'BRIEN: *Anywhere else you'd be right . . . But not here.*

O'BRIEN goes over to the window and raises the blind.

---

[1] Throughout this scene O'BRIEN speaks in English.

O'BRIEN: *They attend to things themselves. Take a look.*

He beckons Jo over.

A high shot of the yard below, where two armed motorcyclists are sitting on their machines ready to leave at a moment's notice. Their motorcycles carry the name of the company: S.O.C.

O'BRIEN, off: *Those guys are mean customers . . .*

Resume on the office. O'BRIEN lowers the blind and turns back to Jo.

O'BRIEN: *. . . Pretty mean . . . Worse than we were because there's no risk in it. Mustn't get sore at me, Jo, I'm the big boss now.*

O'BRIEN is facing Jo, who looks at him resentfully.

O'BRIEN: *By the way . . . Here we're friends, but in front of the others . . . be nice enough . . . Call me Mister.*

O'BRIEN takes Jo *by the shoulder and leads him to the door.*

O'BRIEN: *Get it?*

Dissolve to exterior shot of the S.O.C. compound. We see two men, O'BRIEN and Jo taking leave of one another near the main gate. Jo hurries away.

Jo, in English: *Goodbye, Mr. O'Brien.*

O'BRIEN, in English: *So long, Jo.*

Jo crosses the road and joins MARIO, who is waiting for him.

MARIO: *No dice, huh?*

Jo, furious: *For the moment, no . . . but things are going to change, goddamit . . . It's not possible you can't pick up some dough somewhere.*

The camera tracks in towards them.

MARIO: *Las Piedras is oil. And when the oil stops, there's nothing.*

The two men start walking.

Shot of a stationary lorry belonging to the S.O.C. DICK is standing nearby. He picks up a fag-end.

MARIO: *Look at him. He worked for them and he got thrown out. See what he's reduced to.*

The lorry moves off, revealing some construction workers at work. Shot of LUIGI, who is one of them. He calls to MARIO.

Jo: *Who's that?*

MARIO: *That's Luigi . . . My pal. He's a good guy, you'll see.*

MARIO leaves Jo and goes towards LUIGI, who has left his work

244

and is coming towards him. Jo follows some distance behind.

LUIGI: *A good guy whom you've strangely neglected recently!*
Shot of the two of them.

MARIO: *If you were in our position . . . with all the work we've got.*

LUIGI: *I'd soon change.*

MARIO: *We're working . . .* Tapping his head: *. . . with our heads.*
Jo has come up to them, and looks coldly at LUIGI.

Jo: *How's the building coming along?*
The camera shows each of them in turn.

LUIGI: *Slowly. They could pay us more.*

MARIO: *He's as mean as hell! He's never got enough . . . When he earns two dollars he has to put one aside.*

LUIGI: *I've got to, if I'm ever going to get home.*
Someone whistles in the distance. We see LUIGI's foreman, calling him back to work.

LUIGI: *Sorry! . . . He doesn't like us stopping for a chat.*
LUIGI goes back to work, while the camera pans to follow Jo and MARIO who go off arm in arm.

MARIO: *You see what I was telling you . . . the fat one.* A pause.

MARIO, continuing: *We share a room. Well, he's the one who does the ironing, and the cooking . . . he's a great guy . . . A sucker!*
In the distance, LUIGI waves cheerfully to MARIO and calls him. MARIO turns round, letting go of Jo's arm, and waves back and then goes off again with Jo.

Dissolve to a shot of the patio at the back of the café. Jo is sprawled in a rocking chair, with MARIO seated on the ground beside him. In the background we see a black girl standing naked under an improvised shower made from a jerrycan. (*Still*)

Jo: *What's your bricklayer friend got against me?*

MARIO: *Oh, it's inevitable. Before you came we saw a lot of each other . . . Now I'm always with you he's fed up.*

Jo: *What a mentality!*
In the background, the woman, having finished her shower, reaches down to pick up a cloth to dry herself. She screams. Seen in close up, an enormous scorpion is crawling across the cloth.
MARIO turns round and leaps to his feet.
Close-up of his foot, wearing a worn espadrille, as it crushes

the insect.

MARIO, in Spanish: *Don't be afraid.*

The girl seems reassured and MARIO turns back to Jo, who has come towards him.

MARIO: *They're nasty brutes.*

Shot of MARIO and Jo.

Jo: *Come to the barber's — it's something to do.*

MARIO, running his hand through his hair: *I went there on Saturday.*

Jo: *Never mind, you can keep me company.*

With these words, Jo turns to go, while MARIO stands where he is, embarrassed.

MARIO, hesitating: *I promised Linda . . . today's her day off.*

Jo, annoyed: *Oh, I beg your pardon . . . that changes everything. Fine. Fine.*

MARIO: *Do you mind?*

Jo: *What do you take me for? . . . And who do you think you are?*

Shrugging his shoulders, Jo walks rapidly away, pursued by MARIO, who calls beseechingly after him.

MARIO: *Jo, wait for me, wait for me. Jo, I'm coming . . .*

Cut to LINDA in a white dress, who gives an exclamation as she meets MARIO.[1]

LINDA: *Where are you going? . . . Mario.*

She is wearing her best clothes, with a straw hat in her hand and high-heeled shoes. She gives a little curtsey in front of MARIO.

MARIO, turning round: *I'm going off with Jo.*

LINDA: *But I've made myself a new dress! . . . Look, isn't it pretty?*

LINDA shows off her dress (*Still*), but getting no response from MARIO, quickly picks up a large publicity calendar on which is a photograph of a model wearing a dress more or less identical to her own.

LINDA: *It's the same as this one.*

Annoyed, MARIO takes the calendar without looking at it.

LINDA: *Just the same . . . doesn't it look the same?*

MARIO: *Yes, it's very pretty. If you wear it you'll spoil it.*

LINDA: *Bah! If I spoil it I'll make another one.*

Jo appears beside them, looking inquisitive and a little jealous,

---

[1] The following conversation between LINDA, Jo and MARIO all takes place in Spanish except as indicated otherwise.

in spite of his general ill humour.

Jo, in French: *Are you coming — yes or no?*

LINDA anxiously approaches Jo and pleads with him. A close shot of the two of them is followed by a shot of LINDA's face.

LINDA: *Won't you lend him to me for a bit, Señor Jo? . . . Just one day a month isn't very much.*

Jo: *Mario's old enough to make up his own mind.*

Furious, Jo turns and walks off, his hands in his pockets.

MARIO, in French shouting to Jo: *I'll follow you.*

Jo, in French, without turning round: *No, it's too late now.*

Now MARIO is furious too, and he looks LINDA up and down contemptuously.

MARIO: *Are you satisfied?*

LINDA: *You can hit me if you want to.*

MARIO: *I really don't know why I don't.*

He bows mockingly in front of her, then resigns himself to the situation.

MARIO: *Come on, if we've got to go out, let's go.*

Looking happy, LINDA bends down immediately to put on her high-heeled shoes which she has been carrying in her hand, and teeters after MARIO, who turns back towards her.

MARIO: *And there's no need to look like that.*

The camera tracks rapidly after them.

Dissolve to the barber's shop where Jo is seated back to camera having a shave. Reflected in the mirror opposite, we see his face and, behind him, the barber and the door into the street, which is open. BERNARDO is almost on his knees beside Jo, showing him his passport.

BERNARDO, pleading: *It's terrible, Monsieur . . . My visa expires in a month and I don't have any money for the journey. A hundred dollars, a hundred dollars and I'm saved. Help me, Monsieur, I beg of you.*

While Jo starts to get up, we see MARIO and LINDA passing in the street, reflected in the mirror. MARIO slaps LINDA. Jo is now standing up. He brushes himself down and goes towards the door, followed by BERNARDO, who pleads with him more and more desperately.

BERNARDO: *I'll pay you back Monsieur, I promise . . . My family is*

247

an honourable family. You're an honourable man too . . .

Jo: *Get lost.*

Jo pays the barber and goes into the street.

Dissolve to the main street. Jo passes LINDA as she runs off sobbing, and joins MARIO.

MARIO, in Spanish, shouting at LINDA: *That'll teach you not to start again.*

Jo: *Did you give her a pat?*

MARIO, importantly: *I can't stand all that sentimental stuff.*

Jo, leading him away: *Guys like us aren't meant for the girls.*

Arm in arm, the two men go off in the opposite direction to LINDA.

A jeep belonging to the oil company — the S.O.C. — passes rapidly down the street, splashing them as it goes through a puddle.

Some splashes of mud land on Jo's white suit.

Dissolve to a close-up of someone's hands trying to clean off the splashes from the white suit.

We are in MARIO and LUIGI's room. MARIO is cleaning the suit while Jo sits on LUIGI's bed. A series of shots and reverse shots, following the dialogue.

MARIO: *No good. It'll have to be cleaned.*

Jo: *What am I going to wear in the meantime? I can't walk about bare-assed at my age.*

MARIO: *Don't worry . . . We're well provided here.*

MARIO goes towards a chest of drawers and opens the top drawer, which is full of shirts and other pieces of clothing, neatly arranged. He rummages through them and, throwing aside a few shirts, pulls out a pair of trousers, which he holds up.

MARIO: *You can wear a pair of Luigi's trousers.*

We see Jo, still sprawled on LUIGI's bed. Above him are two photographs of a man and a woman, fairly old, who look like peasants. He takes down one of the portraits.

Jo, ironically: *Is that Calabrian bandit Luigi's old man?*

MARIO: *Yeah . . . great, isn't he?*

Then MARIO goes towards Jo and holds out the trousers to him. While Jo gets up to try them on, the camera pans to follow

248

MARIO as he goes over to his bed in the opposite corner of the room.

MARIO: *You've seen my museum?*

MARIO points at the decoration he has made on the wall above his bed. There is a drawing of the entrance to the Pigalle Metro station in Paris, decorated with photographs of naked women. MARIO points them out very proudly.

Close-up of the ' museum ' and of MARIO, who sits down on the bed.

MARIO: *That's for the women . . . for dreaming . . . To think of something else when you're laying a negress.* He shows a small piece of paper which is given pride of place in the display. *And that's the biggest treasure of all . . . a gem.*

Close-up of a used metro ticket.

MARIO, off: *It's real, you know.*

MARIO holds out the ticket to Jo, who is amazed and overjoyed. A series of alternating shots follows the dialogue.

Jo: *No kidding! . . . I haven't seen one of them for years.* He reads the name on the ticket. *Pigalle! . . .*

MARIO: *It's the last one I took. It took me to the train, and the train to the boat . . . and the boat here! . . . The North-South line goes further than you think.*

Jo, reflectively: *It cost fourteen sous when I left.*

MARIO: *Fourteen sous to leave . . . a thousand dollars to get back. There's no doubt about it — the cost of living is rising.*

During their last exchange, a voice is heard approaching, cheerfully singing *Santa Lucia.*

Cut to show MARIO, who straightens up, then the doorway as LUIGI comes in. He stops in surprise and surveys the open chest of drawers and the general disorder of the room in increasing bewilderment.

A shirt is seen lying on the ground, unfolded. LUIGI bends down and picks it up, then approaches the two men.

Shot of the three men.

LUIGI, in Italian: *Oh, great . . . do just what you want. Give away my clothes . . . After all they didn't cost me much.*

Jo, to Mario: *What's he saying?*

MARIO, in Italian: *Oh, let it go . . . We'll give you your rags back . . .* A pause. *Cleaned and disinfected . . .*

LUIGI, in Italian, throwing down the shirt which he has picked up: *No, you can keep them. You can give them away . . . to him . . . or anyone else. The next time you change friends.*

MARIO, in Italian: *You get on my nerves! We're not married, are we? . . . If you've seen enough of my face, I'm fed up with yours too. I'm changing streets.*

JO: *What does he want?*

    MARIO takes Jo by the arm and leads him to the door. The camera pans with them.

MARIO: *Nothing — he's nuts. Let's beat it before I get angry.*

    Shot of LUIGI, furious.

LUIGI: *That's right . . . Get lost . . . I shan't be sorry!*

    Resume on MARIO who turns in the doorway and gives him an ironic wave of the hand.

    Outside in the street, we see Jo, then MARIO emerging from LUIGI's lodging.

MARIO: *You see how I fixed him!* A pause. He turns back towards the door: *Wait!* He goes back into LUIGI's lodging.

    Camera holds on Jo who does not have long to wait as MARIO emerges again almost immediately, brandishing his metro ticket.

MARIO: *I got it back! . . .*

    They walk nonchalantly off up the street.

    Dissolve to the exterior of the café at night. The camera tracks in towards the façade, on which the words CORSARIO NEGRO stand out in neon lighting in the darkness.

    Medium shot of the café façade and the street, where some Negroes are dancing in the semi-darkness. LUIGI can be seen approaching with a determined step. He is wearing his Sunday best — a clean suit, and a white tie and cap, and he is coming towards the café.

    The camera pans with BIMBA as he joins SMERLOFF on the verandah.

BIMBA, in German, in a low voice: *The bricklayer's coming.*

SMERLOFF, in German: *Really?*

    SMERLOFF immediately throws away the butt of his cigar and goes into the café.

SMERLOFF, in German: *I'll go and warn the others.*

Inside the café, SMERLOFF goes and sits down at the table occupied by his friends (DOC, BERNARDO, DICK, etc.). Jo and MARIO are sitting at the next table smoking and drinking. MARIO has taken a clasp-knife out of his pocket and is playing with a piece of wood. He signals to Jo with the point of the knife. Jo turns round. LUIGI comes defiantly into the café and stops near the bar. He buttons up his jacket, straightens his tie, and looks towards MARIO.

Resume on MARIO, who lowers his eyes and continues to play nervously with his knife.

Very slow circular pan shows all the occupants of the café, who say nothing. The pan ends on HERNANDEZ, brought out of his semi-somnolent state by LUIGI's arrival.

Resume on LUIGI, still looking at MARIO, then back to MARIO and Jo.

We see MARIO's hand as he nervously whittles the piece of wood with his knife; Jo's hand is seen next to it as he puts down his glass.

LUIGI now passes in front of the bar and approaches HERNANDEZ. A shot of the two of them, then of the drawer HERNANDEZ uses as a till; a cosh and a revolver are lying on top of the notes and coins.

Close shot of LUIGI and HERNANDEZ.[1]

LUIGI: *Good evening, Pepito.*

HERNANDEZ: *Getting married?*

LUIGI: *I'm having a little celebration with my friends.*

Looking pleased with his entrance, LUIGI then goes towards the table where his friends (SMERLOFF, BERNARDO, DICK, etc.) are seated, next to that occupied by MARIO and Jo. SMERLOFF welcomes him with open arms . . . and everyone sits down as HERNANDEZ comes over to the table.

LUIGI: *This round's mine, fellers.*

Cut to the table where MARIO and Jo are sitting.

Jo, calling: *Hey, barman! . . . two whiskies.*

Shot of HERNANDEZ; LUIGI seated at his table, holds him back by the arm.

HERNANDEZ, to Jo: *Right away, Señor Jo.*

---

[1] The entire conversation up to LUIGI's final confrontation with Jo takes place in Spanish.

251

LUIGI: *Now then, you jerk, everyone in turn!*
HERNANDEZ, shaking free: *Yeah, I know . . . one lemonade for the five of you.*
LUIGI: *What do you mean, one lemonade? We're not as poor as that!* He gets up, grabs HERNANDEZ by the lapels of his jacket and shouts at him. *Champagne! Champagne! Spumante! . . .*
All the customers laugh and applaud him. LUIGI lets go of HERNANDEZ and goes over to a corner of the room.
He passes LINDA, then the table where MARIO and Jo are sitting, and goes to turn on the radio. Music.
LINDA, in passing: *Are you going to have real champagne, Luigi? You must be in the money . . . Will you let me try it?*
LUIGI: *With pleasure.*
Shot of LUIGI's friends at their table as samba music begins to blare from the radio.
SMERLOFF, in French: *That's right . . . Let's have a bit of music.* He laughs unpleasantly. *That should liven things up.*
Resume on LUIGI who passes Jo and MARIO's table once more, taking no notice of them. Jo is playing patience.
Jo, to MARIO, in French: *Your little pal is beginning to get on my nerves.*
The camera pans with LUIGI as he saunters across the centre of the room.
He bows to LINDA and invites her to dance.
LUIGI, in Spanish: *May I have the pleasure?*
LINDA, in Spanish: *Delighted.*
Both smiling, they dance in the middle of the room, getting more and more frenzied.
Jo and MARIO sit at their table, both looking mystified.
BIMBA is sitting on the bar. He is smoking and drinking, taking in the scene with an ironic and blasé expression.
The camera shows the two dancers, then MARIO and Jo looking tense, then resumes on the dancers. (*Still*) LINDA is smiling more and more radiantly and as she dances she glances towards MARIO.
His nerves on edge, Jo gets up, goes to the radio and pulls the flex out of the back of it. The music stops immediately.
LUIGI and LINDA freeze in the middle of a dance step. After a short pause, LINDA runs off towards the kitchens and LUIGI,

having got over his surprise, begins to smile again. Clapping his hands and singing, he dances back to his table. All those who have been watching the scene sing and clap their hands to accompany him.

Having sat down, LUIGI continues to sing with his friends, banging rhythmically on the table. After a few moments he stops — the others do likewise — and addresses HERNANDEZ.

LUIGI, in Spanish: *Get a move on, waiter. Our tongues are hanging out.*

Rapid close-up of Jo nervously banging his fist in his palm.

MARIO, equally on edge, sweeps the pieces of wood off the table. Resume on Jo who has got up and is going towards HERNANDEZ. The latter is about to take LUIGI his bottle of champagne. Jo takes the bottle from him and shakes it up.

Sitting at his table with his friends, LUIGI sees Jo coming towards them, shaking the bottle and beginning to loosen the cork.

Close-up of Jo's feet advancing slowly towards the table. He walks in time to the singing of the spectators which has now begun again.

Jo stops in front of the table.

Jo, in Spanish: *Here you are.*

LUIGI, in Spanish: *Well?*

Jo uncorks the bottle and an enormous jet of foam spurts out of it. Jo pours it over LUIGI and his companions.

Jo, to LUIGI, in Spanish: *The gentleman is served.*

As Jo walks calmly back towards his own table, LUIGI and his friends get up, soaked. Picking up the empty bottle, LUIGI gets up suddenly, overturning the table.

Glasses crash to the ground and break.

LUIGI's feet kick aside the table; they crush a glass and advance towards the centre of the room.

Jo turns round abruptly and stands threateningly, facing LUIGI.

Close-up of HERNANDEZ's hand taking the cosh out of the drawer of the till.

Resume on LUIGI and Jo, face to face. LUIGI raises the bottle threateningly in the air. A pause.

The camera pans in a circle round the café as the customers watch in silence.

253

Resume on LUIGI and Jo. The latter does not move, and stares intently at his adversary. The camera shows close-ups of each of them.[1]

DICK, to LUIGI: *Go on, what are you waiting for?*

MARIO watches from his table, smiling though somewhat anxious; he still has his knife in his hand.

Resume on Jo, who whips a revolver out of his pocket and sticks the barrel in LUIGI's stomach.

LUIGI raises his arms . . . and finally drops the bottle.

Jo: *Now you're unarmed . . . In my position, I can't afford to brawl like a docker! . . . I'll shoot!*

LUIGI lowers his arms, alarmed and furious.

LUIGI: *It's easy to show off with that thing.*

Jo: *Here.*

With these words, Jo hands LUIGI the revolver. The latter looks in astonishment at the weapon in his hands and aims it at Jo. BIMBA watches smiling, from his place on the bar.

We see a series of shots of the other customers, both black and white, watching the scene.

Jo, after a pause: *Go on — shoot!*

Close-up of LUIGI's face; he is sweating.

We see his hand holding the revolver against Jo.

LUIGI: *I can't . . . just like that . . .*

Jo: *And like that!*

Disregarding the revolver pressed against him, Jo slaps LUIGI violently round the face. A series of close-ups shows: Jo, teeth clenched; LUIGI, having received the blow; he frowns; his hand, on the finger of the trigger moves, ready to press it.

Jo stares at LUIGI.

LUIGI removes his finger from the trigger.

LUIGI's face: he hesitates for a moment longer . . . then lowers his eyes and bows his head slightly.

Shot of the scene. LUIGI thrusts his revolver back into Jo's hand and walks away, shoulders drooping. When he is nearly at the door of the café, he turns and stops as MARIO calls him, off.

MARIO, off: *You look a fine sight now!*

---

[1] The dialogue now continues in French.

Jo: *A revolver's not enough! You've got to have something else too . . .*

Luigi: *I'm not a killer, that's all.*

> Luigi goes out of the café while Mario, having got up, goes over to Jo by the bar.

Jo, to Hernandez: *Now are we going to get these whiskies?*

Mario: *You really had me worried.*

Jo, bragging: *Nothing to it.*

Mario: *You didn't have to belt him. He could have turned nasty.*

Jo, smiling: *That's what they call . . .* He snaps his fingers . . . *imagination.*

> Dissolve to Jo's room. It is dawn. Jo is asleep in bed. Mario, in a hammock beside him, wakes up and gets out. The sound of voices in the street can be heard from the balcony. Mario, who is in vest and pants, puts on his trousers and goes towards the noise. It is broad daylight and the sun is already hot. Having put on his trousers, Mario looks out over the balcony. In a high shot of the street, a group of men and women, mostly natives, are being harangued by an angry woman who is standing on a cart. The camera zooms in on her.[1]

Woman, off at first: *It's not fair, it's always the same. We're the ones who have to pay for it. It's always us who have to die.*

Voices: *She's right.*

Woman: *The Yanks never die! . . . They kill my father or your brother . . . They give you a handful of coins and that's it.*

A Man: *It's true! They killed my brother!*

A Woman: *And my husband too!*

A Man: *Francisco got caught in a machine and lost his leg.*

Another Woman: *But they gave you some money!*

Woman: *Peanuts!*

> Resume on the balcony of Jo's room. Jo comes out in his pyjamas and goes towards Mario. He leans on the balustrade and looks down at the crowd gathered in the street. Mario has stopped half-way down the stairs.

Jo, in French, yawning: *What's going on — a revolution?*

Mario, in French: *A disaster at the oil well — 500 kilometres from here.*

---

[1] The conversation amongst the members of the crowd takes place in Spanish.

255

High angle shot of the crowd. BIMBA shouts to them from some way away.

BIMBA, in French: *One well's been on fire since last night.*

MARIO, in French: *Thirteen victims — they've all got relations round here.*

Once again, the members of the crowd speak in Spanish.

A WOMAN: *The hills are on fire. The flames can be seen from Santo Angeles.*

A MAN: *Who's dead?*

ANOTHER MAN: *We don't know!*

A WOMAN: *We've got a right to know!*

A MAN, shouting: *Here they come!*

Loud noise of engines.

The crowd scatters as a lorry belonging to the S.O.C. drives up escorted by motorcyclists. As soon as the lorry stops, the crowd surges round it again and we can see that it is full of wounded men. People try to clamber up onto it. At first the guards on the lorry hold them back, but they are soon overwhelmed by the invasion. Everyone swarms up onto the back of the lorry, even trampling on the wounded men on the floor.

Dissolve to O'BRIEN's office. In the foreground, seated at his desk, O'BRIEN turns towards the camera to answer a telephone. His desk is behind him and in the background his SECRETARY can be seen through the doorway, following the conversation. O'BRIEN takes a cigarette as he speaks into the telephone, and picks up a piece of paper.

The entire dialogue in O'BRIEN's office takes place in English.

O'BRIEN: *What could I do? . . . A gas pocket . . .* He reads the paper. *Nearly killed an engineer. Hell, the poor boy. One of our men, too . . . foreman named Rayner. Yes, very serious. I'll call you back this afternoon.* He hangs up and calls his SECRETARY. *Get me Camp B., derrick 16.*

He eats and drinks while his SECRETARY, who has come in, calls the number.

SECRETARY: *You've got it on the other line.*

O'BRIEN picks up the phone again.

O'BRIEN: *O'Brien speaking. The safety commission will be out there this afternoon . . . Give them a good meal and plenty to drink and put all the blame on the victims . . . They're done for, they won't feel it, eh? I'll attend to the reporters . . . I'll attend to the witnesses too.*

O'BRIEN eats and talks into the phone with his mouth full.

O'BRIEN: *Don't worry . . . I'll handle it right.*

At these words one of O'BRIEN's assistants — ' TOOTHPICK ' — calls across to him.

TOOTHPICK: *His mother.*

Putting down his telephone O'BRIEN addresses TOOTHPICK furiously.

O'BRIEN: *The hell with her. Cut her short. If he dies we'll call back.*

With these words, O'BRIEN picks up the phone again.

O'BRIEN: *It was Rayner's mother . . . A pause. He's dead? . . . That's a break for him . . . for us too.*

Dissolve to the interior of a hut at the oil well. In the centre of the shot a man is standing, speaking on the telephone. Behind him the flickering light from the oil-well fire can be seen through the open door. He is the CHIEF ENGINEER, who speaks in English, and beside him lies a wounded man covered in bandages — the engineer RAYNER.

CHIEF ENGINEER, answering on the telephone: *Of course . . . of course . . . Sure . . . Obviously. The boss sends you his regards.*

Close-up of the CHIEF ENGINEER on the telephone.

CHIEF ENGINEER: *The material . . . There's not much to save . . . Scherman's attending to it.*

The CHIEF ENGINEER goes up to three naked Indians who are watching the fire. (*Still*)

CHIEF ENGINEER: *What are you doing here? Get out!*

He walks on and jumps without stopping into a passing jeep.

Dissolve to general shot of O'BRIEN's office where five men are engaged in serious discussion around a round table. O'BRIEN seems to be in charge.

The dialogue continues in English.

O'BRIEN: *It goes out like a candle, gentlemen, if you blow on it. Only you have to blow hard.*

MONTY: *A bomb that just grazes the crater . . . a good thousand-pound bomb, like the ones we left on the Ruhr.*

O'BRIEN: *You're going to drive the bus? Oh, I've had enough trouble already. I hate trouble. Besides, even if you tried it wouldn't do any good. The tree has to be cut at the base . . . The explosive charges placed all round, set off all at the same time, a cut of the axe . . . neat and dry.*

BRADLEY: *We have 200 gallons of nitroglycerine left in stock.*

O'BRIEN: *Three times as much as you need . . . it'll be O.K.*

CONOLLY: *It would be O.K. if the tank were down there, but's it's here . . . In order to move it we'd need special trucks . . . and I haven't got any.*

O'BRIEN: *Me neither . . . and I haven't got the time to get them here . . . So . . . Take your two best trucks . . .*

CONOLLY: *You don't mean a ten-ton Curbitt for a hundred gallons weight of nitro . . .*

O'BRIEN: *I said your two best trucks . . . load them and put them on an elastic base, to absorb shocks.*

CONOLLY: *It's murder! With conditions of the roads, your drivers haven't got a fifty-fifty chance.*

O'BRIEN: *We'll keep trying until one gets there . . . That'll be enough.*

BRADLEY: *You think the union's going to let you just go ahead?*

O'BRIEN: *The hell with the union. There are plenty of tramps in town . . . all volunteers. I'm not worried . . . to get the bonus they'll do the distance with the charge on their backs.*

BRADLEY: *You mean you're going to hire those bums?*

O'BRIEN: *Yes, Mr. Bradley . . . because those bums don't have any union, or any family, and if they blow up, nobody'll come bothering me for any contributions.*

CONOLLY: *And besides, they'll work for peanuts.*

O'BRIEN: *You rat!*

> Furious, O'BRIEN bangs his fist on the table, several times. The others do not say a word.

O'BRIEN: *Haven't you guys gone hungry? I know what it's like. They're going to get what's coming to them! I'll see to that! . . . And you're going to pay them, and what's more, you'll thank them for it.*

> The telephone rings. The SECRETARY gets up and goes to answer it. After a moment he holds out the phone to O'BRIEN.

O'BRIEN: *Rayner's dead. He turns towards the* SECRETARY. *Go tele-*

258

phone his old lady . . . and if she faints again, I'll fire you.

Dissolve to the main street of Las Piedras, seen from the café. An S.O.C. van with loudspeaker on top is passing slowly by.

LOUDSPEAKER, in Spanish: *Drivers needed. Well paid. Apply to the S.O.C. offices.*

The verandah of the café, SMERLOFF, having heard the announcement, smiles and claps BERNARDO on the back.

SMERLOFF, in German: *This is it. If it comes, Mister, you'll soon be on your way home.*

Another shot of the village as the van passes through it, repeating the announcement, first in Spanish and then in English.

LINDA is seated on the verandah, reading a magazine. She listens to the announcement, and looks worried.

Shot of MARIO and Jo.

Jo: *You hear that?*

MARIO: *Two thousand dollars each, they say.*

Jo: *In a week's time. We'll be far away . . .*

We see LINDA listening to them, then HERNANDEZ comes out of the café, carrying a tray.

Jo: *And we'll be loaded too.*

He gives HERNANDEZ a friendly slap on the back, and continues in Spanish.

Jo: *And we won't forget Hernandez, who was a really great guy.*

Dissolve to high shot of the S.O.C. compound, where a long queue is waiting patiently in front of the gate.

Inside the employment office, a motley collection of men file past an S.O.C. employee, who signs them in. We recognise SMERLOFF, DICK, MARIO, Jo and others in the queue. The ensuing conversation takes place in English.

EMPLOYEE: *Profession?*

A DEADBEAT: *Truck-driver.*

The queue continues to file past each man giving the same reply. Then it is SMERLOFF's turn.

EMPLOYEE: *Profession?*

SMERLOFF: *Truck-driver . . .* He clicks his heels . . . *professional.*

After SMERLOFF come two more men, quarrelling as to who should go first.

259

Dissolve to the Doctor's surgery. Doc is in the process of examining Luigi, who coughs as the former sounds his chest. They converse in French.

Doc: *Your lungs are full of cement . . . There . . . and here the tips must be completely clogged . . . If you carry on this way, you won't last much longer.*

Luigi: *How long?*

Doc: *A year . . . Six months . . . perhaps a little more.*

Luigi: *Perhaps a little less.*

Doc shrugs his shoulders.

Luigi: *What can I do?*

Doc: *Get out now.*

Luigi: *But how?*

Doc: *How? . . . Yes indeed!*

The camera pans with Luigi as he goes across to the window.

O'Brien's voice fades in.[1]

O'Brien's office, a dozen or so men, including Bimba, Jo, Mario, Smerloff, Dick and Bernardo, are gathered round O'Brien, who is standing beside his desk.

O'Brien: *Atta boys . . . What I have to offer you is not cozy. It's a real tough job. I've got to send a ton of nitroglycerine to derrick 16.*

Close shot of O'Brien, holding a glass beaker in his hand.

O'Brien: *That stuff's nitroglycerine.*

Close-up of O'Brien's hand cautiously holding the beaker. Slowly and very gently, O'Brien tilts the beaker and lets fall a couple of drops of the liquid inside. There is a loud explosion. The men react nervously.

O'Brien looks pleased with himself. General laughter.

O'Brien: *With a ton of that stuff under you . . . the slightest bump, the slightest heat . . . and you're a goner . . .*

Wide shot. O'Brien walks round the room as he speaks. He is now right beside the men.

The camera cuts to show Luigi entering softly.

O'Brien: *There won't be enough of you left to pickle!*

O'Brien stops and looks fixedly at the men standing silently

---

[1] The dialogue in the following scene is in English except where indicated otherwise.

in front of him.

O'BRIEN: *My trucks are plain ordinary trucks. No safety gadgets, no shock-absorbers, nothing . . . You got to do it all with your arms and legs.*

Rapid shot of LUIGI.

LUIGI, in French: *What are you paying?*

Cut to a group of men, with BIMBA in the foreground.

SEVERAL VOICES, in French: *Two thousand dollars.*

Resume on O'BRIEN, standing in the middle of the room.

O'BRIEN: *I see someone tipped you . . . Well, now you've been warned . . . You're taking your lives in your own hands . . .*

At these words, DICK emerges from a group of men and stands facing O'BRIEN.

DICK: *Too risky for me, O'Brien . . .* he advances into the middle of the room. *I was brought up in Texas . . . When I was a kid, I used to see men go off on jobs like this and not come back, but when they did they were wrecks, with their hair turned white and their limbs shaking like palsy. You don't know what fear is! You'll see . . . it's catching, like smallpox, and when you get it, it's for life. So long boys and good luck!* He goes out.

Close shot of several men. There is a general silence.

O'BRIEN: *Did you hear that? If anyone wants to back out there's still time.*

The camera pans round the room, taking in all the men: BIMBA, JO, MARIO, BERNARDO, SMERLOFF, LUIGI and several others. No-one speaks. The camera returns to O'BRIEN.

O'BRIEN: *O.K. . . . have you thought it over?*

Shot of the men.

SMERLOFF: *A guy's got to be crazy to let a chance like that go by!*

The camera tracks in on O'BRIEN as he goes to his desk.

O'BRIEN: *Who's crazy? . . . Maybe Dick, maybe you . . . In any case, not me . . . not the S.O.C.*

He is now at his desk.

O'BRIEN: *There's two trucks to drive . . . we're putting four thousand dollars into each truck. At least one's got to get there. Two drivers by truck. That makes four. I want real truck drivers, and you'll have to prove it to me . . .*

We move to exterior shot of the S.O.C. compound. It is daytime. A small lorry passes, loaded with men. O'BRIEN is sitting beside BERNARDO, who is driving. The lorry brakes at the barrier across the entrance; the barrier is raised. LINDA runs up and shouts to MARIO, who is in the lorry beside Jo and BIMBA.

LINDA, in French: *There you are, thank the holy Virgin! Don't go ... don't go with him ...*

She hangs on to the lorry and runs after it as it moves off again.

LINDA, in Spanish: *Don't go. If you go, you'll die, I know! I don't want you to! ... Don't go with him! He'll only bring you bad luck! ...*

Rapid shot of MARIO, who remains unmoved, then resume on LINDA as she finally lets go of the lorry, out of breath.

LINDA, in Spanish, shouting: *You're all going to die!*

Dissolve to show the lorry, loaded with men, as it moves along a road through the barren countryside.

Close shot of the men on the lorry, then of BERNARDO driving with great care while O'BRIEN watches him critically. We see two men on top of the lorry. One of them takes off his jacket and hurls it down onto the bonnet.

The lorry skids and brakes abruptly.

BERNARDO sits at the wheel, sweating nervously, while O'BRIEN shouts at him:

O'BRIEN, in English: *You little dope! What did you come around for? What I need is drivers! Des chauffeurs ... compris?*

BERNARDO: *But Monsieur, I've got my visa ... I'm really a good driver ... It's because those bastards ...*

Shot of the men on the lorry.

SMERLOFF: *Whose go now?*

BIMBA stubs out his cigarette and jumps down from the back of the lorry, addressing the others as he does so.

BIMBA: *If anyone fools about ... I'll take the first one I lay my hands on and smash his face on this rail — don't forget it's steel.*

SMERLOFF and Jo sit on the back of the lorry, apparently watching BERNARDO as he departs, off-screen.

Jo: *That makes one.*

We move to the interior of O'BRIEN's office. It is evening. O'BRIEN stands by his desk, sorting some papers. Seven or eight other men are standing in the room, nervously expectant, as if they were waiting for the results of an examination. Amongst them are MARIO and JO, standing a little way away from SMERLOFF, BIMBA, LUIGI, JORNET and two others.

Close shot of MARIO and JO. They converse in an undertone.

JO: *You've as good a chance as any . . . you drove like a dream.*

MARIO: *It was nothing . . . compared to you.*

Resume on O'BRIEN. He stamps some papers, then goes to the centre of the room and starts to call out the names of the drivers who have been chosen.

O'BRIEN: *Bimba . . .*

BIMBA goes up to him and takes the paper which O'BRIEN hands him.

O'BRIEN: *Luigi . . .*

Smiling hugely, LUIGI removes his cap and takes his paper.

O'BRIEN: *Mario . . .*

O'BRIEN goes up to MARIO and JO, and gives MARIO his sheet.

JO, confidently: *I told you so.*

As MARIO takes his paper, JO holds out his hand to O'BRIEN also. But the latter ignores him and passes on.

O'BRIEN: *Smerloff.*

SMERLOFF immediately steps forward and clicks his heels as he takes the paper from O'BRIEN.

Several men look disappointed and furious.

JO is dumbfounded.

GROMOFF: *What about me then?*

O'BRIEN goes up to three men who are protesting furiously.

O'BRIEN, in English: *Shut up! It's my dough and my stuff! If you're not satisfied, go home!*

He pushes them out and turns back to the four chosen drivers. JO has also remained, next to MARIO.

O'BRIEN, in English: *You four guys I picked are to be here at three o'clock in the morning, sharp-sure. I know it would have been better to leave earlier . . . But the trucks won't have loaded till just before dawn.*

The camera shows O'BRIEN walking round the room as he speaks, then cuts to MARIO and JO, then to BIMBA, SMERLOFF and LUIGI.

O'BRIEN, in English: *Don't worry about the heat.*

He looks at them all in turn, the camera panning to follow his gaze.

O'BRIEN, in English: *If you don't stop, the sun won't hurt.*

BIMBA and LUIGI move towards the door, and with a wave to the others, go out. O'BRIEN goes up to the remaining men, MARIO, Jo and SMERLOFF.

O'BRIEN, in English: *Now go get some rest, I'll see you later.*

MARIO, to Jo: *Come on . . .*

Jo: *You go on . . . I'll follow.*

SMERLOFF goes over to the door, followed by MARIO.

SMERLOFF, to MARIO: *Don't worry . . . We'll get along.*

They go out, and we cut to Jo and O'BRIEN standing face to face.

Jo: *Now you can cut out the fancy stuff, you're not going to play the big boss with me. There's just the two of us, Bill and Jo, and we're going to have things out.*

O'BRIEN, in English: *Jo, don't ask me . . .*

Jo goes over to the desk and sits on it. O'BRIEN passes him and sits in an armchair.

Jo: *Come on, don't try and stall me . . . We've known each other too long for that. You know what I'm like at the wheel . . . so why?*

O'BRIEN, in French: *You're too old, Jo . . . me too. We've been around too long.* In English: *If we were twenty years younger . . . I'd have gone myself . . . and I'd have gone with you. Bucks is real dough even to me.*

Close shot of the two of them.

Jo: *I don't feel old at all — less old than those jerks who are going to crack up on the way.*

O'BRIEN, in French: *We'll see.*

Jo: *What's the betting?*

O'BRIEN, in French: *Two thousand dollars — the first one to give up — you take his place.*

Jo, thoughtfully: *That changes everything . . .*

Dissolve to the interior of the café, at night. A NEGRO is playing a guitar on the verandah. Other men and women listen to him, humming the tune. The camera pans across to a table where BERNARDO is seated, writing a letter.

Close-up of the letter, which reads (in Italian):

Dearest Mama,

I've found some work at last. Don't worry if you don't hear from me for a little while. Love and kisses. Bernardo.

BERNARDO seals the letter, gets up and goes over to the bar, where we see HERNANDEZ, LINDA, MARIO, BIMBA and DOC.[1]

DOC, in French: *Here's to the heroes!*

They all drink except for BERNARDO.

HERNANDEZ: *To the millionaires!*

BERNARDO: *Linda, please . . .*

LINDA: *Not now!*

MARIO: *Let him say what he wants.*

BERNARDO, beseechingly, in French: *It's very important.*

He holds out the letter to LINDA.

Close-up of LUIGI, who comes forward, looking uneasy and suspicious.

BERNARDO, in Spanish: *Please would you post this letter for me tomorrow morning.*

LUIGI goes up to BERNARDO and claps him on the shoulder.

LUIGI, in Italian: *Cheer up, it'll be your turn next time. Don't cry . . . be a man!*

BERNARDO, in Italian: *You may be men . . . I'm not.*

BERNARDO goes out of the café to the patio.

MARIO, looking at the clock: *What's Jo up to?*

Close shot of LINDA and MARIO, then of MARIO and HERNANDEZ.

HERNANDEZ: *He's upstairs. He came in just after you . . . and went and shut himself in his room.*

LINDA: *You're going and he's staying behind . . .* She looks at the clock . . . *only an hour to go.*

MARIO: *That's enough . . . if you're going to cry, go outside.*

MARIO looks rather tired and disappointed. He glances at the clock again.

Close-up of clock.

Resume on MARIO. He turns to LINDA and shoves her away.

A series of close shots show: BIMBA, by himself; the clock; LUIGI; and finally DOC.

DOC, in French: *An hour can sometimes be a long time.*

---

[1] The dialogue takes place in Spanish except when indicated otherwise.

Dissolve to a shot of the patio of the café. It is night.
The camera follows LINDA as she comes out of the café and
goes over to a wood fire with several Indians seated around it.
She lights a candle and moves away into a dark corner of the
patio.

We see, briefly, a pair of feet hanging in the air.

Resume on LINDA as she arrives in front of a statue of the
Virgin Mary ,and reaches up to place on it her candle and her
rosary. Then she kneels down and prays.

Close shot of her, facing the camera.[1]

LINDA: *Hail Mary, full of grace, the Lord is with Thee. Blessed art
thou among women and blessed is the fruit of the womb. Jesus.
Holy Mary, Mother of God, pray for my sinners* . . .

Low angle close-up shows the body of a hanged man, his bare
feet nearest camera.

LINDA is terrified at the sight of the corpse. She runs screaming
towards the café.

LINDA, shouting: *Quick* . . . *quick* . . . *everybody* . . . *come as quick
as you can* . . .

Camera pans to follow her.

Dissolve to the interior of the café. LINDA arrives in the centre
of the room and bursts into tears. HERNANDEZ goes up to her.

HERNANDEZ: *What's the matter, girl, have you gone crazy?*

LINDA raises her head.

We see MARIO looking alarmed, then resume on LINDA.

LINDA: *He's dead, he's hanged himself in the patio.*

MARIO, starting: *Who, Jo?*

LINDA: *No, the young one* . . . *the Italian, Bernardo* . . .

DICK, getting up: *Mr. O'Brien's first victim!*

Dissolve to the interior of O'BRIEN's office, in the early morning.
BIMBA, MARIO and LUIGI are standing in the middle of the
room, putting on S.O.C. driver's overalls under the benevolent
eye of O'BRIEN.

LUIGI: *We look pretty funny in this gear.*

BIMBA: *You can't go to war without a uniform.*

MARIO: *There's a special dress even for the guillotine.* A pause. *They
dress the guy up before the ceremony.*

---

[1] The dialogue in this scene is again in Spanish.

266

O'BRIEN goes to the window and raises the blind, then turns back towards the men.

Shot of BIMBA as he gets up from the table on which there are four glasses . . .

O'BRIEN, in English: *Still no news from Smerloff?*

BIMBA goes over to LUIGI. O'BRIEN approaches MARIO and fills the glasses with whisky.

O'BRIEN, in English: *Funny, don't you think so?*

LUIGI: *It's not like him to be late.*

BIMBA: *No, it's not his style.*

O'BRIEN, in English: *Five more minutes and I'm gonna replace him.*

MARIO gives one glass to LUIGI and another to BIMBA.

MARIO: *I think I'll ring the Corsario, just in case.*

BIMBA, pricking up his ears: *Wait . . . here he is.*

Noise of footsteps.

The door opens and Jo appears nonchalantly in the doorway.

Jo: *Hi fellas!* Coming into the room and advancing towards the table. *I've come to say goodbye to my pal.*

They all look at him astonished and slightly sceptical.

Jo: *What's up . . . you look like you've seen a ghost.*

Shot of BIMBA, LUIGI and MARIO on the other side of the table.

LUIGI: *You haven't seen Smerloff, by any chance? . . .*

Resume on Jo, who fills the remaining empty glass with whisky.

Jo: *Why? He's not here? . . . That's too bad.*

O'BRIEN is now right next to Jo. They look each other up and down.

O'BRIEN, in French: *Who saw Smerloff last?*

LUIGI: *He had a drink with us . . . and then he went out with Jo.*

Silence. Finally Jo reacts.

Jo: *Yeah, we had a chat . . . there's no law against that.*

O'BRIEN, in English: *And since, nothing?*

He looks round the room, then at the men, and grimaces.

O'BRIEN, in English: *In that case, well . . . I don't think Smerloff will appear now . . .*

There is a loud noise of engines, as the lorries pass close by the office and come to a halt. O'BRIEN goes to the door, followed by LUIGI and BIMBA.

O'BRIEN, in English, to Jo: *So get dressed anyway . . .*

He goes out, addressing LUIGI and BIMBA as he does so.

O'BRIEN, in English: *Come on, it's time.*

Pan with the three men as they go out. Jo remains in the foreground, still drinking his whisky. MARIO starts to go out, then hesitates and turns to Jo.

We see O'BRIEN walking along the corridor which leads to the yard outside, followed by BIMBA and LUIGI, then resume on MARIO and Jo.

MARIO, anxiously: *You don't think we're making a big mistake?*

Jo: *What's the matter with you?*

Jo takes off his shirt and puts on the S.O.C. overalls.

MARIO: *I'm scared.*

Close shot of him.

MARIO: *Yes, I'm scared I won't measure up . . .*

Jo: *Don't worry kid! . . . I'll be there to show you how.*

We move to the compound yard, in the early morning. It is still dark. O'BRIEN, LUIGI and BIMBA go over to the two big trucks, which are standing in the yard, with men busying themselves around them. LUIGI notices with astonishment that they are not yet loaded.

LUIGI: *Where's the stuff?*

O'BRIEN, in English: *Don't worry about the stuff, it's coming.*

O'BRIEN goes up to a MECHANIC who has just been adjusting the engine of one of the lorries, while LUIGI and BIMBA inspect the back of it.

O'BRIEN, to the MECHANIC, in English: *Finished? O.K. Leave your tools, just in case . . .*

The door of a great hangar opens nearby, lighting up the yard. Some men lay a stout plank against the back of each lorry to serve as a gangway and very cautiously begin to load the vehicles with jerrycans of nitroglycerine.

O'BRIEN, in English: *And now beat it . . . There's no reason to take any unnecessary risks.*

O'BRIEN leaves BIMBA and LUIGI, who move a little way away to watch the loading.

A WORKMAN carefully carries a jerrycan very slowly up the plank onto one of the lorries.

Jo, now in his overalls, and MARIO leave the office and go towards BIMBA and LUIGI. MARIO is still holding his glass; he stops for a moment and drinks . . . then looks enviously at the workmen as they move away.

MARIO: *They're off to have their dinner . . .*

Jo: *Don't drink too much, kid — it's bad for the reflexes.*

High angle shot of the two lorries being loaded. The four men look on, LUIGI and BIMBA on one side, MARIO and Jo on the other, together with O'BRIEN, who has just rejoined them. We see the plank leading up to one of the lorries: a WORKMAN advances slowly up it, carrying a jerrycan.

Close-up of his foot as it slips. The WORKMAN quickly regains his balance without shaking up the jerrycan too much.

MARIO and Jo, as they turn their heads at the sound of breaking glass, off.

BIMBA stands sweating nervously, his whisky glass at his feet. Close-up of his boots and the fragments of glass.

Resume on BIMBA. He pulls himself together and goes over to O'BRIEN.

BIMBA, in English, in a strained voice: *I apologise, sir . . .*

O'BRIEN, in English: *Forget it. Get another glass.*

BIMBA passes camera and moves away.

Shot of O'BRIEN as he goes up to LUIGI, tossing a coin in his hand.

O'BRIEN, in French: *Heads or tails, Luigi?*

We see the four men: LUIGI and O'BRIEN, with MARIO and Jo a little way away.

O'BRIEN, in English: *The winner takes the big truck and will leave immediately. The others'll follow in half an hour. It's the safety margin in case . . .*

Close-up of O'BRIEN.

O'BRIEN, in English: *In case . . . of . . . accident. Make your choice.*

MARIO: *What does it matter since we're going anyway . . .*

Shot of Jo.

Jo: *So what the hell . . . we'll toss all the same.*

O'BRIEN tosses the coin in the air and puts his foot over it as it lands. Jo and LUIGI bend over his foot.

Jo: *Heads.*

LUIGI: *Tails.*

LUIGI straightens up.

LUIGI: *I never had any luck!*

Jo: *Can you beat that!*
> A series of shots shows the men as they finish loading. O'BRIEN supervises the work and sees that the load is lashed down on the lorries.

AN ENGINEER, in English: *Everything set?*

A MAN, in English: *We really can't do any better without material.*

O'BRIEN, in English: *I know, Lee, I know.*
> O'BRIEN addresses MARIO and Jo, off.

O'BRIEN, in English: *Hop to it, boys!*
> Shot of MARIO, Jo, BIMBA and LUIGI.

MARIO: *Let's go.*
> Shot of Jo as he goes up to O'BRIEN, who is standing near the door of their lorry.

Jo: *Hold it I said . . . what's the pressure on the tyres?*
> He kicks the tyres.

O'BRIEN, in English: *Don't worry, you're not going to bounce.*

Jo: *If this thing gives out, I'm the one who goes up in smoke . . . so if you don't mind . . .*
> He motions MARIO to the driving seat.

Jo: *Get in, kid.*

O'BRIEN, in French: *Every minute you lose is costing a packet!*
> Ignoring O'BRIEN, Jo walks round to the front of the lorry and calls out to MARIO.

Jo: *Put on the sidelamps . . . the heads . . .*
> The headlamps light up his face.

Jo: *Now the spotlights.*
> Shot of O'BRIEN standing impatiently by.

O'BRIEN, in English: *What are you looking for?*

Jo, getting into the lorry: *If you want to take the wheel go ahead, there's still time.*
> MARIO moves across to let Jo take the wheel.

Jo, to O'BRIEN: *You're not the one who'll be sitting on a bomb . . . Right? . . . So cut it out!*
> He slams the door violently.
> We see MARIO and Jo from behind, inside the cab of the lorry. Jo is about to turn on the ignition when MARIO leans towards him.

MARIO: *Hey. Jo! . . . I brought you something. Here . . . it's for you.*
> Close-up of MARIO's metro ticket as he holds it out to Jo.

270

Resume on Jo.

Jo: *No, you're crazy . . . are you sure?*

MARIO: *In any case . . . it's no longer valid.*

Shot of the outside of the lorry. O'BRIEN looks through the driver's window and addresses Jo.

O'BRIEN, in English: *Ready?*

Jo: *Ready, pal.*

O'BRIEN, in French: *So now I'll say . . . up yours!*

Jo, in English: *Same to you.*

O'BRIEN moves back slightly, motioning to Jo to move off. Resume on the interior of the lorry. Jo tries the starter, which does not work. He tries again. Nothing happens.

Jo, looking through the window: *What's up with your crate? . . . Didn't you put any gas in?*

MARIO pushes Jo's arm aside and points at the dashboard.

MARIO: *The ignition.*

Shot of O'BRIEN coming up to the lorry.

O'BRIEN, in English: *Something wrong?*

Jo: *It's O.K., it's fixed.*

The engine roars into life.

Close-up of one of the wheels as the lorry moves off.

O'BRIEN, in English, off: *Good luck boys! . . .*

Shot of the lorry moving slowly forwards.

Jo, shouting to O'BRIEN: *That's it . . . good luck . . . Coca Cola! . . .*

The camera pans across the compound yard, as seen from the driver's seat, lit by the lorry's headlamps.

The headlamps sweep across the road which leads out of the compound. The lorry's hooter sounds loudly.

Shot of LUIGI and BIMBA, following the lorry with their eyes as it moves off slowly.

LUIGI: *He's certainly taking it easy.*

As BIMBA mutters a non-committal reply, dissolve to another shot of the lorry, still advancing very slowly towards the exit.

A high shot shows the main street of Las Piedras. LINDA, who is reclining on the verandah of the café, hears the noise of the lorry and gets up, while beside her HERNANDEZ cranes forward, trying to make out who are the drivers.

The camera follows LINDA as she runs to meet the lorry, which

271

is now coming up the main street.

The sound of the lorry's engine, its hooter and the siren at the S.O.C. compound all make a deafening racket. LINDA, who is now close to the lorry, puts her hands over her ears, waves and climbs onto the running board on MARIO's side.

The faces of Jo, MARIO and LINDA are seen through the cab window on Jo's side of the lorry. (*Still*)

LINDA, in Spanish: *Mario, Mario my darling . . . why are you doing this? I asked you . . . begged you . . . I would have done any-thing . . . I would have robbed . . . killed to keep you with me.*

Sobbing. *You don't care that I'm unhappy . . .* A pause. *I detest you . . . I hate you . . .*

In a close-up, MARIO grits his teeth and says nothing.

Resume on the three of them, Jo nearest camera.

MARIO, to Jo: *Watch out to the right, there's a gutter.*

LINDA, in Spanish: *Have pity, my darling.*

MARIO, to LINDA, in Spanish: *Shut up and buzz off. Get it?*

LINDA: *Then . . . then goodbye Mario my darling . . . promise you'll be careful . . . take care . . . promise you'll come back.*

Thoroughly fed up with LINDA's pleadings, MARIO opens the door and knocks her off the moving lorry.

LINDA falls and tumbles over on the ground, narrowly missing the rear wheels.

In close shot she gets up and tearfully looks after the retreating lorry.

From the bonnet of the lorry, the camera shows the two drivers. Close-up of the lorry's wheels as it passes over the gutter.

We see the cab of the lorry from the side. The two men have just been jolted by passing through the gutter. Jo breathes a sigh of relief and turns to MARIO.

Jo: *Not this time, I guess.*

MARIO: *Not the next either, don't worry.*

They continue to drive. Jo, who is at the wheel, seems uneasy.

Jo: *Is it hot or cold?*

MARIO: *Rather hot, why?*

Jo: *Oh — I don't know, I'm freezing.*

MARIO: *Did you bring your sweater? . . . Do you want to put it on?*

Jo: *No, not now.*

MARIO picks up a pullover and places it over Jo's shoulders.

Jo: *Thanks, kid.*

A few moments later, Jo begins to look ill; sweat courses down his forehead.

Jo: *Wipe my forehead.*

MARIO: *What's the matter. Something wrong?*

Jo: *I think I must be ill.*

MARIO: *You haven't got a fever, have you?*

Rapid close-up of Jo, still driving.

Jo: *I don't know . . . I'm shivering . . . It's my malaria coming back.*

Shot of the two men from the front.

MARIO: *This is a fine start. Stop and I'll take the wheel.*

Jo: *No . . . it'll pass.*

They continue in silence for a while. Jo blinks.

Jo: *Where are we?*

MARIO leans out through the window and looks back.

MARIO: *About a hundred metres after the turning.*

Jo: *Three thousand times that and we'll be there.*

The light of the headlamps sweeps across the oil pipe-line which runs alongside the road.

Jo and MARIO's lorry, the Curbitt, is moving slowly through a bamboo grove. The weather is dull. The light of the headlamps sweeps across the bamboo stems from left to right.

A long avenue of bamboo stretches away into the distance.

Dissolve to a shot of MARIO and Jo. The lorry is still moving slowly.

Jo: *Can you smell oil?*

MARIO: *No, I can't smell a thing. But the engine may be hot — we've hardly moved out of first in the last hour.*

Jo: *We'll let it cool off for a couple of minutes.*

He turns the wheel and pulls into the side of the road. The lorry has stopped in a clearing in the bamboo grove. Seen from behind, Jo gets out and moves away, while MARIO, having walked round the front of the lorry, comes into frame facing camera and puts his hand on the radiator.

MARIO: *It's hot, but not boiling.*

Jo is busy urinating by the roadside and does not reply immediately.

Jo: *You see, that's better. Let's have a bite to eat.*

Looking pleased with himself, Jo rubs his stomach interrogatively.

MARIO: *Already! We've only done seventeen kilometres . . . we don't want to get behind time . . . they must be anxious to see us with the stuff.*

The camera tilts up with MARIO as he climbs onto the front wing of the lorry to open the bonnet.

Resume on Jo, who reaches into the cab to get their bag of provisions.

Jo: *We don't have to clock in! To hell with the oil. They won't remember you at the end of the year when they hand out the dividends.*

He comes and hangs the bag on the radiator and opens a packet of food. He looks at the label.

MARIO is seated on the wing, looking back along the road.

Suddenly he gives a shout of alarm.

MARIO: *Hey Jo . . . get moving. They're on our tail.*

Jo: *Goddamit, you nearly choked me, yelling.*

The headlamps of BIMBA and LUIGI's lorry shine through the bamboo stems in the distance.

MARIO, off: *You can have your grub later. Come on, let's get moving . . . hurry!*

We hear the doors of the Curbitt slam and the sound of it moving off.

The scene changes to the interior of BIMBA and LUIGI's lorry, the Dodge. Jazz is playing softly. LUIGI reaches towards the radio. Close-up of the radio as LUIGI's hand turns up the volume. The music gets louder.

LUIGI: *You hear that . . . It must be nice to have some cash . . . it's funny, yesterday we were like them . . . like everyone else. We could have fun, sleep, eat . . . we were with other men and women — now there's no one, just the two of us.*

BIMBA: *I can't think enough?*

LUIGI: *Sure . . . for driving a lorry, but I like company sitting at the door in the evening . . . drinking, talking.*

BIMBA: *About what?*

LUIGI: *I don't know . . . anything which comes into one's head . . .*

and then the girls . . . one takes them into a corner, for a bit of a tickle . . . A pause. You don't like corners?
BIMBA: *No.*
LUIGI: *Ah! . . . you've been spoilt.*
BIMBA: *You think so, eh?*
LUIGI: *You're a mother's boy. What did your father do?*
BIMBA: *I'm an orphan.*
LUIGI: *How old are you?*
BIMBA: *A hundred years.*
LUIGI, laughing: *A hundred years! Ha ha! It's not true.*
      Close-up of BIMBA driving.
BIMBA: *It doesn't take long to be a hundred years old . . . a few months . . . you just have to be in the right place at the right time.*

      Dissolve to show Jo and MARIO in the Curbitt, which is now moving. Jo is nearest camera. Looking tense, he sighs deeply.
Jo: *Not even time for a drink.*
      They drive on in silence. After a few seconds, Jo shudders and nervously grips the steering wheel. (*Still*)
MARIO: *What's up . . . is it coming back?*
Jo: *No, I'm all right, I just don't want to be pushed while I'm driving.*
      He changes gear noisily, while MARIO half fills the beaker of their thermos and holds it out to Jo.
Jo: *How do you expect me to hold it?*
MARIO: *In your hand . . . here!*
Jo: *Supposing a tyre bursts . . . we'll skid all over the place.*
MARIO, scornfully: *You must be joking — they're brand new.*
Jo: *It's happened before.*
MARIO: *What shall I do then? Chuck it away?*
Jo: *Hold it for me, can't you.*
      MARIO looks sideways at him, then holds the beaker up to his lips.
MARIO: *Come on then, poppa . . . suck at this . . .*
      Jo drinks, coughs and spits the liquid through the window. The engine splutters. Jo is bent over the steering wheel, his eyes full of tears, but he steels himself to bring the engine up to its proper revs again.
MARIO: *Now what's up? Something wrong?*

Jo shakes his head negatively. He is overcome by nausea. MARIO looks at him anxiously, full of concern.

Jo, choking: *The wheel! Take the wheel . . .*

At the same instance, he leans out of the window and vomits. The lorry veers to the left. MARIO, who is encumbered by the thermos and beaker, grabs the wheel and brings the lorry back on course.

Just as the engine is about to stall, MARIO turns off the ignition and puts on the handbrake. The left hand door opens. The lorry stops on the opposite side of the avenue. Jo gets out and comes towards camera, and sits down on the pipeline at the roadside. MARIO gets out also and comes across to Jo.

MARIO, impatiently: *I told you you shouldn't have eaten.*

Jo vomits between his legs. There is the sound of a horn and a glare of headlights off. He raises his head and looks to the left. The Dodge driven by LUIGI and BIMBA approaches on the left hand side of the avenue. It halts a few yards away from the camera.

LUIGI: *What's up . . . Have you broken down?*

MARIO: *No . . . we're on our way . . . There's a sick man here!*

BIMBA leans out of the other door and sees Jo, slumped on the pipe, vomiting between his legs. LUIGI gets out and comes forward.

LUIGI: *He's sick? He's either drunk or scared.*

MARIO: *Scared? . . . Jo? . . . Just come and say that to his face.*

LUIGI passes in front of MARIO and goes over towards Jo.

LUIGI: *No kidding! . . . Hey Frankenstein . . . we're talking about you.*

Jo, wearily raising his head: *Get lost. . . .*

MARIO reappears and stands in rear view on the left. LUIGI comes back towards the camera.

MARIO: *Just leave him alone, can't you?*

LUIGI: *Don't worry! I'm not going to run off with your pal. I'm not jealous. . . . But get a move on or we'll be here all night.*

MARIO: *We'll move when we're ready . . . we don't have to take orders from a jerk like you!*

LUIGI, who has moved away from camera towards the Dodge, turns back.

LUIGI: *And we don't fancy stopping every fifteen kilometres.*

Jo: *Let it go, but . . . if there is a hurry . . . they can go on ahead.*
LUIGI goes towards the lorry and gets in through the left hand
door. BIMBA, who has got out and is now standing in front of
the bonnet, takes a step forward.

BIMBA: *Orders are orders! You're supposed to keep half an hour
ahead.*
LUIGI takes his place at the wheel of the Dodge.

LUIGI: *Come on. . . . You've seen how they drive. If they get onto
the washboard first, we'll have to trail behind them.*
BIMBA gets in. LUIGI starts the engine and leans out over the
wheel to shout scornfully at the others, while BIMBA shuts his
door.

LUIGI: *You're not drivers . . . you're a couple of goddam cripples.*
The door slams, leaving MARIO looking sad and thoughtful. He
goes towards Jo as the Dodge is heard moving off. The two of
them step over the pipeline to let the Dodge pass, off-screen.
Its headlights sweep across. Camera pans and tracks to show
the Dodge just managing to pass between the pipeline and the
other lorry. Shot of MARIO and Jo as they walk towards their
lorry. Jo sits down on the running board.

MARIO: *They can smash themselves up and good luck to them.*
Jo, uneasily: *Why? Is it bad further on?*
MARIO: *It's O.K. through the bamboo! It's more or less clear to the
little corral . . . only after that there's a nasty stretch of washboard.*

Rapid dissolve to BIMBA and LUIGI, facing camera, in the Dodge.
LUIGI is driving.

BIMBA: *You know what washboard is?*
LUIGI: *It's what they wash clothes on.*
BIMBA: *At home, yes . . . but here it's a bad road surface. It's the
wind that does it — wrinkles the ground like old leather. . . . It
shakes anything that goes near it to pieces.*
LUIGI: *So we're going to get shaken to pieces?*
BIMBA: *Not if you put your foot down. . . . At forty miles an hour
you ride over the bumps and you don't feel a thing. . . . But you've
got to keep your speed up. . . . Below thirty the vibration starts and
goddam . . . that's it.*

Resume on the clearing. MARIO and Jo are still beside their
lorry.

Jo: *How long is it?*
MARIO: *About twenty miles starting from the little corral.*
    Close-up of MARIO's hands as he illustrates what he is saying
with a matchbox.
MARIO: *Look . . . here's the corral . . . and then here's the wash-
board. Pump 6 is in the middle. The Americans have concreted in
front of it . . . but even there you can't slow down, because you
wouldn't have time to get up speed again . . . you've got to keep up
the maximum all the time.*
Jo: *Can't we go at it slowly?*
MARIO: *You'd still get vibration — the ridges are close together. . . .
To be safe you'd have to keep below — oh, I don't know . . . six
miles an hour.*
Jo: *Okay . . . let's do that then.*
MARIO: *You must be joking. It's thirty kilometres — it would take
us at least four hours.*

    Rapid dissolve to shot of LUIGI and BIMBA from behind.
    Through the windscreen, a small bridge can be seen along the
    road ahead.
BIMBA: *Once you're over the little bridge, accelerate . . . we need
to be at forty miles an hour in two minutes. . . .*
    The lorry passes slowly over the hump-backed bridge and
    begins to gather speed as it moves away from the camera, which
    pans to follow it. (*Still*)
    Resume on the two men.
BIMBA: *Go on, put your foot down.*
    LUIGI sighs and puts his foot down.
    We see his foot on the accelerator.
    Close-up of the speedometer. The needle moves slowly round.
BIMBA, off: *Thirty . . . thirty-five . . . forty.*
    Rapid close-up of LUIGI, then resume on the two men, facing
    camera.
BIMBA: *There's the corral. . . . You're there . . . keep listening to
the engine note, and don't let it budge. . . .*
    We see LUIGI, his hands clenched on the steering wheel. He
    suddenly jumps as a backfire is heard behind them.
    Close-up of BIMBA.
BIMBA: *You hear that?*

Luigi wipes the sweat from his forehead with his arm. His hands tremble.

LUIGI: *A bit of dirt in the carburettor.*

The engine continues to run smoothly again.

Resume on the two men.

BIMBA: *You're sure? It's not water in the petrol?*

LUIGI: *Don't tempt providence!*

BIMBA: *Now we're on the washboard. . . . If the motor gives up we're done!*

Dissolve to MARIO and Jo by the Curbitt in the bamboo grove. MARIO looks at his watch. Jo takes a drag at his cigarette.

MARIO: *It's time.*

Jo: *Let me finish my smoke.*

MARIO: *You can finish it on the way.*

Jo: *I don't like smoking at the wheel. You don't get the flavour.*

They get into the lorry.

Dissolve to LUIGI and BIMBA in their lorry — both still very tense.

BIMBA looks at LUIGI.

BIMBA: *Okay?*

LUIGI touches the cross which he wears round his neck.

LUIGI: *Okay.*

At that moment there is another backfire. BIMBA looks at LUIGI and licks his lips.

LUIGI, in a strangled voice: *It's not going to start again?*

BIMBA: *Put your foot right down. Let's get up a bit of speed.*

A series of close-ups shows LUIGI as he puts his foot down; his foot pressing on the accelerator; the speedometer — the speed continues to rise; the lorry's wheels, turning; the accelerator.

The camera shows the load of jerrycans on the back. The engine backfires again.

Resume on BIMBA and LUIGI. The latter's hands are clenched nervously on the wheel.

LUIGI: *We'll have to clean the jets.*

BIMBA: *Once we get to the Yanks' bit of concrete, we can slow down safely.*

LUIGI: *The concrete? . . . If we make it that far.*

Shot of the countryside through the windscreen. There are a couple more backfires, from the engine.

The two men sitting silently, facing camera. There is a volley of backfires and then the engine cuts out completely.

LUIGI pumps the accelerator desperately.

There is no sound but the rumble of the wheels.

Close-up of the accelerator; the starter switch; the speedometer as the needle falls.

Shot of the two men. The engine bursts into life again. BIMBA, who has just pressed the starter, freezes with his hand in the air.

Time seems to stand still.

LUIGI: *Maybe the crap has passed through.*

BIMBA maintains a sceptical silence. The engine begins to backfire again. LUIGI closes his eyes with an expression of pain.

Close-up of the speedometer. The needle begins to drop again.

LUIGI: *What speed do you think we go up at?*

BIMBA: *I don't know . . . thirty, twenty-five perhaps.*

Suddenly he yells.

Through the windscreen, about two hundred yards ahead of the left, can be seen a sign indicating the location of the pump.

LUIGI: *We won't make it. . . . I tell you we won't make it.*

BIMBA: *See the notice? . . . we're nearly there.*

Dissolve to a shot of the Curbitt, which is moving slowly towards the small bridge which LUIGI and BIMBA passed earlier. Jo is driving.

MARIO: *Put your foot down, Jo, it's time.*

JO: *You're sure it wouldn't be better. . . .*

MARIO: *No, I've told you . . . four hours in first . . . twelve minutes if you take it at a run.*

JO: *So long as we don't blow up.*

MARIO: *Touch wood! . . .*

JO, gripping the steering wheel: *Plenty of it around. . . .*

Jo takes a hand off the wheel and reaches for the gear lever. Shot of the lever and pedals; Jo changes into second with a clash of gears.

280

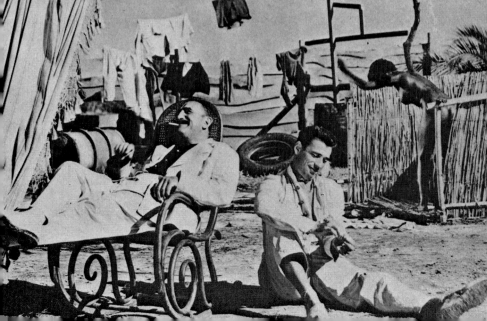

He peers anxiously forward through the windscreen, his jaw set.

MARIO, in close-up, is getting impatient.

Jo is seen from the side. He lifts his foot from the accelerator before declutching; the engine note drops. Jo declutches. We hear the gear change. He presses the accelerator before letting the clutch in again. The lorry is now in third gear.

MARIO: *Get a move on . . . change into fourth . . . we're nearly there.*

Jo lifts his foot from the accelerator.

MARIO: *Don't lift your foot! . . . Put it down hard!*

Shot of Jo as seen by MARIO. His eyes are wild. Through the side window, in the background, the countryside can be seen flying by.

MARIO is seen from Jo's position. He beats his fist in his palm.

MARIO: *More! More! Only a hundred yards to go!*

Shot of the pedals. Jo's right foot hovers between the accelerator and the brake. MARIO's left foot comes into shot and presses the accelerator as he speaks, off.

MARIO, off: *Go on, then! Go on! And the gear change! . . .*

Jo's foot declutches. The engine races and Jo's foot jabs at the brake.

Close-up of the lorry's wheels as it comes to a halt.

In the cab, MARIO makes a gesture of despair and then bursts out angrily.

MARIO: *Are you crazy? Now we're done for. You should have gone on! . . . For Chrissake what got into you?*

Jo has turned off the **ignition**.

Jo: *It's not my fault if this junk-heap doesn't have any push. It's a dud.*

MARIO, cutting in: *It's just not right. A brand new lorry, and only half-loaded. It ought to move.*

Jo: *Perhaps there's a governor on the engine — it's the Yanks' favourite trick! . . . They're so afraid we'll damage their crate for them.*

MARIO, struck by the idea: *If that's what it is they'll hear all about it! . . . And from me!*

MARIO gets out of the cab. Jo tries to hold him back, but is too late. He slumps hopelessly back in his seat and throws an anxious glance towards the jerrycans behind him.

Jo, muttering: *It can't be anything else!*

We see MARIO, who has opened the bonnet, peering down into the engine. He straightens up, shuts the bonnet, jumps down from the wing and walks round the front of the lorry, to appear by the driver's door.

MARIO: *We'll try again.*

Jo: *There wasn't one?*

MARIO: *No, back up a bit . . . two or three yards, that's all.*

The lorry starts to move backwards. MARIO reappears in front of the camera as the lorry backs off the road.

Shot of the tracks left by the lorry. The wheels sink into the ground as it backs.

Resume on MARIO, who has not moved. He signals to Jo to stop, then looks to the right.

MARIO: *Oh! . . . Oh!*

The engine stops.

MARIO: *Come and take a look.*

He points at the tracks.

MARIO: *If we turn on that we'll plough everything up.*

Jo: *So?*

MARIO: *We'll have to back along the tracks.*

Jo turns to face the camera as he looks at the tracks in his turn.

Jo: *Are you crazy? . . . You'll be coming back in the ruts . . . and if you slip out of them and fall back in again, the whole lot'll go up.*

MARIO takes off his jacket.

MARIO: *I won't slip, that's all. Go and guide me back.*

MARIO goes off right. We hear the motor start up, and Jo begins to beckon.

Dissolve to the Dodge, which is parked on the concrete apron by the pump, on the opposite side of the road to the pipeline. At the beginning of the shot, LUIGI is standing by the left hand door, while in the background BIMBA, who has put on a pair of gloves, is bent over the open bonnet rigging up a gravity feed from a jerrycan. LUIGI hurls insults at the vehicle. After kicking the lorry a few times, LUIGI goes round to the front to join BIMBA.

LUIGI: *If I could lay my hands on the son-of-a-bitch who filled it up. . . . He started putting in gas oil, I bet . . . and when he noticed he didn't say anything. The skunk . . . don't move . . . I'll find the jerk and I'll fix his face so his mother wouldn't recognise him.*

BIMBA: *Stop crabbing . . . this time you'll have clean petrol.*

LUIGI: *Hey, I've just thought . . . we don't have room to get up speed again.*

BIMBA: *Too bad, we'll finish at walking pace.*

LUIGI: *And the others — if they're blinding along they won't be able to stop on the washboard . . . they'll drive straight into us.*

BIMBA: *They're taking it slowly — you can be sure of that! . . . If they'd put their foot down they'd be here by now.*

LUIGI: *I think I'll leave a signal for them, all the same.*

LUIGI comes back towards camera and goes off right, by the door of the lorry, while BIMBA shouts to him.

BIMBA: *Go on, while I finish this. Have you got a handkerchief?*

LUIGI turns towards camera and looks to the left, taking a handkerchief out of his pocket.

LUIGI: *A pity it's brand new. . . . Still.* He blows his nose noisily. *At least I've used it once.*

He goes back towards the pump and the pipeline.

The camera pans with the Curbitt as MARIO backs it very slowly from left to right, guided by Jo.

Resume on LUIGI, who looks regretfully at his handkerchief, then squats down and lays it flat in the middle of the road. He anchors each corner with a pebble.

Close-up of the handkerchief.

After a rapid dissolve we see the Curbitt again. MARIO is still backing, guided by Jo.

Jo: *Hold it!*

MARIO: *Okay!*

Jo comes towards camera.

Jo: *You're coming out of the right-hand track.*

MARIO: *Too bad, we're far enough back. . . . Get in!*

Jo, off: *You don't think another hundred yards?*

MARIO: *Get in, we're going now.*

Jo re-enters into picture on the left and goes round the front of the lorry. The two men are seen from the side now seated in cab. The lorry moves off. MARIO settles comfortably in his seat as he changes up into second. Jo sits well down in the seat, with his feet up on the dashboard. MARIO changes into third. Shot of the pedals from the side as MARIO changes gear.

Resume on the two men, facing camera, as MARIO gradually relaxes and leans back in his seat.

Meanwhile in the Dodge, BIMBA sits facing camera, and LUIGI in profile. The lorry crawls slowly along.

BIMBA: *Another mile more and we're out of it.*

LUIGI: *So far so good.*

Shot of the pump site half way along the corrugated section of the road. There is a small hut near the petrol pump, from which a HALF-CASTE emerges and looks at something on the left. It is the handkerchief. The HALF-CASTE bends down and picks it up. As he gets up, the Curbitt appears in the distance, approaching at full speed. The HALF-CASTE waves the handkerchief in greeting. The lorry passes by.

Three-quarter front view of the Dodge, driven by LUIGI and BIMBA, moving slowly along.

Back view of Jo and MARIO as the Curbitt speeds along.

The Curbitt's speedometer reads just over 40 m.p.h.

The Dodge's speedometer reads just over 4 m.p.h.

We see BIMBA and LUIGI, facing camera, in the Dodge. BIMBA is playing the harmonica. Close-up of the two of them.

Dissolve to Jo and MARIO in the Curbitt. Jo has a cigarette hanging from the corner of his mouth. MARIO is relaxed; or rather he has cut himself off from the present. His nerves and muscles are still in control but his mind is elsewhere. His eyes seem to gaze beyond the horizon. Jo is still tense, not letting up for a moment, and so he is the first to notice something on the road ahead. He hits MARIO on the shoulder and MARIO jumps.

MARIO: *Are you crazy? What's the matter?*

Jo: *Can't you see them, ahead, at the bend.*

Through the windscreen, the Dodge can be seen emerging from a bend a long way ahead.

MARIO, off: *Who?*

Jo, off: *Them, the Dodge!*

MARIO, off: *No, I can't see a thing. . . . It's too far for me.*

After a moment.

MARIO: *Hey! The bastards . . . you're right. It's them. What are they playing at. . . . They should have been out of it long ago. . . . Give them a blast on the siren.*

Jo presses the hooter button, and the hooter, in close-up, sounds loudly.

Shot of the right hand door of the Dodge, from the outside.

BIMBA's hand appears through the window shaking the saliva from his harmonica. He hears the hooter and puts his head out of the window.

Rapid shot towards the rear of the Dodge. The Curbitt can be seen approaching in the distance.

BIMBA leans back into the cab.

BIMBA: *God almighty! It's Jo, they're coming, accelerate.*

Shot of the speedometer; the needle rises from 5 to 8 m.p.h.

The steering wheel immediately starts to vibrate.

We return to MARIO and Jo.

Jo: *How far ahead, d'you reckon?*

MARIO: *I don't know . . . about half a mile.*

Jo: *We'll be on top of them in fifty seconds if they're not off the washboard.*

The needle of the Curbitt's speedometer drops from 40 to 35 m.p.h.

The steering wheel starts to vibrate.

Resume on the speedometer; the needle rises from 35 to 40 again.

Facing camera, MARIO and Jo exchange glances.

MARIO presses lightly on the accelerator.

At 45 m.p.h. the vibration disappears abruptly.

Jo: *What are you going to do?*

MARIO: *Nothing! Wait . . . thirty seconds more. . . .*

We return to LUIGI and BIMBA. Having seen the Curbitt approaching in the rear view mirror, LUIGI turns the mirror aside and nervously shuts his eyes.

BIMBA: *Look.*

Shot of the road ahead. The marshland has come to an end. A small roadsign can be seen in the far distance.

BIMBA, off: *You see that little silver point ahead, it's a roadsign.* Close-up of him.

BIMBA: *The end of the washboard. . . . If they leave us another ten seconds, we're saved.*

Jo and MARIO are seen from the front, Jo nearest camera. His eyes are now wide with fear.

MARIO: *Ten seconds, then . . . boom! . . . One . . . two. . . .*

Jo: *Shut up, for Chrissake!*

Shot of the two of them from behind; the back of the Dodge can be seen through the windscreen, about forty yards ahead.

MARIO: *Five. . . .*

Jo puts his hands over his ears.

MARIO: *Six. . . .*

MARIO, who has hitherto remained calm, begins to stare ahead with a hypnotised expression.

Shot of LUIGI and BIMBA facing camera.

BIMBA: *Quick!*

Seen from the back of the Dodge, which appears in soft focus in the foreground, the Curbitt is bearing down on them, a mere twenty yards away.

MARIO: *Ten. . . .*

Jo raises his arm to shield his face and tries to grab the hand-brake with his left hand. MARIO's elbow knocks him brutally aside.

MARIO, off: *Leave that alone.*

Shot of the Dodge, as seen by MARIO through the windscreen of the Curbitt. There is only ten yards between them.

MARIO, off: *Twelve! . . .*

Close-up of MARIO.

MARIO: *Thirteen . . .fourteen . . . look, you fool!*

Jo stares in stupefaction.

MARIO: *They're gaining!*

Seen from the front of the Curbitt, the Dodge is three yards away, moving at the same speed; then it gradually draws away. Jo closes his eyes.

Resume on the front of the Curbitt, which comes to a halt as the Dodge draws slowly away.

MARIO: *We've done it, Jo! We've won!*

He shakes Jo, who opens his eyes and tries to escape a hearty slap on the back from MARIO.

The scene changes to a mountainous countryside with a road full of hairpin bends. LUIGI and BIMBA's lorry, seemingly miniscule, climbs slowly up the road, and approaches a wooden platform erected on the edge of a bend to widen it. There are several quarry trucks standing on roads at the side of the platform. The lorry is the only sign of life in the deserted landscape. Close shot of the cab of the Dodge. LUIGI is eating a banana and looking out through the open window. Just before they arrive at the platform, they pass a danger sign bearing a skull and crossbones. LUIGI throws his banana skin at the sign, then puts his head out of the window and sticks his tongue out at it as the lorry passes by. We see the hairpin bend from a high angle as the Dodge appears and comes to a stop. LUIGI gets out and surveys the situation. He shakes his head and walks towards the platform. BIMBA leans out of the lorry.

BIMBA: *Looks nasty, doesn't it?*

LUIGI: *Not a pretty sight. . . . They're widening the road.*

He surveys the countryside and the bend again.

LUIGI: *You won't get by . . . you'll have to take it in stages.*

Standing on the platform, six feet away from the edge, he gestures to indicate the route BIMBA will have to take.

LUIGI: *You'd better start here . . . go right up to this.* He indicates the rock face on the inner side of the road. . . . *Then back across here.* He points to the platform.

LUIGI stands facing the lorry and signals to BIMBA; the Dodge starts to move slowly forwards.

LUIGI: *Okay. . . . Come on!*

The Dodge passes over the planks.

Close-up of the wheels, narrowly avoiding the edge.

Resume on the lorry as it moves gently up against the rock face while LUIGI moves towards a quarry truck which is standing right on the edge of the platform.

Close-up of LUIGI pushing the truck aside to make room for the lorry. The lorry is now backing slowly onto the platform. LUIGI moves to the right, towards the Dodge, and goes towards the cab, singing *Santa Lucia* to himself in Italian. The Dodge continues to move slowly towards the edge of the platform, which projects out over the mountain side with a steep drop below. Close-up of the lorry's back wheels as a plank suddenly gives way beneath them with a loud crack.

LUIGI immediately bends down to inspect the damage.

LUIGI: *It's nothing — the wood's rotten.*

He picks up a log and jams it under the back wheel.

BIMBA leans out of the cab window.

BIMBA: *Will it hold?*

LUIGI: *Carry on like that.*

The lorry moves slowly forwards.

Close-up of the wheel, which spins, then comes out of the hole. The lorry reaches the point where the platform joins the road. There is a slight step up onto the ground.

The wheel comes up against the edge of the road and slips slowly back again. It starts to slip again. LUIGI jams the log under the wheel.

LUIGI: *Wait!*

This time the wheel bites into the wood and passes over the hump.

The lorry moves forward onto the road and round the bend.

BIMBA stops and gets out, and comes back to LUIGI.

BIMBA: *Thanks, Luigi.*

LUIGI: *Don't mention it . . . a piece of cake. . . .*

BIMBA, looking at the broken plank: *Well, I think we can say. . . .*

LUIGI facing camera, grimaces, then walks round behind the hole, scratching his head. Suddenly the planking gives way beneath his feet and he falls. BIMBA grabs hold of him.

Shot of the two of them, LUIGI sitting by the hole, his feet dangling through into the void, and BIMBA standing beside him.

LUIGI: *What a death trap! . . . We'd better tell the others. . . . How are they going to get round?*

BIMBA: *Let them sort that out for themselves. After all they only had to stay in front.* A pause. *You hear that?*

The sound of an engine is heard in the distance.

LUIGI: *It's them.*

The two of them hurry to the edge of the platform.

The Curbitt is coming slowly up the winding road far below. A low angle shot shows the lorry in the foreground. The noise of its engine is deafening as it grinds slowly uphill. Far above, LUIGI and BIMBA can be seen standing on the edge of the platform, vainly shouting and waving their arms.

Dissolve to interior shot of Jo and MARIO's lorry, as it slowly climbs the hill. The desolate countryside can be seen through the open windows of the cab. They pass a row of black wooden crosses.
Shot of MARIO, who sticks his head out of the window.
The camera follows his gaze as he sees the platform, then the planking and the steep drop beneath.
The rear wheels of the Curbitt pass across the inner edge of the platform. The outside tyre projects slightly over the edge. The lorry, having made a half turn, comes to a halt, and MARIO gets out and looks down at the planking.
Rapid shot of MARIO as he takes a few steps forward. BIMBA and LUIGI have arranged some planks in a cross over the hole.
MARIO removes them as Jo comes up and notices the hole.

MARIO: *What does that mean?*
Jo: *I don't know and I don't care! All I know is that for me this little excursion is over.*

MARIO, who has been crouching over the hole, gets up and goes over to the cable which supports the platform. He jumps up and down to test the strength of the planking.

Jo: *And for you too. . . . How do you think you're going to get a ten-ton lorry round there. . . . You think it can leapfrog the hole I suppose. . . . There's only one thing to do . . . get out, and quick.*

Ignoring Jo, MARIO continues to size up the situation.
MARIO, pointing towards the edge of the planking: *It looks a bit better here, if we take it right to the edge and then turn we should be all right.*

He walks back towards the lorry, while Jo stands in the centre of the platform and shouts after him.

Jo: *You can't drive onto that! It's rotten right through.*

He bends down and drives his knife into one of the planks.
Close-up of the knife. The blade sinks in easily.

Jo, off: *It's not wood, it's like a sponge.*

He gets up and goes back towards MARIO, who is about to get back into the lorry.
We see the two of them, with the lorry behind them.

Jo: *Are you out of your mind?*

MARIO: *The others got by . . . so will we.*

Jo: *They're not half as heavy as we are, and they've already stove in the apron.* A pause. *The nitro's making you drunk. . . . It must be.* Holding up his finger. *Look . . . there at the surface; it's covered in clay . . . it's a skating rink! Even if you don't go through it, you'll skid right off the edge.*

> MARIO, who is about to get into the driving seat, gets out again and grabs Jo angrily by the arm.

MARIO: *Just you listen to me . . . there's two thousand dollars in this job.*

Jo: *To hell with the dough. I'd rather stay alive.*

MARIO: *Too late, pal, you should have thought of that before. I didn't ask you to come, right? I told you I was scared. . . . 'Don't worry kid', you said, 'I'll show you'. . . . Remember? . . . Well now we've got to get through.*

Jo: *It's crazy.*

MARIO: *Crazy, yeah! . . . We were crazy to start on this whole caper. . . . And you're the one who got me into it, don't forget.*

> He pushes Jo aside and gets into the driving seat. Jo gets round the back to keep a look out.
>
> Jo looks nervously at the hole and takes off his cap.

Jo, in an undertone: *You poor jerk. . . . You'll get your medal but you won't be there to receive it!*

> Jo passes round behind the lorry, which backs slowly towards the camera. It moves out onto the platform, still backing.
>
> Rapid shot of the lorry from the side, MARIO at the wheel. The lorry is almost touching the quarry truck.

Jo, shouting: *Hey! . . . Easy! That'll do!*

> The lorry continues to back.

Jo: *Stop, stop, for God's sake.*

> Shot of MARIO facing camera. He shouts out of the cab window.

MARIO: *Right to the edge, I said!*

> The camera remains still, while the lorry continues to back. Seen from the side, the lorry begins to push the truck backwards.

Jo, bellowing: *Stop! . . . Mario. . . . Stop!*

MARIO: *Jo, how much is there left?*

> Shot from the road, the back of the lorry moves away from the camera towards the edge of the precipice. Jo is already hidden

298

behind it. Another side view, as the lorry continues to move, Jo is pinned between the back of it and the truck. The latter falls over the edge, and we hear it crashing down the precipice below. The lorry stops with its wheels right on the edge.

Shot of MARIO, wide-eyed, as he thrusts his head out of the cab window and shouts in alarm.

MARIO: *Jo*. . . .

He gets out of the lorry, rushes to the edge of the platform and looks down into the void below.

MARIO, muttering to himself: *Jesus Christ!*

He sees Jo's cap lying on the debris below.

Seen from below, MARIO jumps down from the platform onto a small outcrop of rock. He comes down further and picks up the cap, looking from side to side.

MARIO: *Jo, Jo, answer me! . . . Stop fooling around!*

He looks at Jo's cap in his hand. He is very shaken.

MARIO: *Jesus Christ!*

He looks up and sees the back of the lorry projecting over the edge of the platform, then he climbs back up again. Having reached the platform, he looks up the mountain side and is outraged by what he sees: Jo is sneaking away on all fours up the side of the mountain.

Resume on MARIO, shot from above.

MARIO: *The sonofabitch!*

Close shot of Jo from behind as he continues to climb.

MARIO, off: *Jo . . . hey, Jo! Don't you hide. I've seen you.*

In a high shot of the platform and the lorry, MARIO, at the bottom of the frame, yells up to Jo.

MARIO: *I can see you. Come down, you bastard!*

He picks up a stone and hurls it towards the mountain side, then goes back towards the lorry.

Shot of Jo hiding behind a broken-down wall.

We look down on the lorry, as seen by Jo, no bigger than an insect. There is an unearthly peal of thunder, off.

Close shot of the lorry from ground level. It advances towards the camera, away from the edge of the precipice.

MARIO is sitting tensely at the wheel.

The rear wheels spin.

Close-up of MARIO. We sense the movement of the cab as the

lorry begins to slip sideways.

The back wheels of the lorry are seen from the right hand side, near the edge of the platform, which is supported by a steel cable running diagonally across the shot. The wheels spin and the lorry slips towards the edge. (*Still*)

MARIO looks tense and puts his foot on the brake.

Close-up of one of the back wheels, which has stopped spinning. It slips a few inches more towards the edge before finally coming to a stop.

Resume on MARIO. He gets nervously down from the cab, glances at the wheels and runs towards a hut at the side of the road.

Jo, meanwhile, is crouching fearfully in his hiding place, chewing his nails.

Seen from above, MARIO arranges some brushwood under the back wheels.

Resume on Jo, who shrugs his shoulders.

MARIO, in profile, is back at the wheel of the lorry, seen through the right hand window. The cab moves forwards. Shot at the back of the lorry from the side. It moves forward, past the diagonal cable supporting the platform. A few feet above the ground there is a turnbuckle, linked to the cable by a hook.

MARIO, in profile, tenses nervously and accelerates.

Rapid close-up of his foot on the accelerator.

We see the hook on the end of the turnbuckle, which is gradually pulled open. The opened hook snaps and the cable parts.

Jo throws himself down, face to the ground.

The right-hand back wheel of the lorry leaves the platform.

Just as he reaches firm ground, a gap opens between the planking and the road. The gap slowly widens.

Shot of the platform from below; daylight can be seen between it and the road as the planking collapses, while the back of the lorry, overhanging the precipice, disappears from view.

High angle long shot from the mountain side. As the lorry moves on round the bend, the platform collapses behind it. The last few planks are seen tumbling rapidly down the slope.

MARIO gets out of the lorry. He looks left, to where the platform was, then walks over and looks down into the void.

High angle shot over the edge of the precipice.

Dissolve to Jo, sitting on the ground, his back to the low wall behind which he has been hiding, his head in his hands.

The noise of the Curbitt's engine is heard off. Jo shoots a furtive glance to the left, then buries his head in his hands again.

The lorry comes up the hill towards camera.

It hoots briefly, twice. Jo gets up slowly and advances towards MARIO, who leans out of the cab window, sneering, and throws him his cap.

MARIO: *Here!*

While Jo is picking up his cap, the lorry moves out of frame to the left.

JO: *Hey. . . . Wait for me, Mario.*

MARIO faces camera, a mocking expression on his face. A large stretch of the countryside can be seen in soft focus on the right. In a shot from behind the lorry, Jo appears in the narrow space between the lorry and the rock face at the side of the road, trying to catch up with the moving vehicle.

As he hurries after it, MARIO gradually accelerates. Jo breaks into a run.

JO: *Mario! . . . Mario!*

He continues to run along beside the lorry.

Jo, beseechingly: *Mario!*

He manages to draw level with the cab.

Close-up of MARIO from the side.

MARIO: *Mario says . . . screw you!*

By now completely exhausted, Jo continues to run for a moment, hanging on to the back of the lorry as it draws ahead again. He finally lets go, stumbles and comes to a stop, panting with exhaustion.

Shot of the back of the lorry as it stops a dozen yards or so up the road.

In the cab, MARIO looks out to the right and lights a cigarette. Jo comes up and drags himself up to the cab window. He does not dare to get in.

Resume on MARIO, who flicks the match he has used to light his cigarette on Jo's face and flings open the door. Jo still hesitates.

301

Close-up of MARIO through the cab window.

MARIO: *Well — are you getting in or not?*

Jo gets in and shuts the door. The lorry moves off.

Shot of the lorry from the front. Seen through the window-screen, Jo sits beside MARIO, who is driving. Apart from two or three alternating close-ups each, the camera remains on the two of them throughout the following sequences.

MARIO: *You filthy, stinking bastard!*

Rather shamefacedly, Jo opens his mouth to reply.

MARIO: *No don't say a word . . . I get it. Monsieur Jo's got the jitters. . . . Yeah, he's just scared out of his wits. Boy, you're a really tough egg. . . . A real Al Capone. Malaria, you say. Screw malaria! I tell you, you're just plain scared to death.*

Jo: *I forbid you to say that. If you'd been through what I've been through.*

MARIO: *Oh, no. Screw your autobiography. You may have been a man once but not since the time of my grandmother. Now all you can do is shoot a guy in the back, when there's no risk, because you don't like risks.*

Jo: *I don't like them because I know them. You're different. You forge ahead without thinking, you think you're invulnerable. I'm always looking out for the stone or the hole which is going to send me up in smoke. I've died fifty times since last night.* He taps his head. *It's going on in here, I tell you. I see myself blown up, torn to ribbons, shattered into bits. It's no joke having a brain in your head.*

MARIO: *You must have that somewhere else, if you ask me.*

Jo: *Say what you like . . . you won't be laughing when you've had them strung from a branch like a pair of cherries.*

Dissolve to a shot of the lorry which, having reached the top of the hill, is now running along on the flat.

The scene changes, and we see the Dodge, coming round a bend towards the camera.

Shot of LUIGI and BIMBA. BIMBA is sprawled over the wheel, looking very relaxed.

LUIGI is leaning back in his seat smoking a large cigar and listening to the radio. He is taking enormous puffs at the cigar and the smoke is making his eyes water, but this appears in no way to diminish his contentment.

302

LUIGI: *Terrific. . . . Want a drag?*

He offers the cigar to BIMBA, who takes a long drag and then hands it back.

LUIGI: *The day after tomorrow I'll buy you one all to yourself . . and we'll each smoke our own.*

The two men watch the road ahead. BIMBA is more tense than LUIGI, despite his outward calm.

LUIGI: *Hey Bimba — why so sad? It's all over. . . . No more cement, no more Corsario. . . . The day after tomorrow we'll be either rich or dead. If we're dead it'll be all over, anyway . . . but if we're not dead it'll be good to get away, right?*

BIMBA: *Get away to where?*

LUIGI: *Somewhere else.*

BIMBA: *A change of mosquitoes? Thanks, the mosquitoes here are good enough for me.*

LUIGI: *Oh, I prefer the ones at home! When I get the bonus, I'll go back to Calabria, buy some hens . . . and marry a pretty girl.*

Rapid shot of BIMBA's face. He suddenly starts and stares forwards through the windscreen.

Dissolve to MARIO and Jo, facing the camera. MARIO is still driving.

MARIO: *If you've got the wind up you can get out. No one's keeping you. This is an oil lorry, not an old folks' home.*

Jo: *No, I'll go on — I need the cash and I'll earn it.*

MARIO: *You'll earn it . . . you'll earn it if your sugar baby does it for you.* A pause. He turns the steering wheel. *Make no mistake, kid, I'm not a charitable institution.*

I'll do the whole job, so my friend Jo can stick his thousand bucks under his belt. Oh, no, that won't do. If you want the dough you got to earn it. You've got to play on both pedals — that's what you're paid for.

Jo: *You think you're paid to drive a lorry? Poor kid, you're paid to be afraid. You just haven't understood. That's the division of labour; I drive and I worry myself to death; you've got the best part of the deal.*

Dissolve to high shot of the Dodge as it comes to a stop a few yards away from a big rock which is blocking the road. BIMBA and LUIGI jump out on either side of the lorry and go up to the rock. LUIGI takes his cigar out of his mouth with a furious gesture.

Close-up of BIMBA.

BIMBA: *That's all we needed!*

He gets up onto the parapet by the roadside to get a better view, while LUIGI goes up to the rock and beats his fists on it angrily.

LUIGI: *It's too much . . . everything's against us. Goddam stone. . . . How did you get here?*

BIMBA looks back at LUIGI from the parapet.

BIMBA: *It came from up there . . . a landslide.* He picks up a stone, examines it and throws it away. *That's from the rock — the stone must be rotten.*

LUIGI, picking up his cap, which he has thrown on the ground, in Italian: *We're right out of luck!*

BIMBA, in German: *That does it, we're finished.*

LUIGI: *Wait.* He mimes the action of lifting the rock with a crowbar. *We each take a crowbar and heave.*

BIMBA: *You're out of your mind — it weighs at least fifty tons.*

LUIGI: *What do we do then?*

BIMBA ponders for a moment, and then his eyes fall on the lorry. The camera pans, following his gaze, to show the word EXPLOSIVES painted on the front.

Resume on BIMBA, who walks with a determined air towards the lorry.

BIMBA: *We'll blow it up.*

LUIGI hurries after BIMBA.

A rapid shot of the two men, then close-ups of each, during the dialogue.

LUIGI: *What with?*

BIMBA: *There's enough there, isn't there?*

He jerks his head at the load of nitroglycerine.

LUIGI, dumbfounded: *You're going to blow up a jerrycan of nitro?*

BIMBA: *A jerrycan! . . . Why not a ton of it!* He climbs cautiously onto the back of the lorry and continues: *Just a little — that's all it needs.*

LUIGI: *But how are you going to get it out?*

BIMBA: *Syphon it out with a rubber tube. Meanwhile you can take that crowbar and make . . .* LUIGI *has a coughing fit . . . and make me a hole in the stone, about two feet deep.*

LUIGI immediately takes a heavy crowbar from the lorry and goes towards the rock. He climbs on top of it, spits in his hands and prepares to chip out a hole.

Resume on BIMBA standing on the back of the lorry. He slings a length of rubber tubing around his neck.

LUIGI starts to chip away at the rock.

Close-up of the rock, which starts to crack.

Meanwhile, BIMBA gently extracts a jerrycan of nitroglycerine from the load, and steps down to the ground with the utmost caution, keeping his eye on the jerrycan as he does so.

Close shot of LUIGI, who has stopped for a moment to watch BIMBA. His face is running with sweat, caused not only by his exertions but also by the fear that BIMBA will drop the jerry-can. Then he starts chipping away at the hole again. Close-up of the crowbar gradually digging into the rock.

Dissolve to show the crowbar as LUIGI withdraws it from the hole, which is now about two feet deep.

LUIGI shows BIMBA the white mark on the crowbar.

LUIGI, to BIMBA: *Is that enough?*

BIMBA: *Yes that'll do. . . . Go and get me the jack handle and a hammer.*

BIMBA has put the jerrycan down on a rock; there is a thermos flask beside him. Very slowly, he dips the rubber tubing into the jerrycan and sucks at the other end to syphon the nitro-glycerine into the thermos.

Dissolve to high shot of the scene. The Curbitt appears around the bend and comes to a stop. MARIO gets out.

BIMBA has just finished filling the thermos flask and he takes the tools from LUIGI and walks towards the rock which is blocking the road. MARIO comes up to him.

MARIO: *Hi, fellers, what's the game?*

BIMBA, indicating the rock: *See that?*

LUIGI: *We're going to blow up the mountain.*

MARIO: *What? You're nuts.*

BIMBA, philosophically: *We've got to clear the road, right? . . . So.*

MARIO turns towards Jo as the latter shambles up to them.

MARIO: *What do you think?*

Jo, shrugging his shoulders: *Me . . . nothing.*

LUIGI: *Everyone's got a right to his opinion here. You can give yours.*

Jo has sat down on the parapet near the jerrycan and is wiping the sweat from his forehead.

JO: *Me? . . . I don't give a damn.*

MARIO: *Hey, don't you think it's a bit risky?* To BIMBA: *You might blow up the whole load and us with it.*

Shot of BIMBA, who has arranged the crowbar and the lorry's jack to form a tripod over the hole which LUIGI has dug in the rock. He now suspends the hammer by a piece of string directly over the hole.

BIMBA: *Of course, we'll have to put the trucks under cover. Yours first, then ours.*

The camera shows MARIO, LUIGI, and Jo, the latter still seated at the roadside.

MARIO, to Jo: *You hear that, chief?*

Jo pulls himself together, gets up looking exhausted, and goes towards the Curbitt.

Seen from behind, he staggers towards the back of the lorry.

LUIGI, astonished: *What's the matter with him?*

MARIO, scornfully: *He's got the shakes! . . . If you want a hard case, take him, you're welcome. Just look at him!* To Jo: *Come on, flat-foot, move!*

LUIGI: *You shouldn't . . . can't you see he's a walking corpse?*

MARIO: *Isn't that what we all are?*

Cut to BIMBA.

BIMBA: *Hey, Mario . . . take the jerrycans as far away as possible. . . . Luigi, bring me the thermos?*

LUIGI: *Maybe too much.*

Close shot of LUIGI, who picks up the thermos flask in both hands and gingerly carries it across to BIMBA. Half way there, he is overcome by a violent fit of coughing. BIMBA looks at him in alarm. The coughing subsides.

LUIGI: *What a set-up!*

BIMBA: *It's quite simple. I light the cord and when the flame gets up to here, the hammer drops in the hole and . . . bang!* A pause. *Go and get a branch off that palm over there.*

Close-up of LUIGI; then we see MARIO, as he carefully carries the jerrycan away to a safe distance.

Jo meanwhile backs the Curbitt round the bend, a hundred yards or so along the road.

Resume on LUIGI as he brings BIMBA the palm leaf he has requested.

BIMBA: *Right, now you can get out.*

LUIGI: *You don't need me any more?*

BIMBA: *First you must back the lorry and anyway . . . there's no need to take unnecessary risks. Goodbye.*

BIMBA goes up to LUIGI and shakes him affectionately by the hand, then watches as he walks away. As he looks down again, BIMBA notices LUIGI's cigar butt lying in a crack in the rock.

BIMBA: *Here . . . your cigar!*

He throws it to him.

LUIGI catches it, grins at BIMBA, and turns back towards the lorry.

MARIO, to Jo, off: *Okay, stop.*

Resume on Jo, who stops backing and gets out of the lorry. He sits down on the running boards and after a moment MARIO joins him.

MARIO: *I think this'll do.*

Cut to BIMBA, who trims the palm leaf until he is left with a long stem.

LUIGI starts to back the Dodge.

Resume on MARIO and Jo.

Jo, mopping his forehead: *It may do. . . . It may do for us.*

LUIGI backs his lorry up close to the Curbitt. MARIO walks forward and guides him.

MARIO: *Okay, straighten up.*

LUIGI stops and gets out. MARIO immediately goes to him and lays a hand on his shoulder.

MARIO: *How's it going back there?*

LUIGI disengages himself and crosses to the other side of the road, where he looks back towards BIMBA, who is out of sight. He seems very tense.

Close-up of the thermos in BIMBA's hand as he slowly tips it up. (*Still*) In his other hand he holds the palm stem, partly inserted in the hole in the rock. Drop by drop, he slowly trickles the nitroglycerine down the stem.

Rapid shot of his face. He is breathing heavily, the sweat coursing down his forehead.

In close-up, MARIO waits nervously by the lorries.

LUIGI chews on his cigar.

MARIO: *It's taking a long time.*

A series of close shots shows:

MARIO's hands fiddling nervously with a box of matches.

The cigar in LUIGI's mouth.

MARIO's hands fiddling with the matchbox.

JO, seated, nervously drumming his fingers on the side of the lorry.

The thermos, with the nitroglycerine trickling down the palm stem.

MARIO's hands fiddling with the matchbox.

The cigar in LUIGI's mouth.

JO's hand as he drums on the side of the lorry.

BIMBA's face, sweating with fear, as he concentrates on what he is doing.

He finally empties the thermos, pushes the stem gently into the hole, and gives a sigh of relief. He then arranges the hammer so that it is hanging just over the hole and the stem, takes out some matches and lights a cigarette.

Close-up of the fuse as he picks it up, the cigarette in his other hand.

Close-up of his face, still sweating, but slightly less tense, as he lights the fuse.

Then he runs for it.

The fuse starts burning.

BIMBA is running down the road; sees LUIGI and MARIO.

BIMBA, shouting: *Take cover!* They start to run.

He notices the lorries.

BIMBA: *God almighty . . . the trucks! . . . If a stone falls on them . . . .*

At these words, MARIO stops and turns around.

MARIO: *I'll back them up.*

At the same time, LUIGI spins round and starts to run back towards the rock.

LUIGI, shouting: *I'll put out the fuse.*

MARIO, shouting: *Don't be crazy . . . come with us.*

Luigi, running towards the rock: *It'll be faster. . . .*

Jo is still sitting on the running board of the Curbitt. He seems done for, and incapable of moving.

Mario and Bimba, as they climb up the mountain side for cover. They turn around.

Mario, shouting to Jo: *Get down, you fool!*

We see the thermos flask standing forgotten near the fuse, which has nearly burnt down to the string holding the hammer. We see Jo from above. He does not seem to have heard Mario. There is a colossal explosion. Jo stiffens and grits his teeth.

High angle, long shot of the scene. The two lorries stand in the road in the centre of the shot, while in the background a large cloud of smoke billows round the bend, filling the valley. Dust, stones and fragments of rock fly into the air.

We look down on the lorries; some stones fall very close to them. Jo sees them and trembles nervously.

He follows one with his eyes as it clatters down the mountain side towards the jerrycan of nitroglycerine which Mario has left by the side of the road.

Close shot of the jerrycan.

Resume on Jo. He closes his eyes and cowers against the side of the lorry.

Resume on the jerrycan. The falling stone is halted by a rock a few yards above it.

The camera shows the smoke-filled valley, then the mountain side.

We see Bimba and Mario, who get up and start to climb down.

Mario, calling: *Luigi! . . . Luigi!*

Luigi is lying face down in the road. Mario and Bimba, having seen him from a distance, rush towards him.

Luigi's face is in the foreground. His eyelids flicker.

Mario and Bimba run up in the background. Mario throws himself down beside Luigi and puts an ear to his back to see if he is breathing.

Bimba: *Is he dead?*

Mario: *No, he's breathing.*

Luigi finally raises his head.

Luigi: *I'm breathing the smell of your feet, you idiots.*

He gets up and feels his ribs.

309

Mario, with a sigh: *That was quite something. Are you hurt?*
Shot of the three of them standing.

Mario: *You really scared us that time. . . . I thought you were dead.*

Luigi: *So did I.*
Luigi and Mario look at each other then burst out laughing, and throw their arms round one another. Bimba pats Luigi on the shoulder and warmly shakes his hand.

Bimba: *Blessed are the poor in spirit! . . . He was just knocked out, that's all.*
In the background, the drooping figure of Jo appears, coming up the road. The others, who are busy joking and congratulating one another, take no notice of him.

Mario: *Knocked out? . . . And so is the stone.* He looks down the road; the rock has disappeared. *Not a bad job, eh?* He addresses Bimba, shaking him by the hand. *Congratulations.*
Still ignoring Jo, who has stopped nearby, the three of them move up the road to the place where the rock was.

Bimba: *There's nothing left.* He picks up the crowbar, which is twisted and bent. *You see that?*

Luigi: *It's twisted to hell.*
Jo comes up, grumbling.

Jo: *You're a bunch of bandits.*

Mario: *We're all here, aren't we? . . . So shut up.*
He starts to undo his flies and moves away, beckoning to Luigi.

Mario: *Come on, this calls for a celebration.*
Luigi follows suit.

Luigi, in Italian: *Piss with your friends and make amends.*
Bimba does the same.

Bimba: *We'll bring down the mountain.*
He joins Mario and Luigi as they urinate over the steep drop at the roadside. (*Still*)
Shot of Jo, who is left by himself. He becomes indignant.

Jo: *Aren't I invited?*
The other three, back to camera, do not react.
Resume on Jo, who moves off in the opposite direction, unbuttoning his flies.

Jo: *Then I'll have to do it alone.*

310

He stands back to camera and suits the action to the words.[1]

Dissolve to a close shot of LUIGI and BIMBA, facing camera, in the Dodge. The lorry is rolling smoothly along. BIMBA is having a shave, while LUIGI drives. He finishes lathering his face, much to LUIGI's amazement, then opens a cut-throat razor, applies it to his face, and leans carefully forwards to look in a shaving mirror which is perched on top of the dashboard.

BIMBA, to LUIGI: *Watch out, hah? . . . No bumps.*

LUIGI, admiringly: *What a guy!*

A pause. He shoots sideways glances at BIMBA as he drives.

LUIGI: *Mario's got a nerve. I've got a little less, and Jo's got none at all. But you . . . I don't know. . . . You just don't seem to realize.*

BIMBA: *Did you ever work in the salt mines? The Nazis kept me there for three years. I was half dead when I got out. Compared with that, nitroglycerine is nothing!*

LUIGI: *Of course! But even so . . . why are you shaving?*

BIMBA: *Before he was hanged, my father asked if he could take a shower. . . . It's a bad habit in our family. I never sat down at the table without washing my hands. If one's going to be a corpse, one might as well be a presentable one.*

Dissolve to Jo and MARIO in the Curbitt. MARIO is at the wheel, eating dry biscuits from their rations, and a flaked cereal which Jo pours into the palm of his hand.

MARIO: *You ought to have a bit.*

Jo: *My mouth's as dry as dust. . . . I couldn't get it down. . . . But I wouldn't mind a strawberry Vittel at the bar. . . .*

He reflects on the idea.

Jo: *. . . in the Ballon des Ternes! Want a smoke?*

MARIO: *Yes, roll me one, will you?*

Jo pulls out a bag of the maize leaves which serve as the local tobacco. He starts to make a cigarette, singing to himself as he does so.

Jo, singing: *'The weed you take in your fingers and roll. . . .' You know that one?*

---

[1] The original script included at this point some long scenes of a nearby village full of Indians, who are terrified by the explosion. However, Clouzot did not shoot this sequence.

MARIO: *No, but you're out of tune.*

JO: *Because my conscience is clean!*

MARIO, ironically: *No kidding! . . .*

Through the windscreen, we suddenly see a brilliant flash of light.

Close-up of Jo's hands, holding a cigarette paper full of tobacco, about to roll it. The tobacco is blown away by a sudden blast of air.

We see Jo staring in amazement.

Then MARIO, alarmed by the sound of a distant explosion.

A cloud of smoke appears over the mountain ridge above them.

Shot of the two men. Jo's mouth falls open.

MARIO: *Luigi! . . .*

JO, very quietly: *No more Luigi. . . .*

MARIO drops his head between his arms and rests it on the steering wheel, then raises it again with a start.

JO: *Hell, it was bound to happen. You keep playing the fool, you always get it in the neck. It might have been us; the poor guy!*

MARIO: *Forget it. They took the risk and then lost. That's the way it goes.*

JO: *You're a sympathetic fellow; your pal goes up in smoke and that's all you can find to say?*

MARIO: *What difference would it make?*

MARIO turns on the ignition again and starts the engine. Jo immediately turns off the ignition again.

MARIO: *If you start that again, I'll smash your face in.*

He starts the engine again and moves off.

JO: *You're crazy. . . . Don't do that. . . . Stop!*

He opens the door in panic.

MARIO: *Shut it. . . . I don't like draughts.*

JO: *I've had enough.*

He jumps out of the moving lorry onto the side of the road.

Shot of the Curbitt as it grinds to a halt. MARIO leaps out and the camera pans, following his gaze, as he watches Jo running off through the undergrowth. MARIO immediately runs after him.

Tracking shot of Jo running, pursued by MARIO.

Jo, who is a little ahead of MARIO, arrives at a bank of stones and runs down it.

MARIO appears about four yards away. Jo turns to face him, picks up a stick and raises it threateningly.

MARIO stands on the heap of stones, with Jo threatening him, back to camera in the foreground. MARIO bends down and picks up a large stone and makes as if to throw it at Jo.

MARIO: *Drop your stick!*

Jo: *Drop your stone!*

MARIO: *You first.*

Reverse shot, Jo facing camera. He throws down the stick.

The two are seen in close-up as MARIO throws his stone off-screen and it hits Jo full in the face.

MARIO looks pleased with himself.

Resume on the two of them, face to face. Jo belatedly raises his hand to protect his face. His nose is bleeding profusely, the blood dripping down onto his vest.

Jo: *Bastard!*

MARIO: *It may not be very sporting, but I'm the stronger. So we save time.*

Jo sinks to the ground, overcome with pain. MARIO looks mercilessly down at him.

MARIO: *Get up.*

Jo, pathetically: *Why are you such a rat with me?*

As he gets up, MARIO kicks him violently in the stomach, and slaps him round the face.

MARIO: *Just get it through into your skull. I need you . . . there's only the two of us left . . . so you'll come along quietly — right to the end.*

He motions Jo to walk in front of him. Jo drags himself miserably along, turning his bloodied face back to MARIO.

MARIO: *Go on, back to the truck!*

Jo: *You're lucky I'm old! I'm worn out. . . . I'm a coward!*

MARIO: *Faster!*

Dissolve to show the road running through a forest. The lorry passes across the shot.

The lorry comes towards the camera. In the foreground can be seen branches of a partially burnt tree which is blocking the road. The lorry stops.

Shot of MARIO and Jo.

MARIO: *It must have been some explosion. . . . Just look at that.*

313

Jo quickly gets out to move aside the tree. MARIO gets out also, and the camera tracks with him as he goes towards a large pool of thick black liquid which has filled the crater made by the roadway explosion.

Rapid shot of Jo, who has laboriously dragged aside the tree and laid it down at the roadside.

Resume on the crater. We now see that the explosion has shattered the pipeline running along beside the road, which is slowly pumping out oil into the crater.

In a low angle shot, the camera pans across burnt and shattered trees standing out against the sky.

MARIO looks round at the scene, then returns his attention to the crater. Jo approaches.

Jo: *You'd think they'd slipped down the hole! . . . Look! . . . The tracks come just to the edge, then there's nothing.*

MARIO turns round. The faint wheeltracks of the Dodge run as far as the edge of the crater, where they suddenly stop, and do not continue on the other side.

MARIO: *It's funny. . . . It's as though an aircraft had taken off.*

Shot of the two of them.

Jo: *That's just what happened. They took off.*

They look upwards at the blasted trees.

Jo, in bewilderment: *What can have happened to them?*

MARIO, nervously: *How do I know!*

Jo: *We'll never know. . . . They probably didn't know themselves. . . .*

Jo and MARIO are still standing beside the crater. MARIO picks up a stone and throws it into the middle of the pool of oil. Jo picks up a stick and tests its depth.

Jo: *It's not even very deep.*

MARIO: *No, but the level will rise.*

He shows Jo the broken pipeline pumping out oil.

MARIO: *Look at that. . . . In half an hour it'll be one big oil tank.*

With these words he moves towards the lorry, swearing viciously.

MARIO: *We've fallen into every single, sodding, bastard trap we could!*

As MARIO passes in front of him, Jo looks down. . . .

BIMBA's cigarette holder is lying at Jo's feet.

314

Jo bends down and picks up the holder.

Jo: *Look — Bimba's cigarette holder!*

MARIO passes in front of Jo again, and looks around him as though he were looking for some other trace of the dead men.

Jo: *There's no point in looking! That's all there is left.*

MARIO: *Right, we're not going to stick around here. . . . In an hour, you'll need a boat to get across.* He points at the pool of oil. *Get in there and see how deep it is. I'll fetch the crate.*

MARIO goes off up the road, between the trees.

Jo, back to camera, walks into the pool of oil, poking around with the stick to test its depth.

MARIO, walking back towards the lorry, turns round.

MARIO: *Drag it with your feet. I'll be there in two minutes.*

Close shot of Jo. He looks to the right, then shrugs his shoulders and throws away his stick before replying.

Jo: *Yeah. . . . In five minutes or next year. . . . What's the differ-ence.* He shrugs again. *Two minutes or next year. It's all the same.*

He moves away from the edge of the pool, slightly towards the broken pipeline, dragging his feet through the oil. We hear the noise of the Curbitt's engine, off. Jo knocks into some-thing. He bends down and fishes out a branch dripping with oil, which he throws to one side.

The Curbitt comes slowly forwards through the trees.

Rapid shot of MARIO at the wheel.

MARIO: *Well?*

We see Jo in the pool of oil.

Jo: *It's okay, but it's slippery. If you stop you won't be able to start again. . . .*

MARIO: *Too bad, we'll have to go through.*

Jo: *Make sure you don't stop, that's all.*

The camera pans with Jo as he walks on through the pool.

We see the left hand front wheel of the lorry as it comes towards the camera and enters the oil.

Shot of the warning flag on the left hand front wing of the lorry.

Jo is seen from behind. The ground drops and he goes down, the oil coming half way up his thighs. He turns round.

Jo, shouting in alarm: *It goes down here!*

The lorry advances through the oil.

315

MARIO: *What's that?*

Jo, cupping his hands and bellowing: *There's a dip!*

MARIO, at the wheel of the lorry, is seen from inside the cab.

MARIO: *Go on!*

The camera tracks out in front of Jo as he walks on, the front of the lorry following behind. Jo almost falls over, but regains his balance and continues behind him. There is a loud crack and a large branch rises out of the oil just behind Jo and turns over. He pulls at the branch, trying to swing it to one side, but it topples over, and Jo falls backwards into the oil. He tries to get up.

We see the lorry, advancing on Jo, who is now only a few yards away.

Jo: *Stop! . . . Stop!*

Rapid shot of MARIO as he shouts desperately at Jo.

MARIO: *Get out of the way, for Chrissakes. . . . Get out of the way. . . . For Chrissakes, out of the way!*

Close-up of Jo.

Jo: *I can't. . . . I'm stuck!*

He tries to move to the left.

Resume on MARIO as he shouts again.

MARIO: *Get out of there!*

Jo is lying back in the oil, the front wheel of the lorry moving towards him in the foreground. Instead of doing as MARIO says, he tries to crawl away to the left. Suddenly he jumps and bellows with pain as the wheel passes over his leg under the surface. (*Still*)

Jo: *My leg. . . .*

Close-up of MARIO; gritting his teeth, he keeps the lorry moving. We see the front of the lorry as it starts to climb the other side of the crater.

Jo is lying limply, floating in the oil. His face and body are covered with the black sticky liquid. He groans.

Slowly the lorry continues to advance.

The back wheels move past Jo.

MARIO puts his head out of the window, then turns back to the wheel again. The lorry reaches the other side of the pool of oil.

Close-up of the wheels. Just before reaching dry land, they start to spin, and slip back into the oil again.

MARIO gets out and stands on the running board, surveying the situation. He jumps down and stands thigh-deep in the oil, looks at the wheels of the lorry, then glances towards Jo. Finally he goes back and lifts him up.

Jo: *Oh! My leg! It hurts!*

MARIO: *You should have got out of the way! Aren't we in the shit enough as it is?*

He pushes him towards the edge of the pool, where he props him with some difficulty against a tree. Jo bellows with pain. Close shot of the two of them. We can see one of the legs of Jo's trousers, completely flattened half way up the thigh. MARIO seizes hold of Jo and shakes him brutally.

Jo: *You rat. You saw you were going over me, didn't you? And you went on just the same. Over your pal!*

MARIO: *Pal or no pal, I had to get by.*

Jo: *You've hurt me!*

MARIO: *It's your fault! I shouted at you to get out of the way. If I hadn't hesitated. . . .*

Jo: *You hesitated. . . .*

MARIO: *You bet I did . . . and if I hadn't, we'd be across by now! Thanks to you, all our acrobatics have done us no good at all. We're out of the running.*

Shot of the two of them. MARIO gets up and looks furiously across at the lorry.

MARIO: *And we didn't even blow up! . . . We're bogged down. . . . Stuck like a pair of idiots! And pretty stupid we look too!*

Jo takes no notice; he is too occupied with his own pain.

Jo: *I'm hurt. . . . Do something . . . look at me . . . you don't know what's it like!*

MARIO goes off to the right.

MARIO: *You think I've got time for that?*

Jo, beseechingly: *Oh . . . I'm hurt!*

Shot of Jo propped up against the tree, his face contorted with pain.

Jo: *Mario, where are you going? . . . It hurts!*

MARIO, who is on his way back to the lorry, turns round.

MARIO: *Well, now you've won, I hope you're pleased.*[1]

We see MARIO, at the edge of the pool. He drives a stout crowbar with a cable attached to it into the ground in front of the
lorry. Then he comes back towards the rear wheels and gropes
around in the oil. Finally he takes a deep breath and plunges
down into the oil in order to attach the cable under the wheels.
MARIO surfaces again, having fixed one end of the cable to each
of the wheels.
Shot of the bar stuck in the ground, with the cable attached
to it.
Jo meanwhile takes off his belt and tries to make a tourniquet
for his thigh.
Resume on the lorry as it moves slowly forwards with MARIO
at the wheel.
The crowbar gives slightly under the tension of the cable.
The wheels spin.
Jo sits looking on. He sips from a thermos flask standing on
the ground beside him. (*Still*)
Shot of the wheels, still spinning.
Resume on the crowbar. It gives further in the ground and
then starts to bend.
MARIO spins the steering-wheel to keep the lorry on course.
The wheels finally reach firm ground.

Dissolve to long shot of the road. The lorry appears in the
distance. Beside the road is a signpost indicating that the S.O.C.
oil well is not far off.
In the background is a stony plain, with derricks scattered
across it.
The lorry comes towards camera.
Shot of MARIO and Jo in the cab, both black with oil.
MARIO is still at the wheel, while Jo sits with his head leaning
against MARIO's shoulder and his leg suspended horizontally in
an improvised sling attached to the windscreen and the open
window of the door. The tension between them seems to have

---

[1] At this point, the original script contained a very long scene in which Jo is
almost on the point of death, and he begs for water and tries to cajole
MARIO. Although it was partly shot the scene does not appear in the copies
of the film now available.

relaxed, but Jo appears completely exhausted.

MARIO: *I'm not bumping you too much?*

Jo: *Oh, don't worry, I'm not nitro. I'm not dangerous . . . at least not any more. My leg stinks, doesn't it?*

MARIO: *You think so? It just smells of oil, that's all.*

Jo: *Oh no! . . . I'm beginning to smell like a corpse.*

MARIO: *Shut up, will you!*

Jo: *It's not funny, rotting alive. . . .*

MARIO: *If you start to panic, you're done for.*

> Jo looks at his hands.

Jo: *Hey, look at my nails . . . they're violet . . . that's the end.*

> MARIO starts; he is now genuinely alarmed.

MARIO: *Hey, quit fooling about, will you. . . . You're not going to die now!*

Jo, with a sigh: *That's one time when you don't get a choice.*

> Shot of the road outside. The lorry passes a hut, outside which three Indians are squatting on the ground, watching it go by. Resume on MARIO and Jo, in the cab of the lorry.

MARIO: *Talk to me, Jo! . . . Say something. . . .*

Jo: *I want to go to sleep.*

MARIO: *Don't do that. . . . Once you're asleep, you're not resisting any more.*

> Jo's eyes are closed and his face is twisted with pain. He can hardly speak, but manages to force out a few words.

Jo: *I'm so tired.*

MARIO: *Never mind. Make an effort, Jo.*

Jo: *What do you want to talk about?*

MARIO: *Oh, I don't know. . . . Where did you live in Paris?*

Jo, in a whisper: *Me . . . in the rue Galande.*

MARIO: *No kidding? I know it, you know.*

Jo: *A long time ago. . . .*

MARIO: *Isn't that funny? You remember there's a tobacconist on the corner.*

Jo: *Is it still there?*

MARIO: *You bet it is! Then there's a paint shop.*

Jo: *In my time there was a hoarding. It must have been built since then.*

MARIO: *No . . . you're right . . . it's the hoarding first.*

Jo: *The hoarding. . . . I never knew what there was behind it.*

MARIO: *There's nothing . . . a bit of waste ground.*
Shot of the road through the windscreen. The lorry passes an Indian on a donkey, coming in the opposite direction.
Resume on the two men in the cab. MARIO is carefully watching the road.
Dissolve to the same shot, some time later.
Dissolve to show the lorry with its headlamps on. It is night. The lorry continues to travel smoothly along.
Resume on MARIO at the wheel and Jo, who has his eyes closed. When he speaks, it is in a faint croak; he is nearly finished.
MARIO: *Something wrong?*
Jo, with a great effort: *I'm okay. . . . A pause. What a long road this is. . . . I'm quite out of breath.*
We see the small warning flag on the front of the lorry as it advances through the night.
Dissolve to the same shot of the flag; the countryside ahead has changed.
Resume on the cab. Jo is dozing, his head lolling slackly on MARIO's shoulder.
MARIO, in close-up, looks down at Jo's hand.
The hand tries to scratch the improvised bandages on Jo's broken leg.
Rapid shot of the pipeline at the roadside, running past outside.
MARIO: *Hey, Jo . . . don't let yourself go . . . it's not far now. A* pause. *Are you asleep?*
Jo: *No, I'm trying to remember.*
MARIO: *What?*
Jo: *The hoarding. A pause. What there was behind the palissade.*
MARIO: *I told you . . . nothing.*
Close-up of Jo's face. His mouth drops open. His hand stops scratching his leg and falls inert. He is dead.
MARIO faces the camera; his eyes are fixed on the road ahead and he has not noticed anything wrong. He blinks wearily, then suddenly stares forward through the windscreen.
The glare of the burning oil well is now visible in the distance.
Resume on MARIO, who immediately turns to Jo.
MARIO: *Look, we've won. . . . Thinking that Jo is asleep: That's right . . . have a little nap.*
MARIO turns his attention to the road for a moment, then looks

320

at Jo again. The lorry stops. Jo's lifeless eyes stare into space. Close-up of MARIO, who now realises that he is dead. He seizes hold of Jo's head and closes his eyes.

MARIO: *Not like that . . . you scare me. . . . Shut your eyes.*

MARIO sighs, then turns back to the wheel, switches on the ignition and starts the engine, with a slightly vacant expression. Close-up of him at the wheel; his face comes rapidly towards the camera as the lorry moves off again.

Dissolve to a shot of some burning oil derricks. They topple over in the darkness, lit by the gigantic flames from the burning oil well.

Another derrick over a bore-hole is seen silhouetted against the flames. The camera tilts up to show the platform at the top.

A man passes on a bulldozer, trying to check part of the fire. (*Still*)

Several men are seen moving to and fro near the fire.

Shot from the platform on the derrick. Down below, some men can be seen working round the drilling machinery.

A man on the platform turns round and looks up. He is sweating under his safety helmet. He goes to the corner of the platform, away from camera, to have a drink. As he tilts his head back to do so he notices something off-screen.

The camera tracks forward along the platform, tilting down to show the headlights of the Curbitt, as it arrives by the signboard at the entrance to the camp.

Resume on the man, who hurriedly puts down his bottle and grabs the field telephone.

He scrambles down the ladder from the platform as fast as he can.

Cut to the entrance to the camp. Three peons armed with torches are waiting for the lorry to arrive. They light their torches, which drip burning particles, and raise them in the air as they see the Curbitt coming towards them. The lorry comes at snail's pace towards camera.

The peons come into view, holding their torches in the air, and are immediately followed by four others. Two of them go to Jo's side of the lorry, five towards MARIO's.

Another shot. The lorry appears from the right. The peons crowd round and open the door in great excitement.

VOICES, in Spanish: *Fantastic! . . . Fantastic. . . . Say, how was the trip?*

MARIO gets out, completely done for. He only manages to utter a single word.

MARIO: *Cigarette!*

He walks forward, and lifts a trembling hand while one of the men pokes a cigarette into his mouth. As MARIO lights the cigarette, the camera pans across to a NEGRO WORKER who goes up to the cab of the lorry.

We see Jo lying dead on the seat. The NEGRO takes off his safety helmet.

Shot from the other side of the lorry. Two men have opened the door and now stand motionless in front of Jo's body. They take off their helmets. Two other peons have done likewise. A tall NEGRO comes into shot and crosses himself.

Resume on MARIO, leaning back against the lorry with his eyes closed, smoking. He is surrounded by the peons. The CAMP MANAGER and an ENGINEER come into shot.

The ensuing conversations, until MARIO leaves the camp, all take place in English.

CAMP MANAGER: *Good work Mario, you made it.*

MARIO: *Yes . . . but alone.*

CAMP MANAGER: *What about the others?*

MARIO: *All dead. . . .* He jerks his head towards the cab and adds: *This one too.*

Then he pushes aside the people surrounding him and staggers off.

The CAMP MANAGER and the ENGINEER take a couple of steps forward.

CAMP MANAGER: *He looks dead beat.*

ENGINEER: *Yes. The two of 'em . . .* He crosses his fingers . . . *were pretty close.*

Everyone looks in the direction taken by MARIO.

He is seen from behind, staggering like a drunkard towards the camp. He veers towards the fire then suddenly trips and falls to the ground.

The engineers and workers run towards him.

322

Close shot of MARIO lying on the ground. The others run up from the background and stand around him, the ENGINEER on the left. The CAMP MANAGER bends over MARIO.

ENGINEER: *What's wrong?*

The CAMP MANAGER straightens up.

CAMP MANAGER: *Nothing, he's sound asleep.*

MARIO lies on the ground, watched by the two men, the raging fire in the background.

Long dissolve to an exterior shot of the camp the next morning. The BOSS ENGINEER comes out of the camp office and goes towards the CAMP MANAGER, who is standing talking to MARIO. The latter is now clean and dressed in fresh clothing.

The BOSS hands him a cheque; MARIO takes it and looks at it, grinning.

BOSS: *I made it for four thousand dollars.*

CAMP MANAGER: *Your share . . . and your buddy's. The way he would have liked it.*

MARIO: *He was one hell of a guy. . . .*

BOSS: *And tough, too. . . .*

MARIO: *Yeah . . . he had guts, all right. . . .*

The CAMP MANAGER passes in front of MARIO, while the camera pans to show the Curbitt, also cleaned and newly serviced, which has just come to a halt nearby.

BOSS: *Here is the truck.*

MARIO: *Right away.* He waves the cheque. *I want to arrive before the banks close.*

He gets into the cab.

The ENGINEER appears and comes towards the others.

ENGINEER: *If you're tired, keep the driver.*

Shot of the lorry as seen by the two men. The DRIVER gets out and MARIO takes his place.

MARIO: *No thanks. I'm scared if someone else is driving.*

He slams the Curbitt into gear and moves off abruptly. As it moves out of frame, the helmeted camp workers are revealed, standing and waving goodbye.

The scene changes to the bar in the café in Las Piedras. HERNANDEZ is behind the counter, talking on the telephone.

323

LINDA is washing glasses at his side. HERNANDEZ hangs up and, with a sigh, comes round into the foreground to make an announcement to the customers, off-screen.

The ensuing conversation takes place entirely in Spanish.

HERNANDEZ: *Bad news. Luigi and Bimba got blown up. Jo's dead.*
LINDA comes fearfully up to him.

LINDA: *And Mario? . . . And Mario?*

HERNANDEZ, smiling: *He'll be here in two hours.*

LINDA: *Really? Are you sure?*

She throws her arms joyfully round HERNANDEZ then runs across the room. The camera tracks after her as she goes over to DOC's table. HERNANDEZ's radio is blaring the 'Blue Danube' waltz. LINDA curtseys before DOC.

LINDA: *You hear that Doc! In only two hours.*

DOC rises ceremoniously to his feet, bows to LINDA and sweeps her into a waltz.

Dissolve to show MARIO's hand reaching towards the dashboard radio in the lorry. Beside it is Jo's metro ticket.

Rapid close-up of the ticket.

Resume on the radio. MARIO turns it on and we hear the 'Blue Danube' waltz, as in the café.

MARIO rocks his head from side to side in time with the music. We see his hands on the steering wheel as he swerves the lorry from side to side, following the rhythm of the waltz.

Resume on *El Corsario*. LINDA is now dancing gaily with HERNANDEZ. All the occupants of the café are dancing with them. The lorry comes towards the camera. The music continues over. The Curbitt swerves to and fro, waltzing round the bends in the road.

In *El Corsario*, LINDA is now dancing with SMERLOFF.

We see a high shot of the whirling dancers.

MARIO smiles. He turns the steering wheel first one way, then the other, humming the 'Blue Danube' as it blares from the radio.

Rapid shot of the café. The dancers are whirling round faster and faster.

Close-up of the steering wheel from the side, with MARIO's hands still turning it in time with the waltz.

The lorry is seen from outside. The road is now winding along the side of a mountain.

As seen by MARIO, the scenery outside waltzes to and fro. MARIO tosses his head from side to side in time with the music.

A high shot of the dancers in El Corsario. In the centre, LINDA suddenly faints into the arms of her partner, who lays her down gently on the floor.

Close-up of her face, her eyes closed.

MARIO in close-up, suddenly looks alarmed and jerks the steering wheel round.

The lorry is swerving wildly from one side of the road to the other. It narrowly misses the parapet once, then finally crashes into it.

The lorry plunges over the precipice beside the road.

At the wheel, MARIO stares wildly.

The lorry crashes down the precipice, and is completely smashed to bits. (*Still*)

As it comes to rest, the battered hooter on the roof of the cab, seen in close-up, starts to wail with an ear-splitting noise.

Close-up of MARIO's face, seen through the flying dust, as he lies dead, his eyes wide open. The camera passes along his arm. It comes to rest on his hand, holding the metro ticket . . . and, as the hooter continues to wail, the words THE END appear on the screen.

CRITICAL APPENDIX

The Italian Straw Hat

The Italian Straw Hat established the maturity of René Clair as a film maker. Though the gay stage farce by Labiche and Michel on which the story is based is turned into a satire, a strong element of fantasy remains to lighten the attack on the social posturing of a foolish middle-class society and sweeten it with laughter which has no trace of bitterness. Successful satire is usually the mark of maturity in an artist, since he has to keep his sense of humour alive at the very moment when his desire to attack the evils of society is at its strongest. Clair's previous films, *Paris qui dort, Entr'acte, Le Fantôme du Moulin Rouge, Le Voyage imaginaire* and *La Proie du vent* showed his versatility and, in some instances, his refined sense of visual humour (as in *Entr'acte* and *Paris qui dort*). But *The Italian Straw Hat*, which also gained Clair a certain notoriety because some sections of society found its satire objectionable, will remain one of the permanent " classics " of the silent cinema.

Paul Rotha gave it high praise in *The Film Till Now* (1930): " I certainly suggest that *Le Chapeau de paille d'Italie* is the most brilliant satirical comedy produced in Europe to be grouped with Lubitsch's *The Marriage Circle* and Chaplin's *A Woman of Paris* ". It is, he writes, " a brilliant comedy deep in bitter satire of French middle-class life, and realised with a high degree of intelligence and cinematic skill. Around a simple dual theme of a man who was a little hard of hearing and the destruction of a lady's straw hat, Clair wove a film that was not only exceptionally witty, but a penetrating commentary on the pettiness and small-mindedness of the bourgeoisie who constitute such a large proportion of the French population ".

Writing in 1932 in *Scrutiny of Cinema*, the late William Hunter says of the film:

" It is a superb study in general stupidity. It is thoroughly French in spirit, though by no means local in treatment. It is set in a dead and ridiculous epoch, but also in an epoch whose pettiness still survives and will never be wholly stifled. Clair's attitude is that of an intelligent and sensitive person, a critically satirical attitude, but human, tolerant, and without bitterness. He has pointed out futility by drawing attention to detail, he has satirised an epoch, and, still more, he has satirised the perennial and undying elements of that epoch and intensified the awareness of his audiences."

Bardèche and Brasillach make a further comment which many critics have endorsed. " Clair's realism ", they say, " is . . . that of the ballet. He puts his characters in fancy dress and provides them with the appropriate accessories, but at the same time he stylises them, simplifies their outline and leads them into that world which is peculiarly his."

The Italian Straw Hat is made up of a succession of episodes linked together by the slender story of a young bridegroom whose horse eats part of a married lady's straw hat while she is preoccupied with a lover behind a bush in the Bois de Vincennes. The incident might have been smoothed out with reasonable diplomacy, had not the bridegroom been on his way to his wedding and the young lady's safety been dependent on returning home with her hat, if not her honour, intact. Her lover is a fierce and foolish officer, intent only on revenge and immediate reparation. This pair pursue the bridegroom throughout his wedding and the subsequent celebrations. They loll about in his house and send him threatening messages by means of his terrified valet. He must replace the hat before they will consent to go. There is no other plot-link to the film except the coincidence that the deaf uncle of the bride, Mon. Vézinet, is discovered to have brought her the present of an Italian straw hat. This is given to the errant wife, the bride and groom are reconciled, and the deceived but suspicious husband is tricked into submission.

Clair has a happy time with this delightful situation, which provides the motivation for his incredible collection of 1895 bourgeois characters. The realism of the film lies in the settings and in the formalities of the wedding, in all those things people do to make them seem important and dignified in their own eyes. The bride's father is fat and self-opinionated, a provincial market-gardener in comfortable circumstances, stuffing his body into tight clothes and struggling with his boots. Everyone who arrives is kissed on both cheeks. A stupid bearded uncle, hen-pecked by his tall and pretentious wife, wears a made-up tie which constantly drops loose from his collar. This drives his wife to distraction and eventually provides the funniest scene in the film. The climax of the kissing formalities comes in a shot directly looking down upon the bald heads of the men and the monstrous feathered hats of the women, all dipping together in the movements of mock ballet. All these social activities take place

330

against the fussy backgrounds of the knick-knack nineties so ably assembled by the late Lazare Meerson, who was Clair's art director.

As a piece of story-telling the film moves slowly enough, but it contains so much carefully contrived humour and is so well acted by the excellently chosen cast that it survives repeated viewings, at any rate so far as I am concerned. Clair learned from Chaplin, for whom he has the greatest admiration, the value of " building " and timing his visual gags, developing them under the scrutiny of the camera with a certain affectionate regard for their rich humour. The best of these gags, in my opinion, is the scene during the Mayor's oration after the civil wedding-ceremony. The bearded uncle's made-up tie slips once more from the socket of his collar. He is leaning forward intent on the Mayor's sentimental oratory: his wife delivers him a series of nudges, but he is too stupid to take the point; he moves along to give her more room, so starting a chain-movement until the man at the end of the row nearly falls off his seat, a time-honoured subsidiary gag. But the aunt's nudges grow in violence, and she grimaces and gestures to make him understand. He does nothing, but the infection has begun; the Mayor fingers his tie, so does his Deputy, so eventually does every man in the company, though the Mayor's oration still flows on. Eventually the aunt can bear it no more, and with a great French shoulder-shrug of exasperation, she herself shoves the offending tie violently back into place. With mild annoyance her husband sinks back into a listening posture. The Mayor's tedious oration never ceases.

All through the film episodes as carefully conceived as this are worked out with little need for captions or dialogue. That the film is both too slow and too long for popular entertainment I have no doubt, and the characters of the officer, the fainting wife and the bridegroom's sorrowful valet become repetitive and tedious. For it is the elderly folk who distinguish this film. They are comic types, no doubt, but wickedly apt and typical in their behaviour. The deceived husband, standing upright and indignant in a footbath, still wearing a frock-coat but without any trousers, is perhaps the funniest portrait of all. While searching the bridegroom's apartments for his lost wife he is the image of stupid suspicion, looking behind doors where the lovers had been hiding only after he had given them every chance to escape. It is characters like these which give the film its final right to survive as one of the richest and most meticulously made comedies of the silent period of film-making, almost in fact, without equal, except for the best work of Chaplin and Lubitsch.

— ROGER MANVELL

Grand Illusion

A NOTE FROM JEAN RENOIR

The story of *La Grande Illusion* is absolutely true and was told to me
by some of my comrades in the war . . . I am obviously referring to
the war of 1914. In 1914, Hitler had not yet appeared. Nor had the
Nazis, who almost succeeded in making people forget that the Germans are also human beings. In 1914, men's spirits had not yet been
warped by totalitarian religions and racism. In certain ways, that
world war was still a war of formal people, of educated people — I
would almost dare say, a gentlemen's war. That does not excuse it.
Politeness, even chivalry, does not excuse massacre.

MY FIRST MEETING WITH JEAN RENOIR

Of all the film directors I have met in the course of my chequered
career, I have admired a few and worshipped one. I worshipped
D. W. Griffith the way that someone can worship the man who has
taught him everything, who has lavished the treasures of genius on
him without holding back. He was the greatest of his day; this is not
a personal opinion, all those who ever worked for him agree with
me. But there was another man for whom I felt, from the very first
moment, an irresistible sympathy, and that was Jean Renoir.

I must admit that, before meeting him, I was on my guard; I had
just had several unfortunate experiences with American colleagues,
and had had to leave that country as well as give up my job.

There had already been a lot of repercussions, the result of petty
jealousies or even full-scale hatreds. So I was very nervous at the
prospect of meeting my future director. I waited for him in the
partly-furnished office, where the company backing *La Grande Illusion*
had arranged for us to meet. I heard footsteps in the corridor, the
door opened. A heavily-built man in baggy clothing was standing in
the doorway. I could not describe his face; I will only say that I was
struck by his eyes. Not that they were beautiful, but that they were
incredibly blue and sharp with intelligence. Before I knew it, he had
walked up to me and had kissed me firmly on my cheeks. As a rule
I am not overfond of such demonstrations of affection. In fact, I
loathe even a handshake with a member of my own sex. Yet I

returned this unexpected show of friendliness without the least hesitation.

Then, Renoir caught me by the shoulder and held me at arm's length to take a better look at me. Finally, never taking his eyes off me, he told me in German how much he liked my past work and how glad he was that I was going to work with him — he said ' with ' not ' for ' him. There was no need to beat about the bush; I understood that all would go well. The only thing that upset me was that I could not return his compliment, for, alas, I had not seen any of his films. But I warmly expressed my delight at working for him.

We began chatting and I noticed with pleasure that he was very familiar with my films; he even remembered some of them much more clearly than I did, recalling things in them that I had completely forgotten. But we were there mainly to talk about *La Grande Illusion* and the part I was going to play. I had been sent a first, hasty draft of the script which I had read, and — being incorrigible — I began making a few hesitant suggestions. Now that I knew what sort of man Jean Renoir was, I could speak up without fear. That man was incapable of taking offence at what more narrow-minded souls would have considered crimes of impertinence. I could talk to him as openly as to a brother, without hedging. And he was not stalling for time, waiting for a future opportunity to say a more or less veiled ' no ' to my overtures. He examined the subject we were discussing with an enthusiasm that brought tears to my eyes. He had given me a pleasure which I had forgotten for some years.

All the work I did with Renoir turned out to be as friendly as that first meeting. I have never met a man with greater self-control. I saw him at Upper Koenigsburg while he was shooting the most important scenes of *La Grande Illusion*. Everything seemed to be against him, even God, for it began to snow in the middle of a scene — it snowed for so long that Renoir had to change the film script in order to justify this untimely snowfall.

For five days and five nights, Renoir worked without a break. On the sixth day, the sun came out and, in less than a hour, the snow melted. An impressive amount of film was thus suddenly rendered useless. Renoir did not bat an eyelid. He calmly went about arranging for some plaster, naphthaline and boric acid to be sent over, then settled down to wait for its arrival.

He is incredibly patient. Without ever raising his voice, he asks over and over again until he gets what he wants. His politeness towards everyone he works with was a source of endless amazement to me, especially as I personally cannot say three words in succession without swearing in whatever language I am using.

Jean Renoir could have been an excellent diplomat as well, for he has more finesse and ability in his little finger than any professional has in what he calls his brains.

— ERICH VON STROHEIM

GRAND ILLUSION

Grand Illusion was filmed in 1937 during the Popular Front period in France when Renoir was regarded as the leading director of the political Left. The threat of a new European war and Renoir's own pacifist leanings led him to develop the film as a moving humanitarian plea against war. In addition, a superb script and outstanding performances from a cast which included Erich von Stroheim, Pierre Fresnay, Jean Gabin and Marcel Dalio had an obvious appeal to audiences during the thirties and proved the greatest international success of Renoir's career.

The film's solid and intelligent script was the product of a close collaboration between Renoir and Charles Spaak, who had worked with Renoir on his previous film, *Les Bas Fonds,* which also starred Jean Gabin. (Spaak could claim to be regarded as the leading French script writer of the thirties having collaborated on three films of Duvivier, Feyder and Gremillon in addition to the two films with Renoir.) But most important of all, *Grand Illusion* represented a personal venture into the past for Renoir, drawing upon his own knowledge and experience of World War I. Although never taken prisoner, he served as a reconnaissance pilot, and much of the film is based on the experiences of his friend and fellow pilot, Pinsard, whom he met again while filming *Toni* in 1934. (As with so many of his projects, the two-year delay in beginning the film reflected his difficulty in finding a backer.)

Most of the film takes place in various German prisoner-of-war camps, and without ever showing the combat itself, Renoir is able to adopt a broad historical perspective. Through the counterpointed relationships and conversations between the main characters one

335

gains a full appreciation of the manner in which the War has forced a rapid transition from the 19th into the 20th century and represents the beginning of the "modern" era. The age of the aristocratic gentleman-soldier is over, for the modern army is mechanised and drafted from the civilian population. The great transformation which took place during the War is reflected in the experience of Renoir himself: he entered the War as an officer in the cavalry and finished as a pilot in the French Air Force. And the changes at home were also far-reaching. These were best summed up in the film, in typical Renoir fashion, by the soldiers' reactions when they first learn of the new feminine fashions — of short hair and short (knee-length) dresses.

The published scenario of *Grand Illusion* (in *Jean Renoir*, by André Bazin, Simon and Schuster, 1973) is quite similar to the final version of the film and suggests that there were relatively fewer alterations made during the shooting than was the case with other films of his. But many of the changes appear to fit into a particular pattern. The basically linear form of the original has been subtly transformed through the developing of more distinctive qualities for each of the three separate episodes or stories. The scenario was almost certainly written before the casting of a number of important roles, including Rosenthal (Dalio), Elsa (Dita Parlo) and especially von Rauffenstein (Stroheim). Stroheim's impressive appearance as the commandant of the fortress prison and the increased importance of his role gives a new and distinctive meaning to this, the second episode. Similarly, the final section of the film originally included many short sequences depicting the escape journey of the two prisoners, and their encounter with the German farm wife was merely one of many brief incidents. The casting of Dita Parlo was matched by a fuller treatment of the farm setting and the relationship which develops between her and Maréchal (Gabin). The entire final part of the scenario was eliminated, including Maréchal's shooting of the lone sentinel barring the way to the Swiss border, the arrival in Switzerland and an epilogue set at Maxim's in Paris. Also left out were a number of linking sequences earlier in the film, including the initial reconnaissance flight, crash landing and capture by the Germans and a sequence showing the characters travelling from camp to camp (which was filmed but not included in the final version).

In addition, in casting the film Renoir was able to assemble a superb and varied group of actors to occupy the " block " in the first prison camp so that this first episode was defined by the " ensemble ", in contrast to the other episodes. And finally, the casting made possible a new pattern of character pairings. Whereas the scenario presents a simple counterpoint between the aristocratic Bœldieu (Fresnay) and the mechanic Maréchal, the final version of the film includes a great variety of relationships: Bœldieu-von Rauffenstein and Maréchal-Rosenthal as well as a briefer matching between Maréchal and a German mechanic and between Maréchal and a French engineer (Modot). (Renoir was to make even fuller use of these same principles of counterpointing the shifting relations between the various male characters in *Rules of the Game* two years later.)

Thus, the pattern of the film's evolution from the scenario through the casting, shooting and final editing can best be understood in terms of the film's structure. And if *Grand Illusion* appears somewhat fragmentary and lacking in the kind of unities of time, place and character found in Renoir's other films, in fact, each of the three individual episodes *do* maintain such a unity.

The film's prologue set in the French and German officers' canteens introduces themes which are more fully developed later. The opening shot shows Maréchal arranging a lift to the nearby town where his girl is waiting for him. But his plans are interrupted by the arrival of Capt. Bœldieu from the General Staff. And this sets in motion a series of events — a reconnaissance flight (during which their plane is shot down), capture by the Germans and confinement in a number of prisoner-of-war camps from which the two men attempt to escape — constituting the major portion of the film. (After Maréchal's eventual escape, only made possible by the death of Bœldieu, his relationship with the young German widow brings the film full circle recalling that missed rendezvous of the opening sequence.)

Like a real gentleman, von Rauffenstein invites the two French officers to join him at lunch, after shooting down their plane. He and Bœldieu develop an immediate rapport, while Maréchal finds himself seated beside a German officer who has worked as a mechanic for a French firm in Lyons. This theme, of the affinity which exists between men of similar backgrounds surmounting barriers of language and nationality, is briefly alluded to at this point, but will be more fully developed later in the film.

The first episode of the film is set at Hallbach, a prisoner-of-war camp where Maréchal and Bœldieu find themselves sharing a " block " with a group of French officers who are digging an escape tunnel, and the story of the two men is integrated with that of the " hole ". The feeling of camaraderie and the natural interrelating of the various members of the group in this, the longest of the three episodes, is closely related to *The Vanishing Corporal* and *The Crime of Monsieur Lange*. Along with Gabin and Fresnay the block includes a number of regular Renoir collaborators. The presence of Modot, Carette and Dalio brings together the three actors who will fill out the main subplot in *Rules of the Game* two years later. The casting of Dalio meant an expansion of his role, as envisaged in the original scenario, and an introduction of the Jewish theme into the film. Merely by including a Jew among the French officers as part of that typical cross-section which includes an actor, teacher and engineer, and without falsifying the World War I setting, Renoir made the film particularly topical for the late thirties. Similarly, a Senegalese officer is included in the group at the fortress prison — one of those African characters who appear in various of Renoir's films of the period including *Toni* and *La vie est à nous* and draw attention to the genuinely international qualities of Renoir's *œuvre*.

The comradeship of the French prisoners first develops, appropriately enough, over a lavish dinner provided by Rosenthal's food parcels. But there is no mention of the tunnel until the following day when the engineer (Modot) is alone with Maréchal and questions him about whether Bœldieu can be trusted. Their conversation is concluded by a cut to the normal nightly routine in the block: as soon as roll call is over they barricade the door with a chair and screen the window with a blanket before setting to work on the tunnel. And this activity unites the group in a common endeavour which is both amusing and serious, a digging game with the risk of suffocation or of getting caught — for which the penalty is death.

The next morning they secretly dispose of the earth accumulated from the previous night's digging. A number of crates of clothes arrive for use in the show which they plan to put on. During one sequence they converse about home and their reasons for wishing to escape, while working on the costumes. And Renoir here makes use of a flexible camera technique and depth of field in bringing the scenes to life and allowing free interaction between the various characters. Interior is related to exterior in a manner which recalls the apartment sequences in *Boudu sauvé des eaux* and giving visual

338

expression to that superb line spoken by Bœldieu: " On one side, children playing at soldiers. On the other, soldiers playing at children." Bazin writes in *Jean Renoir,* " For certain interior scenes which could have been shot in the studio, Renoir had movable partial sets constructed in the courtyard of the actual barracks used on location. This permitted him to have his actors ' inside ' and at the same time show the bustle of the camp through the window (e.g. the scenes of the young recruits exercising)."

The simple but moving climax to the episode, however, occurs during the performance, with the spontaneous announcement of Maréchal that French troops have recaptured the fortress of Douaumont, followed by the singing of the Marseillaise, photographed in one long take by Claude Renoir. The camera observes the English " girls " as they remove their wigs to join in the song (recalling that moving sequence earlier in the film when the men suddenly fall silent on seeing a soldier dressed as a woman for the first time). Then the camera pans around the room taking in the group of prisoners singing, while the German officers leave hastily. The camera pans after them as they leave, then returns to the men still singing happily in the hall.

Stylistically this episode presents a marked contrast to the following story, set in a fortress perched on a mountain where the prisoners are more strictly confined to their rooms. In the series of shots of the German countryside seen from the train as the prisoners move from camp to camp, there is a subtle change in the terrain which gets gradually more hilly and then mountainous. As suggested by the name " Wintersborn ", the atmosphere in this castle prison is cold, unfriendly and claustrophobic — dimly-lit corridors, stone walls and staircases, and an absence of windows. This episode is filmed in shortish takes, and the occasional longer (mobile) shot — such as the introduction to the commandant's quarters or the search of the prisoners' rooms — is concerned more with objects than with people.

As if to make up for the more limited visual possibilities, this episode includes a variety of interesting aural effects. Background music is used effectively to accentuate the theme of the end of the era of the gentleman-soldier as expressed in the words of Rauffenstein, in conversation with Bœldieu; and their relationship also demonstrates Renoir's sensitivity to the subtleties of language. Throughout the film all the characters speak their own language —

French or German — but Bœldieu and Rauffenstein also converse in their own private language, English. And when Bœldieu acts as a decoy for his two fellow-prisoners, he refuses von Rauffenstein's repeated requests to him, *in English*, to come down from the ramparts of the castle where he continues to play on a solitary flute. James Kerans writes (in *Film Quarterly*, Winter 1960): "The exchange leading up to the shooting of Bœldieu is in English, which puts it beyond the listening soldiers, in a world of cosmopolitan isolation."

The castle episode is shorter than the opening one, and Renoir concentrates on the relationship between Bœldieu and von Rauffenstein. The initial sequence introduces Rauffenstein, the commandant of the fortress, in the old chapel which serves as his living quarters. His extremely altered appearance results from the fact that his plane was shot down; not only was he badly burnt, but his backbone was fractured in two places and mended with silver plates, in addition to a silver strut in his chin and a silver knee-cap. All this is carefully enumerated by him at one point in the film, an example of the kind of realistic detail for which Stroheim was famous in his own films. Apparently the idea of transforming the appearance of von Rauffenstein in this manner was first suggested to Renoir by Stroheim, who also served as military adviser and contributed some of the dialogue. In fact, Rauffenstein presents a striking and memorable appearance, and the outstanding acting of Stroheim means that he tends to dominate this episode of the film.

The development of Rauffenstein's relationship with Bœldieu during this episode and particularly a long conversation between them in the old chapel draws attention to the central themes of the film: the affinity between men of the same class in spite of national barriers and the fact that aristocratic soldiers like themselves have been made redundant by modern techniques of warfare and replaced by the new generation of civilian soldiers like Maréchal and Rosenthal.

In the first episode the experiences of Maréchal were blended with the digging of the escape tunnel. His release from the camp prison coincides with the completion of the tunnel, but before the men are able to make use of it, they are transferred to another camp. (Maréchal attempts to tell a group of newly arrived English officers of the hole in one last, futile, gesture.) Similarly, the story of

Bœldieu and Rauffenstein in the second episode is integrated with that of the successful escape of Maréchal and Rosenthal. And the episode concludes, appropriately, with a moving scene between Rauffenstein and Bœldieu at the latter's deathbed in the chapel.

The third, and shortest, episode shows the escape journey of Maréchal and Rosenthal, and it differs stylistically from the other stories for much of it takes place out-of-doors. In spite of the privations suffered by the two men and the bleakness of the land-scapes, there is a feeling of " release " after the confinement of the prison camps. And, as usual, Renoir uses the settings extremely effectively.

The sequences set at the farm have an optimistic and liberating feel, anticipating the final escape across a snowbound landscape into Switzerland. In the farmhouse the sunlight streams through the doors and windows which frame the action. And there is one superb sequence of two shots as the three characters prepare for bed. The camera follows Maréchal as he turns off the gramophone and says " Good night " to Elsa, who stands in the middle of the room with eyes lowered. He goes toward Rosenthal's door, then back to blow out the candles on the Christmas tree before entering Rosenthal's room to say " Good night ". Cut to him leaving by the side door into his own room adjoining. He eats an apple as he walks about the room and the camera follows him, showing, at the same time as he notices it, that the door leading from his room to the central dining room is still ajar. In the background Elsa is still standing where he left her. She raises her face and he takes her in his arms. The couple are framed by the doorway as they kiss. Fade out. Not a word needs to be spoken. Maréchal's relationship with Elsa provides the final, optimistic touch in this film on Franco-German relations. And whereas Gabin, as the solid, dependable engineer, appears a bit dull through much of the film, he comes much more to life in these final sequences at the farm.

The stylistic differences between the three episodes provides an excellent example of Renoir's ability to integrate style and content within each individual story without destroying the unity of the film as a whole. Such is the power of Renoir's cinematic vision that the film lives up to its reputation as one of the enduring classics of the cinema.

— JOEL FINLER

La Ronde

INTERVIEW WITH OPHULS (1950)

Meeting Max Ophuls again, twenty-five years seem obliterated in a whiff and the exciting atmosphere of the twenties, with their errors and enthusiasms, is recaptured. Despite the greying temples, he is, in his 47th year, as youthful and as lively as he might have been on that day when, at the age of 18, he defiantly refused to accept a crown-princely position in his father's department store in Saarbruecken and ran away from home to become an actor.

Listening to the tale of his eventful career is like sitting in that fake train-compartment in his *Letter From An Unknown Woman* and watching the romantic scenery rolling past the window. The only difference is that the painted back-cloth suddenly becomes alive with the colour and life-blood of genuine adventure.

Max Ophuls possesses the rare quality of understanding people not only intellectually but emotionally, of listening to them and absorbing their ideas in a way that makes them immediately feel " at home ". And this includes all kinds of people: from the practically minded studio carpenter to the sophisticated scriptwriter or the self-important production magnate. This is a clue to his success in half a dozen different countries. In each of them he arrived as a stranger, lonely and forlorn, but when circumstances forced him to continue his pilgrimage, he left behind everywhere genuine friends and admirers.

The element of human warmth and absolute sincerity is striking, both in his work and in his talk.

" Why I wanted to become an actor? — It's simple," he says. " Apart from the fascination of all the classical plays which I regularly watched from ' the gods ' of our Saarbruecken Stadt-Theater, my imagination was fired by the crowds of young girls waiting at the stage door every night. I might have achieved this ambition in my young days in Aachen and Dortmund, but I am afraid that I have never been a really good actor. That is why I became a director.

" I never played very important parts. Just what the others left for me. The Dauphin in Shaw's *St. Joan* was my favourite part in my acting days, but only later, when I produced the play in Berlin,

342

I discovered how much better it could be played.

" But I really became a producer by accident. One night I flopped so terribly in a dramatic part that the next day the Manager of the Dortmund Theatre summoned me to his office. As I was paid for playing both comic and dramatic roles, he told me, I would have to take a 50 per cent salary cut. To soothe my indignation he hesitantly suggested an alternative. I could stop playing altogether and become a *Regisseur,* a director, keeping my original salary. My actor's pride was deeply insulted — but a few days later I accepted ". To justify the acceptance to himself, he argued at the time that in his new position he would make actors play their parts exactly the way he himself would have played them. " So through the actor I'll prove that really and truly I should have played the part myself and that I am a much better actor than anybody had thought . . .". But he had not the slightest inkling then that within the next ten years he would produce something like 180 stage plays.

Quick as he is to announce his failures with a humorous twinkle, he passes over his successes with a few hasty remarks. The fact, however, is that they were outstanding and numerous.

The most explicit proof of the quality of his productions was supplied by a sensational offer from the Vienna Burg-Theater to engage him on a long-term contract at a high salary. To appreciate this, one has to remember the old dignified tradition of the Burg-Theater, where everything was time-honoured and the most youthful actors in their fifties. In the long history of this world-famous theatre there had never been a director aged 23 — except Max Ophuls.

His comment on the appointment was:

" All through the time in Vienna I felt like a passenger in a fast elevator: dizzy! — Fate had plonked me down in a magnificent gilt rococo carriage drawn by four matched horses — while what I really wanted was to ride on a motor-cycle ".

The longing for a break with convention drove him back to Germany. In Frankfurt, Breslau and finally Berlin he found a wide field for his talent. His deeply rooted sense of social obligation led him to a purposeful hobby: in his leisure time he visited prisons and played or recited to the inmates. The rapidly spreading net of broadcasting gave him a new outlet, and soon not only his name but also his voice became familiar over the air.

343

But up to the beginning of the thirties Max Ophuls, who had always been in love with the theatre, used to look upon the cinema (excepting only Charlie Chaplin) as a cheap fairground attraction, and despised it all the more for being a dangerous rival to the live stage.

The first " talkie " he saw, with bad and hardly intelligible dialogue, made the first breach in his armour of indifference. He saw great possibilities in the proper use of the sound-track and conceived a vague idea that one day he might try to make a picture.

Significantly enough, he began his work in this new field by becoming a dialogue director for Anatol Litvak, whose poor German was as little understood by the UFA actors as his native Russian. The film was called *No More Love*. Max Ophuls' way of dealing with actors must have impressed the UFA executives. They suggested to him the production of a 40-minute featurette and offered him the freedom of their script-library. The result was a delightful little comedy called *Dannschon Lieber Lebertran* (*Codliver-Oil Preferred*). The author of the original story was the German poet Erich Kaestner (author of *Emil and the Detectives*), while the shooting-script was written by the same Emeric Pressburger who to-day heads the " Archers " with Michael Powell. The picture was given a cautious trial run in a suburban cinema: the public's reaction was such that after two days it was transferred to the biggest UFA theatre in the west end of Berlin.

This long forgotten miniature triumph marks the birth of Max Ophuls, the film-maker.

In *The Bartered Bride* which followed, the newly established director had not only the great advantage of employing the opera star, Jarmilla Nowotna (to-day at the Metropolitan Opera in New York, and also the mother in *The Search*) but also of the greatest possible freedom of action. He caused quite a stir by building a whole Czech village among the hills of Geiselgasteig and by engaging real fairground people and local inhabitants to act in the film. As the finished work turned out a success and not just another " filmed opera " his prestige increased accordingly.

While still shooting the last scenes of *The Bartered Bride* half his thoughts and all his heart were already on another subject: Schnitzler's *Liebelei*, which was to make him widely famous.

Here he proved his brilliance, his singleness of purpose and his independence. Instead of accepting the producer's over-sentimental approach and a cast-list full of box-office names, he refused to co-operate and decided to produce the picture himself.

" I saw the opportunity of making a picture with young people as yet unspoiled by stardom," he says. " Not an easy task, certainly, but fascinating. I believe that most young actors have to be steered through great dangers. Wealth, publicity, a higher standard of living — it all happens far too quickly. The shyness and reserve that constitute the appeal of youth, are easily lost . . .".

To eliminate these dangers he sent Wolfgang Liebeneiner, then an almost unknown actor (and now a film director in Germany) for three months to a lonely place in the mountains and made him promise to keep his assignment a secret. Despite the grumbles of the business manager, who disliked " paying for an actor's holiday ", the experiment proved more than successful.

An experiment with the feminine parts was still less orthodox and more daring. Magda Schneider, a gay and popular musical-comedy star, seemed to envy slightly Luise Ulrich for her semi-tragic role, while the latter proved to be naturally light-hearted by temperament. Following a sudden inspiration Max Ophuls made them exchange parts; and the result was startlingly successful.

Another minor sensation was the fact that a number of secondary parts were played by top-stars, including Gustav Grundgens and Olga Tchekowa. " They did it for Schnitzler's sake " — is the director's modest comment. It is only a fair guess that his own personality must have had something to do with it.

So well prepared was the picture that shooting was completed in less than four weeks. Once it was screened there were many who said it would become a " classic ".

All this happened in 1932. A year later, the advent of the Third Reich forced Max Ophuls to abandon his work and Germany. He had never denied his Jewish faith, and his friends knew very well that he had changed his name from Oppenheimer for one reason only: in order not to " disgrace " his Saarbruecken family through his acting career.

Max Ophuls went to Paris, but the fame of *Liebelei* had preceded him. Soon an independent company was formed with the one and only aim of making a French version of it. Most of the principal actors came to Paris for the purpose, disregarding possible Nazi reprisals and not even first asking how much they would be paid.

This was a good start to a series of films made in France, which their maker himself assesses as follows:

On a volé un homme. — " A pot-boiler. Not my cup of tea! "

Divine (Script by Colette). — " My biggest flop ".

Le Tendre ennemie. — " It was awarded the Prix Lumière and one French paper called it ' René Clair without snobbery '. But many people dislike me for it ".

Yoshiwara (a Maurice Dekobra story). — " The Japanese Sessue Hayakawa and his wife-to-be speaking broken French. Very international ".

Sans lendemain. — " I have never yet seen an uncut version of the picture. And what I was not allowed to show was precisely what I liked best of all. Edwige Feuillère is a great actress! "

In between those Max Ophuls made one film in Holland, *The Comedy of Gold,* put Isa Miranda on the screen in *La Signora di Tutti,* shot in Rome, and accepted an invitation to Soviet Russia on condition that he would only sign a two-year contract if he liked the country. After two months stay he returned to Paris.

He was just shooting the last scene of *From Mayerling to Sarajevo,* that graceful historical film with Edwige Feuillère, with a remarkable closing sequence of the assassination at Sarajevo, when most of his technicians put on uniforms and went off to the Maginot Line. Very soon he was drafted into the French Army too — as a private.

It was a long and very adventurous road that led him from the French battlefields of 1940 to the United States. One of the tragic stops on his way was the Zurich Theatre, where he produced some Shakespeare plays. He could have stayed on if he had satisfied the Swiss police by signing a declaration that he was a French deserter. . . .

" America certainly was not as I had imagined it, and for quite a time I was very depressed," he confesses. " Some people turned my head with easy promises, but for three years or so I was completely idle. I couldn't quite understand the workings of Hollywood machinery, till one day a big-time executive said to me with a friendly pat on the shoulder: ' Our studios are producing a lot of cheaply made money-spinners just now: thrillers, Westerns and so on. But one day the Board of Directors may decide to embark on

Quality Production. That is when we shall need you '. His words were true, which meant that waiting for my chance I might well starve.

"But my chance came unexpectedly, when Preston Sturges one day by accident came across *Liebelei* and rediscovered me. I was first assigned to the scripting of Prosper Mérimée's *Colomba* for Howard Hughes (a picture unfinished yet, as far as I know), then worked for Douglas Fairbanks on *The Exile*. Then I made *Letter From An Unknown Woman* for Universal-International, *Caught* for Enterprise, and finally *The Reckless Moment,* produced by Walter Wagner for Columbia, which attracted some attention in America and led to the project of *La Duchesse de Langeais.* I actually came to Paris to shoot this famous novel with Greta Garbo and James Mason. As nothing came of it, I finally got tired of drawing my salary in idleness and I enthusiastically seized the chance of filming another famous Schnitzler subject: *Der Reigen,* a favourite story of mine ".

Max Ophuls took me out to the St. Maurice studio to show me the rough-cut of *La Ronde.* Not to overstate my case, I cautiously say that is seems to be a completely worthy successor to his best achievements. I didn't try to conceal my elation, but when we were sitting in the car again, I asked him, whether he had thought of censorship at all, American or English — when he was making the picture.

Of course he had not. It would have seemed to him a profanation of Schnitzler's work and spirit.

"Do you really think that the British censor would not pass those love scenes?" he enquired with a note of genuine anxiety in his voice. "That would be a blow to me, because little as I know it — I have a profound feeling for England. If it weren't for the war, my son would have been educated in England, and possibly I might have made a film there. . . .

"I am delighted to be in Europe again," he continues, speaking of his plans. "It is my spiritual home, after all, and at my age it is almost impossible to become 100 per cent American. I have a vague idea that I should turn to good use the proverbial American efficiency by making a few pictures over here which would reflect European spirit and European stability. Even in the States there is an ever-growing market for such films.

347

" Laurence Olivier has really broken new ground with his *Hamlet*. But I believe that, for instance, a film adaptation of Giraudoux's *La Folle de Chaillot*, in English of course, might well attract the same crowds . . . ".

When Max Ophuls talks about something that is important to him, the inflexions of his voice betray a depth of feeling rather unusual in a man who by reason of his profession and after a life full of pitfalls might have become a cynic. Fortunately he is far from it. His faith in the cinema is unbroken; and his youthful enthusiasm still fires the imagination of his friends and fellow-workers who see in him not only an outstanding film-director, but also a good European.

— FRANCIS KOVAL

The Wages of Fear

The Wages of Fear comes to London with a Grand Prix from Cannes and an immense reputation. It turns out to be at once more and less impressive than one had expected. As a thriller it is violent, exciting and, on the whole, excellently sustained; as a serious dramatic work expressing a significant *Weltanschauung* — its reputation and heavily grandiloquent style demand that one look at it in this light — it is inconsistent and trite. It might be described as a scorcher with pretensions.

The film opens with a close-shot of two beetles locked in combat; the camera tilts up to show that they are on strings being manipulated by a small boy. This image sets the key to the atmosphere of the setting — a small mushroom town in Central America, sprung up around an American-run oilfield. Its inhabitants are out-of-work adventurers, lazy, tough, disillusioned, wanting only to get away. A fire in an oilfield several hundred miles away offers a chance of escape. A load of nitro-glycerine is to be taken by lorry to the burning well — a dangerous mission, since the slightest jolt will send the whole load into the air. The bait is $2,000, and four of the desperadoes get the job: Jo, a tough, weary, middle-aged gangster; Mario, Jo's mate in the first lorry, an amiable drifter who idolises Jo; Luigi, a jolly Italian bricklayer; and Bimba, Luigi's companion, a mysterious German refugee. The two lorries meet terrible obstacles — the drive takes up some threequarters of the film — and three of the drivers die. Luigi's and Bimba's lorry blows up; and Jo, who has lost his nerve under the strain, is wounded in a violent accident caused by Mario and dies before the lorry reaches its destination. Mario, the only survivor, sets out to return to the small town with his reward and, in his joy, recklessly crashes over a precipice. The lorry's siren, released by the crash, screams with a piercing note over the end title.

The story of *The Wages of Fear* offers great possibilities for physical excitement, and Clouzot exploits them for all that they are worth. With his flair for violent action and his eye for the most lurid detail any situation has to offer, he has produced a remarkably sustained adventure film. Yet though one is gripped for most of its length — there are two scenes which stretch one's credulity too far — the excitement is somehow impersonal, like that of watching a trapezist in a circus. The characters, unlikeable and superficially portrayed, excite no sympathy. *The Wages of Fear,* with its heavy, overcharged style, its ponderous rhythm and hysterically composed images, tries to inflate its subject into something larger than a thriller. But what? Clouzot is fascinated by evil and takes pains to show it at its most sensational: a character amuses himself by throwing stones at a chained dog; Mario waves cheerfully to his girl as she disappears into her employer's bedroom; and so on. The director isolates the ugliest details of his situation — we get close shots of Jo's putrefying leg, of his oil-drenched face, long close-ups of agonised faces — and passes on to the next. Yet with all this he makes no real statement about his characters; nowhere does he commit himself to any sympathy (much less compassion) which might have given point to the stress he lays on physical and mental anguish. The portraits of the four riders are brushed in with crude, gaudy strokes: Bimba shaves half-way through the journey because he wants to go to his death looking his best; Mario hurls a rock at Jo's head " to save time ", saying that he could have beaten him in a fair fight but it would have taken longer. All four change their characters during the voyage — the swaggering Jo succumbs to panic; the other three, established as weak, gain strength — but they do so without explanation. They do not develop: the first impression of depth turns out really to be a lack of focus.

The Wages of Fear is realised with the technical virtuosity one expects from its director. Armand Thirard's photography is hard and brilliant, Auric's score economically used and powerful. Charles Vanel, Folco Lulli and Peter van Eyck give admirably tight performances, and there is a terrifying portrait of a flabby bully from Jo Dest. Only Yves Montand (Mario), with his single tight-lipped grimace denoting toughness, and his tendency to fall into casually elegant stances, lets down the standard of performance.

On its appearance in Cannes, *The Wages of Fear* was described by some critics as a communist propaganda film disguising under its adventure story an attack on American capitalism. The comment is misleading. The film is admittedly anti-American, but it would be unfair to single this out for special mention, for *The Wages of Fear* is unselectively and impartially anti-everything.

— KAREL REISZ